Michèle Barrett

NLB

15 :D

Women's Oppression Today

Problems in Marxist Feminist Analysis

© Michèle Barrett, 1980

Verso Editions and NLB,
7 Carlisle Street, London W1

Filmset by Villiers Publications Ltd,
Ingestre Road, London

Printed in Great Britain by
Redwood Burn Ltd,
Trowbridge and Esher

**British Library
Cataloguing in Publication Data**

Barrett, Michèle
    Women's oppression today.
    1. Feminism
    2. Communism
    I. Title
    301.41'2   HQ1154

    ISBN 0-86091-033-4
    ISBN 0-86091-730-4 Pbk

Contents

For Mary McIntosh

Preface and Acknowledgments

This book explores a question that has recently acquired new political urgency. Is it possible to develop an analysis of women's oppression in contemporary capitalism that represents a genuine synthesis of Marxist and feminist perspectives? It starts from the position that no such reconciliation has yet occurred and that any attempt to create a coherent 'Marxist feminist' analysis must confront serious theoretical and political issues. These problems may prove a stumbling block to any alliance between the women's liberation movement and the left, and may demand compromises on both sides if they are to be resolved; but they should, surely, be confronted rather than glossed over.

It is impossible to understand why the question of a reconciliation between Marxism and feminism has recently been raised again without considering the political context in which the women's liberation movement and the left now struggle to achieve their respective political goals.

There are a number of reasons why socialists might at present be looking towards such a rapprochement. The left has been forced by the evident failures of social democracy into a reassessment of its aims and strategy. In Britain the collapse of the Labour government and the election, in a period of deepening recession and rising unemployment, of a right-wing Conservative administration has created the conditions for collective self-criticism. Socialists have become more aware of the problems of factionalism and sectarianism, and have evinced a desire (almost a desperation) to seek popular alliances. The women's liberation movement presents itself, along with popular anti-racist movements, as an instance of a political mobilization that has used, with some success, methods and ideas different from those traditionally employed on the left. One rather uncharitable reading of the present interest of socialist organizations in feminism is that this new movement has succeeded in politicizing a formerly isolated and conservative constituency which can now be recruited for the 'real' struggle.

More constructively, there has been a recognition among socialists that the ideas and practice of the women's liberation movement provide a critique of deficiencies in the traditional conceptions of the left. In particular, the insistence of women's liberationists on the political character of personal life has made a profound impact on many socialists and injected a heightened sense of personal political authenticity into socialist struggle. The enormous interest displayed in the feminist critique of hierarchical forms of socialist organization presented in the book *Beyond the Fragments*[1] is an indication of a newly open and reflexive disposition in the left. In addition, there has been a welcome increase in attention to the divisions within the working class that militate against building a united revolutionary movement. Of these, the division between men and women has been recognized as particularly divisive and disabling. The left's political interest in feminism is underwritten by the critique of economism that has dominated the Marxist intelligentsia in recent years. A new political generation, reared on a rather selective reading of Louis Althusser and Nicos Poulantzas, and even more significantly shaped by the revival of interest in the work of Antonio Gramsci, has been disposed to see the reduction of all political and ideological phenomena to their supposed economic determinants as the worst and most vulgar error of

---

1. Sheila Rowbotham, Lynne Segal and Hilary Wainwright, *Beyond the Fragments: Feminism and the Making of Socialism*, London 1980.

Marxism. So when the autonomous women's liberation movement sprang up in the late nineteen sixties — as far as socialists could see, out of nowhere — no wonder it was seized on as a walking falsification of economism.

But what has socialism to offer women's liberation? This question is more divisive, since while feminism appears, at worst, as a 'bourgeois diversion' to some socialists, the counter-charge laid against socialism by some women's liberationists is the graver one of betrayal. In order to understand the relationship between the women's liberation movement and the left we must look at the various influences that have played a part in constructing the political practice of contemporary feminism.

On the one hand there is an important grouping of women in the women's movement with an independent (and often biographically prior) commitment to the struggle for socialism. From this has sprung not only a disillusioned critique of sexism on the left, but also an interest in the role women, and feminism, have played in revolutionary movements. In particular, the lives and work of socialist feminists such as Alexandra Kollontai have been retrieved and re-examined.[2] This forms part of a more general effort, sustained by feminism's politicization of personal life, to challenge the separation of feminist and socialist activity and to understand the relations between the struggle against capitalism and the struggle for women's liberation.

At the same time, however, there has also been a shift towards a socialist analysis by feminists who feel that the women's liberation movement is, precisely, *not* grounded historically in a relationship with the left. I am rather suspicious of the view, which socialists are wont to assume as a fact of history, that feminism is naturally and inevitably associated with the left. The British women's movement draws also on a tradition of feminist activity that goes back to the nineteenth century and which, throughout the

2. See Sheila Rowbotham's *Women, Resistance and Revolution*, Harmondsworth 1974, for a general discussion.

Ref to diff types of fem

In This Book

a bit new

supposedly 'dead' decades of this century, continued to achieve liberal reforms of many kinds. This indigenous tradition of democratic feminism provides an important reference point for contemporary activism. In addition to this, the British movement was massively influenced at the outset of the present phase by American radical feminism. The ideas of radical feminism are for the most part incompatible with, when not explicitly hostile to, those of Marxism and indeed one of its political projects has been to show how women have been betrayed by socialists and socialism. Yet for many feminists, and particularly for those women (like myself) whose first involvement with women's liberation was through contact with radical feminism these ideas represent an irreducible core of truth and anger which forms the obstinate basis of feminist politics. The arguments of this book in fact rest on the assumption that, to some extent at least, the feminism addressed is that of radical rather than socialist feminism.

Yet for some of us, the reason why radical feminism was unsatisfactory lay in its failure to provide an adequate analysis of the oppression it denounced with such certainty, and its parallel silence about an adequate political strategy for change. In posing women's oppression simply as the effect of male domination, it refuses to take account of the widely differing structures and experience of that oppression in different societies, periods of history and social classes. Most importantly, in so far as women's oppression is inevitably embedded in relations between men and women, the strategy of separatism sometimes advocated by this current is no strategy at all, for it can never change things. Even in the areas where it has contributed most, such as the analysis of sexual politics, radical feminism refuses to attend to issues that cannot be incorporated into the elemental model of male supremacy.

These comments are necessarily partial, and I am sure that others, certainly other socialist feminists, would identify a different range of landmarks on their various political maps. Nevertheless it seemed essential to attempt to

specify what I see as the political context in which the
questions that concern us here have arisen. However, the
book is only indirectly about the possibility of socialist
feminism. It attempts to explore the analytic and historical
questions currently in dispute, and in this sense it is a
general book about Marxism and feminism rather than a
strategic discussion of revolutionary socialism and women's
liberation. It is a 'reflective' rather than an 'angry' book,
written for those who do not need to be convinced that
women are oppressed. The reality of women's oppression is
assumed rather than argued throughout; the object of the
book is to analyse and understand it. Some feminists may
well disapprove of this studied calm, but it rests precisely on
the achievements of the last ten years in demonstrating the
facts of oppression.

Another basic assumption of the book is that the issues at
stake cannot be resolved at the level of theory alone. Two
central questions recur throughout the discussion, since I
regard them both as underlying much of the debate: Can we
see women's oppression in capitalism as independent of the
general operation of the capitalist mode of production? Do we
see women's oppression as taking place exclusively at the
level of ideology? Neither of these questions is likely to be
resolved by some 'correct' formulation that encapsulates the
problem and specifies its answer by juggling with the terms
'capitalism', 'patriarchy' and 'articulation'. Hence the book
considers these questions from an empirical and historical
point of view. Some basic conceptual problems are dealt with
in the opening chapter; others are discussed as they
subsequently arise. In adopting this approach I am not
attempting to write an account of women's oppression in
capitalism from a feminist historian's point of view. For one
thing I am not competent to do so. The questions that
concern me are the how and why of women's oppression
today, but I am sure that the answers to these questions
cannot be deduced in strictly theoretical terms. Accordingly,
I argue for an historical approach to these questions,
drawing on the work of feminist historians, without claiming

6

to provide a systematic historical account.

The frame of reference of the book is limited in certain specific ways. The argument deals mainly with the oppression of women in contemporary capitalism through a consideration of gender division in Britain. It is indebted to work undertaken in the context of the United States and Western Europe, but touches only briefly on other societies. Although the analysis engages with some work in the Marxist and feminist traditions, as well as with recent 'Marxist feminist' ideas, it does not attempt to provide a systematic exposition of either Marxist thought on 'the woman question' or the history of feminist theory from Mary Wollstonecraft to the present.

It is customary, somewhere in the 'acknowledgments', for an author to assume responsibility for the text that follows, and I hereby exonerate the people mentioned below for all errors of fact or judgment in this book. It needs to be stressed, though, that a book so immediately located in current debates must be more than usually indebted to people I have listened to and work I have read.

A number of people read drafts of particular chapters and I am grateful to them for their comments and encouragement. They include people whose work I have disagreed with and I am especially grateful to them for their constructive and clarifying responses: Veronica Beechey, Cynthia Cockburn, Rosalind Coward, Rosalind Delmar, Terry Eagleton, Catherine Hall, Annette Kuhn, Terry Lovell, Karen Margolis, Angela Martin, Julia Naish, Rebecca O'Rourke, Jeffrey Weeks, Elizabeth Wilson, Janet Wolff and AnnMarie Wolpe. It was useful to have American responses to the overall project and I would like to thank all those I discussed it with, particularly Barbara Rosenblum and the *Socialist Review* collective. Chapter 2 is indebted to some fascinating conversations with Peter Stallybrass in the USA.

Perry Anderson, Olivia Harris, Mary McIntosh and William Outhwaite read the entire draft (some of them more than one draft) and their heroism and comments are very much appreciated. The book went through NLB's editorial process in a very constructive and painless way and I am grateful to Francis Mulhern for presiding over this; also to Maxine Molyneux and Fred Halliday for their initial encouragement.

Underlying the book are some years of teaching 'sexual divisions' courses in sociology. Having to organize my views and argue with students was an enormous stimulus to my work in this area and I would like to thank students taking these courses at Hull University and The City University, London. The Department of Social Science and Humanities at City University was extremely helpful in providing secretarial help and funds for research expenses; my thanks to Ruth Newton for her excellent typing and to Maria Papatheodoulou and Maggie Millman for their help with references and indexing.

Friends such as Julia Naish, William Outhwaite, Elizabeth Wilson, Victoria Greenwood and Barry Atkinson contributed in various ways to the book and the pleasantness of my life while I wrote it. I must particularly acknowledge Julia's provision of that wonderful Italian stationery that transforms writing from work to pleasure. I would also like to take this opportunity of thanking my mother, Helen Barrett, for her constant support and encouragement of my work.

Finally, I come to the debt that this book and I personally owe to Mary McIntosh. Our work together on the questions the book deals with, and our many discussions of my arguments, have contributed enormously to its overall character. The dedication is an appropriate mixture of the personal and the political, reflecting not only my own feelings but a recognition shared by others of the political and intellectual contribution she has made to the development of socialist feminism.

1
Some Conceptual Problems in Marxist Feminist Analysis

It is relatively easy to demonstrate that women are oppressed in Britain, as in other contemporary capitalist societies, but more contentious to speak of a 'Marxist feminist' analysis of their oppression. In recent years attempts have been made to develop a theoretical perspective that might confidently be termed 'Marxist feminist', yet the work so generated remains fragmentary and contradictory, lacking a conceptual framework adequate to its project. This, perhaps, is only to be expected, given the magnitude of the task and the obstacles that any synthesis must overcome.

The problem faced by any such analysis can be put simply in terms of the different objects of the two perspectives. Marxism, constituted as it is around relations of appropriation and exploitation, is grounded in concepts that do not and could not address directly the gender of the exploiters and those whose labour is appropriated. A Marxist analysis of capitalism is therefore conceived around a primary contradiction between labour and capital and operates with categories that, as has recently been argued, can be termed 'sex-blind'.[1] Feminism, however, points in a different direction, emphasizing precisely the relations of gender — largely speaking, of the oppression of women by men — that Marxism has tended to pass over in silence. Of course, just as

1. See Heidi Hartmann, 'The Unhappy Marriage of Marxism and Feminism: Towards a More Progressive Union', *Capital and Class*, no.8, 1979, and Mark Cousins, 'Material Arguments and Feminism', *m/f*, no.2, 1978.

there are many varieties of 'Marxism' so there are many 'feminisms' and indeed one task of any 'Marxist feminism' must be to identify which version of the one is being bracketed with which version of the other. But what is clear is that any feminism must insist on the specific character of gender relations. Some forms of feminism may pose these relations as the primary contradiction of social organization, just as Marxism poses the labour/capital contradiction as primary in the analysis of capitalism, but all must surely pose them as distinct.

What then might be the object of Marxist feminism? In the most general terms it must be to identify the operation of gender relations as and where they may be distinct from, or connected with, the processes of production and reproduction understood by historical materialism. Thus it falls to Marxist feminism to explore the relations between the organization of sexuality, domestic production, the household and so on, and historical changes in the mode of production and systems of appropriation and exploitation. Such questions are now being addressed by Marxist feminists working in anthropology, the sociology of development, and political economy.[2] This book, however, deals with the relations of gender and the oppression of women in a contemporary capitalist society. In this context a Marxist feminist approach will involve an emphasis on the relations between capitalism and the oppression of women. It will require an awareness of the specific oppression of women in capitalist relations of production, but this must be seen in the light of gender divisions which preceded the transition to capitalism and which, as far as we can tell, a socialist revolution would not of itself abolish.

It is immediately clear that these questions must be treated historically. Although the chapters that follow could not attempt to provide a systematic historical account of the topics considered, they do point to the need to look at definitions of sexuality, the structure of the household and so

2. See, for instance, the special issue of *Critique of Anthropology*, vol.3, nos. 9/10, 1977.

on in concrete historical and empirical terms. Before moving on to more detailed areas we need, however, to discuss the theoretical framework in which the development of a Marxist feminist approach has been located. In order to do this I am going to consider the different uses of three concepts that have proved central to the debate: those of 'patriarchy', 'reproduction' and 'ideology'. These three concepts, as they have been developed in Marxist feminism, bear directly on two issues that have recurred consistently in the discussion. 'Patriarchy', drawn primarily from radical feminist writings, and 'reproduction', drawn from Althusser's emphasis on reproduction of the relations of production, have both been used to address the question of the independence of women's oppression from the general operation of the capitalist mode of production. Developments in the concept of 'ideology', and its use in specific trends of Marxist feminist thought, lead us straight into the question of whether the oppression of women takes place at the level of ideology, and what such a claim would entail.

Patriarchy

The concept of patriarchy is perhaps the crucial one with which to begin. The editors of a recent collection entitled *Feminism and Materialism* insist that it 'be seriously addressed in any theoretical practice which claims to be feminist'[3] and indeed the term is used extensively in the women's liberation movement. To get an idea of its theoretical and political force we need to look at the context in which the concept has been used.

The term 'patriarchy' was taken up by the sociologist Max Weber to describe a particular form of household organization in which the father dominated other members of an extended kinship network and controlled the economic production of the household. Its resonance for feminism, however, rests on the theory, put forward by early radical

3. Annette Kuhn and AnnMarie Wolpe, eds., *Feminism and Materialism*, London 1978, p.11.

feminism and in particular by American writers such as Kate Millett, of patriarchy as an over-arching category of male dominance.

Millett locates male domination in the following terms: 'groups who rule by birthright are fast disappearing, yet there remains one ancient and universal scheme for the domination of one birth group by another — the scheme that prevails in the area of sex'. She argues that the political power which men wield over women amounts to the fundamental political division in society. Our society, like all other civilizations, is a patriarchy in which the rule of women by men is 'more rigorous than class stratification, more uniform, certainly more enduring'. Millett confronts the thesis that in capitalist society the domination of women by men is mediated by class differences between women, and argues that such differences are transitory and illusory, that 'whatever the class of her birth and education, the female has fewer permanent class associations than does the male. Economic dependency renders her affiliations with any class a tangential, vicarious and temporary matter'. Millett's position here implies that class divisions are relevant only to men; she denies that significant class differences exist between women. Her project is to establish a fundamental system of domination — patriarchy — that is analytically independent of the capitalist or any other mode of production.[4]

Millett's theory of patriarchy resembles that of Shulamith Firestone insofar as it gives not only analytic independence to male domination, but analytic *primacy*. Firestone, however, grounds her account more firmly in biological reproduction, her aim being 'to take the class analysis one step further to its roots in the biological division of the sexes'. Firestone's theoretical goal is to substitute sex for class as the prime motor in a materialist account of history. She paraphrases Engels as follows: 'all past history...was the history of class struggle. These warring classes of society are

4. Kate Millett, *Sexual Politics*, London 1971, pp.24, 38.

always the product of the modes of organization of the biological family unit for reproduction of the species, as well as of the strictly economic modes of production and exchange of goods and services. The sexual-reproductive organization of society always furnishes the real basis, starting from which we can alone work out the ultimate explanation of the whole superstructure of economic, juridical and political institutions as well as the religious, philosophical and other ideas of a given historical period'.[5]

Although Firestone emphasizes the need to revolutionize reproductive technology in order to free women from the burden of their biologically determined oppression, her account of this determination itself falls into biologistic assumptions.[6] This raises a problem which is often encountered in these early radical feminist uses of the term 'patriarchy': not only do they invoke an apparently universal and trans-historical category of male dominance, leaving us with little hope of change; they also frequently ground this dominance in a supposed logic of biological reproduction. This has paved the way, as we shall see later, for a consideration of patriarchy that tends to stress male supremacy as male control over women's fertility, without a case being made as to why and how men acquired this control. We need to ask whether such an emphasis on the importance of the division of labour between men and women in the reproduction of the species does not amount to a form of biologism, and if so whether 'feminist' biologism escapes the arguments that can be put against other forms of biological explanation of social relations.

Biologistic arguments can be challenged on a number of different grounds. In philosophical terms they tend to be reductionist, in that they subsume complex socially and historically constructed phenomena under the simple category of biological difference, and empiricist, in that they assume that differences in social behaviour are caused by the

5. Shulamith Firestone, *The Dialectic of Sex*, London 1972, pp.20-21.
6. This is particularly clear in her discussion of 'the biological family' as a natural entity, which is considered in Chapter 6 below.

observed biological differences with which they correlate. The history of social science provides us with examples of various attempts to explain social behaviour with reference to biological determinants — two notorious instances being the alleged connections between criminality and body-type and between intelligence-test scores and racial differences. All such attempts have subsequently been discredited, and psychological findings concerning supposedly innate sex differences have now been subjected to a stringent critique.[7] Furthermore, the political and ideological role of such arguments is inevitably reactionary, since if particular social arrangements are held to be 'naturally' given, there is little we can do to change them.

Although it is important for feminist analysis to locate the question of biological difference in an account of male-female relations, the slide into biological reductionism is an extremely dangerous one. It is regressive in that one of the early triumphs of feminist cross-cultural work — the establishment of a distinction between sex as a biological category and gender as a social one[8] — is itself threatened by an emphasis on the causal role of procreative biology in the construction of male domination. In practice, too, such an analysis may well lead to a feminist glorification of supposedly 'female' capacities and principles and a reassertion of 'separate spheres' for women and men. These dangers are not exclusive to radical feminist analysts of patriarchy — they have surfaced in feminist politics and culture from other sources too[9] — but they are perhaps particularly characteristic of these early radical feminist works.

It has, however, been possible to frame an account of patriarchy from the point of view of social, rather than biological, relations, and a major achievement of the work of

---

7. For a feminist critique of this field see Dorothy Griffiths and Esther Saraga, 'Sex Differences and Cognitive Abilities: a Sterile Field of Inquiry?', in O. Hartnett *et al*, eds., *Sex-Role Stereotyping*, London 1979; for a more exhaustive and general review see E. E. Maccoby and C. N. Jacklin, *The Psychology of Sex Differences*, London 1975.
8. See Ann Oakley, *Sex, Gender and Society*, London 1972.
9. This is discussed in more detail in Chapters 2 and 3.

Christine Delphy and others has been the development of a more properly materialist analysis of women's oppression. Delphy points to the example of the divorced wife of a bourgeois man as illustrating a system of patriarchal exploitation that cuts across class relations: 'even though marriage with a man from the capitalist class can raise a woman's standard of living, it does not make her a member of that class. She herself does not own the means of production. ... In the vast majority of cases, wives of bourgeois men whose marriage ends must earn their own living as wage or salaried workers. They therefore become concretely (with the additional handicaps of age and/or lack of professional training) the proletarians that they essentially were'.[10] Delphy argues that women's class position should be understood in terms of the institution of marriage, which she conceptualizes as a labour contract in which the husband's appropriation of unpaid labour from his wife constitutes a domestic mode of production and a patriarchal mode of exploitation. Hence she argues that the material basis of women's oppression lies not in capitalist but in patriarchal relations of production. The difficulty here, however, is that the category of patriarchy is assigned analytic independence *vis-à-vis* the capitalist mode of production, but we are not led to a systematic consideration of the relations between them.[11]

A general problem with the concept of patriarchy is that not only is it by and large resistant to exploration within a particular mode of production, but it is redolent of a universal and trans-historical oppression. So, to use the concept is frequently to invoke a generality of male domination without being able to specify historical limits, changes or differences. For a Marxist feminist approach, whose analysis must be grounded in historical analysis, its use will therefore present particular problems.

10. Christine Delphy, *The Main Enemy*, Women's Research and Resources Centre, London 1977, p.15.
11. See Michèle Barrett and Mary McIntosh, 'Christine Delphy: Towards a Materialist Feminism?', *Feminist Review*, no.1, 1979.

Before we turn to some general attempts to use the concept of patriarchy in a Marxist feminist theoretical framework, it is worth considering certain specific uses to which the term might be put. Gayle Rubin, for instance, makes the fruitful suggestion that the term patriarchy would be a more valuable one if its use were restricted to societies (and here she cites the nomadic tribes of Abraham's era) where one man wielded absolute power through a socially defined institution of fatherhood.[12] Similarly, it would be possible to argue for a use of the term to describe the ideological aspects of relationships that are predicated on the paradigm, for instance, of a father-daughter relationship. Thus Maria-Antonietta Macciocchi's analysis of female sexuality in the ideology of Italian fascism[13] seems to me to describe an ideological construction of women that might be termed 'patriarchal'. Perhaps Virginia Woolf's account of the pathological attempts of bourgeois fathers to insist on their daughters' dependence, financial and emotional, on themselves, also represents a legitimate use of the term.[14]

These examples, however, are relatively rare in recent theoretical work, which abounds with attempts to represent, more generally, contemporary capitalism as 'patriarchy'. These pose two major problems, as I shall try to illustrate below. First, patriarchy is posed as a system of domination completely independent of the organization of capitalist relations and hence the analyses fall into a universalistic, trans-historical mode which may shade into the biologism discussed earlier. Where attempts are made to constitute patriarchy as a system of male domination in relation to the capitalist mode of production, these frequently founder on the inflexibility and claims to autonomy to which the concept is prone. This problem persists even in the recent, sophisticated formulations of materialist feminism which

12. Gayle Rubin, 'The Traffic in Women: Notes on the "Political Economy" of Sex', in R. R. Reiter, ed., *Toward an Anthropology of Women*, New York 1975, p.168.
13. 'Female Sexuality in Fascist Ideology', *Feminist Review*, no.1, 1979.
14. *Three Guineas*, London 1938.

attempt to incorporate a psychoanalytic perspective. Second, the concept of patriarchy as presently constituted reveals a fundamental confusion, regrettably plain in discussion of it, between patriarchy as the rule of the father and patriarchy as the domination of women by men. Both of these problems can be seen in recent attempts to use the concept of patriarchy in conjunction with a Marxist analysis.

Zillah Eisenstein's collection, *Capitalist Patriarchy and the Case for Socialist Feminism*, includes under this rubric some interesting work on women's oppression and capitalism but ultimately reaches the dilemma of how to reconcile two theoretical approaches with rival claims. Eisenstein herself defines patriarchy as preceding capitalism, as resting today on the 'power of the male through sexual roles', and as institutionalized in the nuclear family. However it is unclear to what extent patriarchy, defined in this way, constitutes an autonomous system, since Eisenstein goes on to refer to it simply in terms of its functions for capital. 'Capitalism uses patriarchy and patriarchy is defined by the needs of capital.'[15] Such a statement can hardly co-exist with the claim that capitalism *is* a patriarchy, and in fact Eisenstein's ensuing analysis of domestic labour is couched extensively in terms of its functions for capital. Her use of the concept of patriarchy, therefore, is one that does not resolve the problem of the analytic independence of 'patriarchy' from capitalism: the analysis vacillates between the assertion of patriarchy as a system of male power external to capitalism and the argument that the organization of patriarchal relations is functional for capital.

Roisin McDonough and Rachel Harrison attempt explicitly to use the concept of patriarchy in a materialist context. Their editors write: 'although it is true that simply to address patriarchy as a concept is in some sense to take its

15. 'Developing a Theory of Capitalist Patriarchy', in Z. Eisenstein, ed., *Capitalist Patriarchy and the Case for Socialist Feminism*, New York 1979, p.28.

validity for granted, the aim in taking it up here is to displace it, to move the terms of its discussion away from the terrain of universalism and to reappropriate it for materialism, for an approach to women's situation in its historical specificity'. McDonough and Harrison regard patriarchy as requiring a two-fold definition: first, 'the control of women's fertility and sexuality in monogamous marriage' and second, 'the economic subordination of women through the sexual division of labour (and property)'. They argue that the patriarchal family as such has been eliminated but that patriarchy can be said to exist at present in the operation of these two processes. Their central thesis is that patriarchy as a concept can be historicized through the argument that, in capitalism, patriarchal relations assume a form dictated by capitalist relations of production: 'though women are placed simultaneously in two separate but linked structures, those of class and patriarchy, it is their class position which limits the conditions of the forms of patriarchy they will be subjected to'.[16] In practice this formulation reduces to an argument that the oppression of women in capitalism presents different contradictions for women, depending upon their social class. Social class, moreover, is ill-defined in this analysis, resting neither on a Marxist nor on a sociological foundation, for the authors argue that 'a woman inhabits her husband's class position, but not the equivalent relation to the means of production'. It is not clear to me what is being claimed here for the concept of patriarchy. For if patriarchal relations assume the form of class relations in capitalism, then however centrally the authors may pose patriarchal relations in the subordination of women, they do not resolve the question of the effectivity of patriarchy as the determinant of women's oppression in capitalism.

Annette Kuhn's paper, 'Structures of Patriarchy and Capital in the Family', from the same volume, constitutes an ambitious attempt to resolve some of these problems. Kuhn argues rightly that many analyses of women's oppression

16. 'Patriarchy and Relations of Production', in *Feminism and Materialism*, pp.11, 40, 36.

designate the family as the crucial site of oppression and yet reduce it to an entity that is itself the product of the playing out of forces whose real operations lie elsewhere. This tendency she ascribes to functionalism, which characterizes both sociological and Marxist accounts of the family. Such analyses, while claiming a crucial role for the family, in practice 'relegate it, paradoxically, to the status of what may be termed an empty signifier'. Kuhn's project is to demonstrate precisely the reverse, that the psychic and economic mechanisms of the family have an autonomy (or at least a relative autonomy) from capitalist relations. Patriarchy unites psychic and property relations, she argues, and it is by this means that the family gains its autonomous effectivity. Kuhn then presents an analysis of the psychic relations of the family, drawn from psycho-analytic theory, and an account of property relations in the family similar to that of Delphy. She argues that 'the family may be defined exactly as property relations between husbands and wives and those property relations in action', and she concludes that 'the family so defined provides the terms for psychic relations, for the production of sexed and class subjects for representations of relations of patriarchy and capital, that is, for the constitution of subjects in ideology'.

However, there is a fundamental difficulty in Kuhn's attempt to marry a psychoanalytic account of the construction of the gendered subject with an account of the family in terms of a labour contract between husbands and wives. This difficulty lies in a confusion as to whether patriarchy refers to the dominance of men over women or the rule of the father as such. Delphy argues straightforwardly that it is the exploitation of wives' labour by their husbands that constitutes patriarchy, and indeed she explicitly opposes the psychoanalytic position that women's oppres-sion lies in the rule of the father. Kuhn, in common with other writers using the concept of patriarchy, glosses over this central definitional problem, as can be seen in the following passage: 'patriarchy — the rule of the father — is a structure written into particular expressions of the sexual division of labour whereby property, the means of production of exchange values, is appropriated by men, and whereby this property relation informs household and family relations in such a way that men may appropriate the labour and the actual persons of women'.[17] This ambiguity as to the referent of the concept of patriarchy is a serious one. Although the concept may well describe forms of social organization in which economic and social power is vested in the father as such, it is not necessarily a helpful concept with which to explore the oppression of women in capitalist societies, and the difficulties with Marxist feminist work on patriarchy and capitalism illustrate this point. The use of the concept is more consistent in psychoanalytic writing, although the status of this perspective as an account of women's oppression is problematic and will be discussed in Chapter 2. It seems admissable in some contexts to refer to patriarchal ideology, describing specific aspects of male-female relations in capitalism, but as a noun the term 'patriarchy' presents insuperable difficulties to an analysis that attempts to relate women's oppression to the relations of production of capitalism. Rather different problems are presented by the concept of 'reproduction', to which I shall now turn.

Reproduction

The concept of 'reproduction' has in recent years been used as a crucial mechanism for relating women's oppression to the organization of production in different societies. There are, however, a number of serious problems attached to its use, not least perhaps (as with the concept of patriarchy) the difficulty in arriving at some consensus about its definition and object. The starting point of these analyses itself raises a difficulty in that what is proposed resembles at times a rather crude juxtaposition and conflation of two very different processes — the biological reproduction of the

17. 'Structures of Patriarchy and Capital in the Family', in *Feminism and Materialism*, pp.45, 65.

species and the need of any social formation to reproduce its own conditions of production.

Interest in the question of social reproduction has received a very strong impetus from Louis Althusser's 'Ideology and Ideological State Apparatuses'.[18] On the opening page of this essay, Althusser draws attention to Marx's letter to Kugelmann of 1868 in which it is remarked that 'every child knows that a social formation which did not reproduce the conditions of production at the same time as it produced would not last a year'. This passage, combined with Engels's formulation from *The Origin of the Family* — 'the determining factor in history is, in the last resort, the production and reproduction of immediate life. But this itself is of a twofold character. On the one hand, the production of the means of subsistence, of food, clothing and shelter and the tools requisite therefore; on the other, the production of human beings themselves, the propagation of the species'[19] — has led to a consideration of the extent to which women might occupy a specific role in the reproduction of the forces and relations of production.

There is clearly a problem in arguing that it is women's role in biological reproduction that underwrites their significance for social reproduction. Hindess and Hirst have objected that this revolves around 'an astonishing play on the word "reproduction"' and Mark Cousins has repeated this charge: 'the argument that a theory of reproduction must include childbirth is based simply on a pun'.[20] This criticism has cogency when applied to the undoubtedly sloppy uses of this concept found in some work, but it has perhaps been overcome in the attempt by Edholm, Harris and Young to clarify and separate the different levels of analysis in which the concept of reproduction can be used.[21]

18. Louis Althusser, *Lenin and Philosophy and Other Essays*, London 1971.
19. Frederick Engels, *The Origin of the Family, Private Property and the State*, New York 1972, p.26.
20. Barry Hindess and Paul Hirst, 'Mode of Production and Social Formation in PCMP: a Reply to John Taylor', *Critique of Anthropology*, no.8, 1977; Mark Cousins, 'Material Arguments and Feminism'.

These authors argue for three analytically distinct referents of the concept — social reproduction, reproduction of the labour force and human or biological reproduction. Although this separation is clearly useful — I would argue that it should be followed — it does not resolve the remaining theoretical problems. These concern first of all the danger of functionalism, into which such analyses frequently (although not necessarily) fall, and I shall deal with this problem below. Second, the question remains as to how far any such analysis can adequately explore the relationship between reproduction (in all three senses) and production. This problem is particularly acute where it is argued that relations of reproduction (presumably referring to biological reproduction) can be described as patriarchal and existing outside of capitalist relations of production.

These problems can be seen more clearly by looking briefly at some attempts to use the concept of 'reproduction' in an account of women's oppression. Marxism's traditional emphasis on the exploitative wage-contract at the heart of capitalist social relations, and its corresponding political emphasis on the exploitative wage contract at the heart of challenged by the development of a body of work exploring the significance of domestic labour as a form of work not governed by these relations. Wally Seccombe, an early contributor to what has become known as 'the domestic labour debate', argues that women's unpaid work in the home serves to reproduce both the forces and the relations of production: at an economic level the housewife's labour reproduces on a daily and generational basis the labour power of the worker, and at an ideological level it reproduces the relations of dominance and subordination required by capitalist production.[22] One of the chief problems of this argument, as critics were soon to point out, is that it underplays the extent to which 'the housewife' is often also a wage

21. Felicity Edholm, Olivia Harris and Kate Young, 'Conceptualizing Women', in *Critique of Anthropology*, nos. 9/10, 1977.
22. Wally Seccombe, 'The Housewife and her Labour under Capitalism', *New Left Review*, no.83, 1974.

labourer too, and hence does not deal with the contradictions between these two spheres of work.[23] Furthermore, although Seccombe himself did not formulate the problem in unduly reductionist terms, the type of analysis put forward in his essay did pave the way for a mechanical account of 'the functions for capital' of women's domestic oppression.

An example of this is the discussion provided by Olivia Adamson and her co-authors, who pursue the argument to the point where women's oppression is seen as both functional for, and created by, capitalist relations of production. Distinguishing between women's role in pre-capitalist societies, where their labour was an integral, direct part of social production, and capitalism, in which their labour in the home is privatized and outside social production, they argue that 'the struggle against capital *is* the struggle against domestic work and the struggle against domestic work *is* the struggle against capital'. Asserting that 'women's oppression derives not from family life as such, but from the capitalist relation itself', they conclude that a politically autonomous women's movement is symptomatic of petty-bourgeois reformism and regret the fact that 'the radical left has abandoned the leadership of this movement to the feminists'. This attempt to demonstrate a Marxist perspective on women's oppression simply conflates the sexual division of labour with the requirements of capital at different stages of capitalist accumulation. The authors explicitly oppose any argument that a sexual division of labour preceded capitalism, and do not address the problem of women's oppression in societies that have undergone socialist revolutions. Their argument rests on unpaid domestic labour and insecure, low-paid wage labour as the twin mechanisms whereby capitalism exploits not only women, but also the entire working class. Their assertion that the interests of women are identical with those of the working class rests on the argument that the low wages and dispensability of women wage workers enables capital to

23. See Margaret Coulson, Branka Magaš and Hilary Wainwright, 'Women and the Class Struggle', *New Left Review*, no.89, 1975.

'drive down wages below the value of labour power'.[24]

This analysis presents us in an extremely clear way with the problems of a reductionist Marxist approach to women's oppression. In charity, it should be seen in the context of a history of Marxist thought in which questions of gender relations and male dominance have long been ignored and marginalized. Reductionism and functionalism are difficulties that will recur in many analyses, and it is worth considering the general objections to formulations of this kind. Functionalism, where it occurs in Marxist as in other explanations, presents various dangers. Aside from the generic difficulty of establishing the imputed 'function' of a particular social process, there is the tendency to assume that any such function, once established, can explain the very existence of that process. This is the error of teleology — the view that the explanation of an object lies in a search for its original 'purpose'. It precludes the possibility that *no* purpose, or function, is relevant to our understanding, and it also precludes the possibility that the function an object now has is different from one it may have previously had. Hence, a functionalist approach necessarily militates against an historical account of social structures and processes. More importantly, from a Marxist point of view the danger of functionalist approaches lies in their over-emphasis on the smooth, at worst conspiratorial, reproduction of dominance and subordination and their failure to recognize the concrete historical conflicts and contradictions that characterize the formation and development of social relations. In seeing, as in their Marxist guises they normally do, the exploitation of one group by another as the unfolding of an inevitable plan, functionalists tend to ignore the historical struggles that have led to their own analyses in the first place.

These are clearly serious problems, but they should not in my view lead to the conclusion that any formulation couched in terms of functions is necessarily incorrect. As I shall try to

24. Olivia Adamson, Carol Brown, Judith Harrison and Judy Price, 'Women's Oppression Under Capitalism', *Revolutionary Communist*, no.5, 1976, pp.12, 42, 32.

show later, some processes are most usefully understood in these terms, if we can locate them in their historical context. Reductionism, however, has been a more fundamental problem in Marxist analysis of women's oppression. This consists in arguing that such and such a phenomenon may appear in one set of terms, but is really only explicable in another. The problem with the argument that 'women's oppression is functional for capital' is not so much functionalism as *reductionism* — in this case because gender relations are reduced to an effect of the operation of capital. This reduction is perhaps most commonly encountered in the style of analysis now known as economism, in which phenomena of an ideological kind are reduced to their supposed economic determinants. In the case of women's oppression, this reduction is particularly fraught. It is not clear why any relationship should obtain between specific forms of male dominance and, for instance, the interests of capital, or at least this cannot be seen as self-evident in any existing Marxist analysis. Furthermore, the existence of different forms of a comparable male dominance in other modes of production and periods of history makes such a reduction implausible. So when any argument is put forward along these lines we need to be very clear as to the grounds on which such a reduction is made and these, as yet, remain unconvincing. More frequently, in fact, the reduction is assumed, or asserted, rather than argued or justified.

Although this problem of reductionism has characterized what we might legitimately regard as 'vulgar' Marxist explanations of women's oppression, it remains, perhaps, a residual danger in more consciously feminist attempts to use the concept of reproduction as an analytical tool in an account of the position of women. Veronica Beechey's work on female wage labour represents a decisive break with earlier Marxist formulations and constitutes an impressive, and influential, attempt to construe the problem in distinctively feminist terms. For while she argues, forcefully, for an analysis of female wage labour in terms of the advantages such a cheap and flexible source of labour power presents to capital, she stresses that this analysis will only hold if we presuppose a particular form of the family: 'the existence of the sexual division of labour which consigns women to the family and the patriarchal ideology embodied in it must be presupposed in order that female labour can constitute these advantages to capital'.[25] Although Beechey does not specify the 'patriarchal' character of the sexual division of labour it is clear that her position represents an important distance from those formulations of Marxism which conflate the oppression of women with the needs of capital.

Beechey correctly criticizes Marx for uncritically connecting the employment of women (and children) with the development of machine production requiring less muscular strength from its workers. Citing the fact that in some societies women traditionally undertake heavy physical work, she points to the 'naturalistic' assumptions underlying Marx's argument. Her own argument makes several important points. Female wage labour is advantageous to capital because it is very cheap. Women's wages reflect a situation where women are paid at a rate below the value of labour power, and/or the value of women's labour power is lower than that of men. That this is advantageous to capital is obvious, since it depresses wage levels overall. Beechey stresses that the existence of the family must be presupposed for women to present these advantages to capital, and goes on to argue that the position of married women workers is analogous to that of semi-proletarianized or migrant workers.

This argument hinges upon a notion that the wage paid to women and migrant workers does not cover the costs of their reproduction. In the case of migrant workers the position has been succinctly stated by Berger and Mohr,[26] who draw

25. Veronica Beechey, 'Women and Production: a Critical Analysis of Some Sociological Theories of Women's Work', in *Feminism and Materialism;* and 'Some Notes on Female Wage Labour in the Capitalist Mode of Production', *Capital and Class,* no.3, 1977.
26. John Berger and Jean Mohr, *A Seventh Man,* Harmondsworth 1975.

attention to the fact that it is the poorer rural society that pays for the production and reproduction of the workers until the age of, say, eighteen, and again becomes responsible for their maintenance if they are returned to the subsistence economy by illness or redundancy. In the case of the married woman worker, given the National Insurance and Social Security arrangements by which she is assumed to be the dependant of her husband, her costs of reproduction are met in times of unemployment from the husband's wage. Hence the individual capitalist who employs a married woman, exploiting the assumption that such work is secondary to her main role as wife and mother, can pay wages so low that they do not even cover the day-to-day costs of reproducing her as a worker. Women, because of the existence of a family structure and ideology which renders them financially dependent on their husbands (or cohabitants), can be paid wages lower than the value of labour power.

Beechey's argument represents an interesting and fruitful advance in the attempt to theorize women's work in capitalist production, and usefully insists on the connection between women as wage workers and the history and ideology of the family. There are, however, crucial questions unresolved in this analysis, and they hinge on problems entailed in the concept of reproduction. First, it is unclear to me why it should be in the interests of capital generally to pay women wages that require the payment of a larger wage to their husbands to enable them to support their wives. Although it may be in the interest of an individual capital to employ women in this way, it is the capitalist class as a whole which ultimately supports this arrangement. This point highlights an important difference between the case of migrant workers and married women workers. For although metropolitan capital clearly benefits from the temporary labour of migrant workers from peripheral rural economies, the advantages are less clear where the costs of female reproduction are borne by capital and the state (and cannot be met outside the economy altogether). Nor is it clear precisely why it should be women who occupy this disadvantageous position as wage workers. As in the case of low-paid black and immigrant workers, an understanding of the mechanisms of exploitation does not necessarily constitute an explanation of why it should be this particular category of workers that is exploited in this way. This would surely require far more detailed analysis of the extent to which, particularly in the crucial struggles over wages in the nineteenth century, the interests of women workers were subsumed under and defeated by those of the organized male working class.[27]

Analysis of the concept of reproduction has pinpointed certain dangers in Marxist feminist analyses that employ it. It tends to conflate women's role in the biological reproduction of the species with the historically specific question of their role in ensuring the reproduction of male labour power and in maintaining the relations of dominance and subordinacy of capitalist production. Furthermore, it has not yet adequately explained how and why it is that *women* should be assigned any special role in these latter two processes of reproduction.

One way in which these problems might be avoided is to insert a discussion of gender relations, even of 'patriarchy', into the analysis of social reproduction. Maureen Mackintosh, in a review of Claude Meillassoux's book, *Femmes, Greniers et Capitaux*, argues that Meillassoux fails to consider, in his analysis of the use to capitalism of domestic production of a pre-capitalist type, the extent to which relations of reproduction are in fact 'patriarchal'. She states quite clearly that 'the characteristic relation of human reproduction is patriarchy, that is, the control of women, especially of their sexuality and fertility, by men'.[28] Mackintosh is correctly arguing against the reduction of

27. See Michèle Barrett and Mary McIntosh, 'The "Family Wage": Some Problems for Socialists and Feminists', *Capital and Class*, no.11, 1980.
28. Maureen Mackintosh, 'Reproduction and Patriarchy: a Critique of Meillassoux, *Femmes, Greniers et Capitaux*', *Capital and Class*, no.2, 1977.

struggles over human reproduction to an analysis of social production and reproduction. But if this reduction is a problem, so too is the separation of these two sets of relations. Lucy Bland and others, in their suggestively titled paper 'Women "Inside and Outside" the Relations of Production', push this separation yet further, to the point where the reproduction of labour-power is construed in different terms from capitalist production. They argue that 'women's overall responsibility for the maintenance and reproduction of the labour force cannot be adequately "thought" through the categories of capital alone. Women's role in the home, from the point of view of capital, cannot be understood without attention to the specific historical and ideological articulations of the sexual division of labour, in relation to particular forms of "the family" through which women's sexuality is organized for reproductive ends, and the effectivity, in the construction of femininity, of the ideologies of domesticity and romantic love'.[29] This formulation highlights the problems inherent in a Marxist feminist use of the concept of patriarchy, as well as the difficulty of using an analysis of social reproduction in conjunction with an account of patriarchy. Are we really to separate reproduction from reproduction in this way, but also to elide biological production (seen in terms of gender relations) and social reproduction (seen in terms of the conditions of existence of capitalist production)?

The problem here might be defined as one of analytic 'dualism'.[30] Certain aspects of, say, household and familial organization can be analysed with a feminist concept of patriarchy (sexuality, fertility, ideology), while others can be slotted into an analysis of the need to reproduce the labour force on which capitalist production depends (domestic labour, child-rearing, socialization). My own view is that a

29. Lucy Bland, Charlotte Brunsdon, Dorothy Hobson and Janice Winship, 'Women "Inside and Outside" the Relations of Production', in *Women Take Issue*, edited by the Women's Studies Group of the Centre for Contemporary Cultural Studies, London 1978.
30. See, for instance, Veronica Beechey, 'On Patriarchy', *Feminist Review*, no.3, 1979.

coherent dualistic formulation would be preferable to this rather arbitrary separation of different elements of reproduction into two distinct explanatory frameworks, with the inevitable slippage that occurs when the two are brought together.

Attempts to combine an analysis of social reproduction with an analysis of patriarchal human reproduction represent the fundamental problem Marxist feminism faces. The concept of social reproduction, as so far elaborated, is so closely tied to an account of class relations at the root of capitalist production that it cannot, by fiat, be rendered compatible with a serious consideration of male dominance. The problem carries with it a contentious history of dispute between Marxism and feminism, and in every formulation we hear the echoes of voices on either side claiming analytic primacy for class or for gender. One obvious way in which the controversy surfaces is in the discussions over how women should be located in an account of the class structure. Are the class affiliations of women as tangential as Millett claims, or can we say that women's oppression is materially different between the different classes of capitalist society? These questions are taken up in detail in Chapter 4, but it is here, in the historic debate between Marxist and feminist interpretations of society, that they have their intellectual origin and divisive political force.

Ideology

It has been argued that recent developments in the theory of ideology provide a route out of this impasse. The feminist insistence that Marxism must take account of women's oppression, and develop arguments concerning its specific form under capitalism, has coincided historically with a revolution in the Marxist theory of ideology. Feminists have taken issue with the position of Engels that the entry of women into production could of itself end male dominance, and have argued against the view that the family as the site of women's oppression is merely a relic of the pre-capitalist era.[31] They have argued to the contrary that the oppression of women and the sexual division of labour are entrenched in capitalist relations of production and must be analysed in that light. Marxist feminists have argued that Marxism must take account of women's domestic labour, their poorly paid and insecure position as wage-labourers, and the familial ideology which contributes to their oppression.

At the same time there has been a fundamental shift in Marxism's theoretical approach to the concept of ideology. Here again, the work of Louis Althusser has been crucial to this development. Althusser rejects equally the notion of ideology as a distortion or manipulation of reality by the ruling class, and the view that ideology is simply a mechanical reflection (in ideas) of a determining economic base. He locates ideology as a practice enjoying relative autonomy from the economic level (which, however, is determining 'in the last instance'). He stresses ideology as 'lived experience', as representing 'the imaginary relationship of individuals to their real conditions of existence', and emphasizes that individual subjects are constructed and reproduced in ideology.[32]

Of course Althusser's contribution to the attempt to rethink the concept of ideology forms only one part of a wide-ranging challenge to economism that has reverberated within Marxism for a number of years. Indeed this has gone beyond the confines of Marxism itself, as can be seen in the rise and popularity of subjectivist sociologies (phenomenology and ethnomethodology, for example) seeking to explain 'reality' in terms of the negotiation of inter-subjective social situations. Some of these last developments have claimed to be particularly helpful in describing male-female transactions, and to be relevant to an understanding of gender identity and gendered interaction.[33]

The feminist challenge to Marxism and the critique of

31. See Margaret Benston, 'The Political Economy of Women's Liberation', *Monthly Review*, September 1969.
32. See 'Ideology and Ideological State Apparatuses' and 'Freud and Lacan', in *Lenin and Philosophy and Other Essays*.

economism in Marxism have not merely 'coincided' historically. There has been a tendency to locate the oppression of women principally at the level of ideology, and it is easy to see how arguments for the importance and autonomy of ideological processes have been seized on by feminists concerned to emphasize the importance of gender division in the capitalist social formation. The rejection of economism has led to a radical re-prioritizing of ideology, in which the question of gender division can apparently be situated. Hence it has become possible, within a new form of Marxism, to accommodate the oppression of women as a relatively autonomous element of the social formation.

The influence of this theoretical revolution on Marxist feminist work has been considerable. It has opened up for 'legitimate' discussion the question of the construction of masculine and feminine subjects and the relation of the sexual division of labour to capitalist production. It has facilitated the feminist challenge to an orthodox Marxism that relegated the oppression of women to the theoretical, and hence political, sidelines. This influence has been demonstrated in the emphasis given in recent Marxist feminist work to the ideological construction of gendered subjects and the attempt to rethink psychoanalytic theory from a Marxist feminist perspective. This work has taken two major directions: the exploration of familial relations and the development of masculine and feminine subjectivity, and the analysis of representations of gender difference in cultural production. As I suggest in Chapters 2 and 3, much of this work is enlightening and promising, yet it has not to date been adequately historicized and one may view with a certain suspicion its claims to be a materialist account. In the absence of work relating these processes to specific historical relations of production, it remains subject to the risk of universalism.[34] Moreover, the processes being described tend to be located at the level of ideology, albeit an ideology which

33. See H. Garfinkle, *Studies in Ethnomethodology*, New Jersey 1967; and J. H. Gagnon and W. S. Simon, *Sexual Conduct: The Social Sources of Human Sexuality*, Chicago 1973.

has materiality and at least a relative autonomy, and the weight one gives to such accounts must depend upon whether or not one accepts the underlying theory of ideology.

If it is the case that developments in Marxist feminist theory are indebted to the Althusserian and post-Althusserian shift in the theory of ideology, it is perhaps also true that this influence has remained largely unremarked. These developments have been assumed, and drawn on, rather than discussed explicitly in terms of their relevance to a feminist approach. One person who has attempted such a discussion, laying bare for comment a relationship between the two developments, is Rosalind Coward. In *Language and Materialism* Coward and her co-author, John Ellis, argue for a new object of knowledge, 'the scientific knowledge of the subject', in a new 'materialist theory of signification'. They correctly object both to the transposition of conventional Marxist categories on to the terrain of psychoanalytic work, and to the view that psychoanalysis can be 'tacked on' to Marxism as an account of gender construction. They see ideology as a practice of representation; it is the way an individual lives his or her role in the social totality. Ideology therefore participates in the construction of that individual, and it succeeds insofar as it can produce acceptance of existing power relations as 'natural'. Coward and Ellis reject economic determinism as 'the idea that economic practice is more important than political or ideological processes in the social process'; and they favour an attempt to see the articulation of the three practices (political, ideological and economic) as depending upon the specific historical conjuncture.[35] In seeing the three practices as equally important, Coward and Ellis reject not only the strong form of economic determinism (ideology as a reflection of the

34. Some recent American work looks more promising in this respect. See Nancy Chodorow, *The Reproduction of Mothering*, Berkeley 1978; and Dorothy Dinnerstein, *The Mermaid and the Minotaur*, New York 1977 (published in England as *The Rocking of the Cradle and the Ruling of the World*).

35. *Language and Materialism*, London 1977, p.69.

economic base) but also any determinate relationship between the economic and the ideological — and hence, the Althusserian formulation of determination by the economic 'in the last instance'. Theirs is in fact an argument for absolute rather than relative autonomy of the ideological, as is made clear in Coward's recent discussion of the work of Cutler, Hindess, Hirst and Hussain.

Coward's article is worth discussing in some detail, since she makes explicit the connections between the work of Cutler and his collaborators and some important recent Marxist feminist work.[36] Coward argues that these writers, although not dealing with feminism, are 'potentially exciting for socialist feminism'. They 'may provide a space theoretically, and, hopefully, politically, for women's political struggles to assume a centrality which has not been possible before within socialism'. Now why should this be the case? Coward sketches out the limitations of previous Marxism, which marginalized women in two ways. First, in insisting on the primacy of the labour/capital contradiction, it rendered women irrelevant unless they were engaged in productive wage labour. Second, in insisting on economic determination, it saw women's oppression as merely an (unimportant) ideological effect. Coward argues that the rejection of economic determination is premised on certain theoretical advances which are important for feminism. In this argument the only thing to be presupposed is definite social conditions of existence; the concept of 'mode of production' is harmful and misleading, and the primacy of the economic is no longer politically necessary. All this is based on a point taken up forcefully by Coward, that we have no need of recourse to 'epistemological theories' (such as 'determination in the last instance'). She defines epistemological theories as follows: 'epistemological theories are theories of knowledge. They presuppose a distinct realm of concepts and a distinct realm of objects, existing outside the

---

36. 'Rethinking Marxism' (Discussion of Anthony Cutler, Barry Hindess, Paul Hirst and Athar Hussain, *Marx's 'Capital' and Capitalism Today*), *m/f*, no.2, 1978, pp.96, 91, 92.

realm of concepts but knowable by them. They therefore assume a definite and privileged knowledge-process, by which these objects are presented in discourse'. Coward rejects epistemological theories as either empiricist or rationalist, in that they assume a 'real' world which can be reflected in some corresponding discourse. She argues that this rejection has important implications for feminist analysis, since it provides a route out of the fruitless debate (as to whether the position of women serves the interests of capitalism) which does not have recourse to problematic concepts like patriarchy. 'The family, for example, need no longer be seen as a monolithic unity with a correspondence or not to the capitalist mode of production. Instead it becomes possible to analyse sexual division appearing in different institutions, and practices — state (welfare) legislation, employment legislation, sexual practices — some of which may be deemed to provide the conditions of existence of the relations of production which now exist... There is no general and essential economic existence of the relations of production — there is only the particularity in which they are secured, a particularity in which the conditions of existence are all-important.' Coward argues that, according to this perspective, 'struggle within political and ideological instances assumes an importance which no other socialist theory has ever offered'. This might of course be true, but it is hardly good reason to accept the underlying theoretical position if it is otherwise untenable. The first problem to note is that within the terms of the theory itself, although the privilege of economic relations has been rejected, there is a tendency for 'conditions of existence', however carefully particularized, to assume a similar status. More importantly perhaps, we can question whether problems of determination, either between the economic, political and ideological 'levels', or between the capitalist mode of production and the oppression of women, are to be resolved by simply abandoning any notion of 'reality'. The position taken by Cutler, Hindess, Hirst and Hussain, and endorsed by Coward, is based on the logical necessity of rejecting the distinction between 'knowledge' and 'the real'. Now there is clearly a problem here, since the categories through which we appropriate 'the real' in thought are discursively constructed rather than given by the real. It is therefore correct, although tautological to the point of banality, to observe that *our knowledge* of the real cannot exist outside discourse. But it is a very long way from this to the argument that, as Rosalind Coward puts it, to privilege one discourse as reflecting the real is inevitably dogmatic.

This is partly a matter of emphasis: Cutler and his associates are not suggesting that nothing exists outside discourse (which would be a rejection of ontological realism), but that we cannot reliably build a knowledge which enjoys a truthful relationship to the real (a rejection of epistemological realism). From an analytic point of view, however, the concession of ontological reality is useless if we can do nothing with it in terms of our knowledge of the real world, and hence it is easy to see how objective reality is consistently denied in this approach. Such a claim does not stem from analytic modesty, but from an extraordinary arrogance. Timpanaro, although writing in a different context, makes a pertinent point here: 'the results of scientific research teach us that man occupies a marginal position in the universe; that for a very long time life did not exist on earth, and that its origin depended on very special conditions; that human thought is conditioned by determinate anatomical and physiological structures, and is clouded or impeded by determinate pathological alterations of these; and so on. But let us consider these results as mere contents of our thoughts as it cogitates or of our activity as it experiments and modifies nature, let us emphasize that they do not exist outside our thought and our activity, and the trick is done: external reality has been conjured away, and not by an antiquated humanism hostile to science, but instead with all the blessings of science and of modernity'.[37]

It should be noted that this rejection of 'the real' represents

37. Sebastiano Timpanaro, *On Materialism*, London 1975, p.36.

a radical break with the Marxism of Althusser, and does not necessarily follow from his reconceptualization of ideology. Indeed it heralds a reversion to phenomenologism in such a strong form that its compatibility with any recognizable form of Marxism is dubious. For the problem which characterizes all social science — that is, our 'knowledge' is itself an object of inquiry — cannot be overcome by dissolving the knowable real world into our discourse about it. Indeed the position put forward here by Coward is no resolution or reconciliation of Marxism and feminism, since the 'Marxism' that it invokes has departed so radically from a materialist analysis of history as to constitute a quite different body of ideas.[38]

One way of approaching this question is to consider the place of 'the real' in Marxist theory. It has been argued that Marxism is essentially a 'realist' science. It is in a fundamental sense predicated upon the notion that there exist real relations in the world of which we can have reliable knowledge. Indeed it is hard to see that Marxism's political claims could be advanced were this not the case. Roy Bhaskar and others have argued, from the point of view of the philosophy of science, that Marxism necessarily represents a realist science whose object is the analysis of relations and the collective expressions of those relations. Bhaskar argues, in my view correctly, that society, as an object of inquiry, cannot be read off the empirical world or reconstructed from subjective experience. It consists of structures of relations which individuals reproduce (albeit unintentionally): 'the conception I am proposing is that people, in their conscious activity, for the most part unconsciously reproduce (and occasionally transform) the structures governing their substantive activities of production. Thus people do not marry to reproduce the nuclear family or work to sustain the capitalist economy. Yet it is nevertheless the unintended consequence (and inexorable result) of, as it is also a necessary condition for, their

38. This is not a proprietorial statement on my part — some adherents of this approach now agree (verbally) that it is 'not Marxist'.

activity'.[39] Bhaskar argues that such an analysis, based on the reproduction or transformation of structures of relatively enduring relations, allows for an account of historical change (as well as clearly allowing for society as a possible and legitimate object of knowledge).

From this position it can be seen that the definition of concepts is crucial. A first step in the direction of any realist analysis must be the construction of definitions that have an explanatory rather than descriptive character. In a sense the various problems and confusions discussed in the uses of concepts such as 'patriarchy' and 'reproduction' result from the absence of systematic definitional work and the *ad hoc* usages that are its result. Marxist feminist theory is at present attempting to constitute a coherent perspective from various fragmentary bodies of work, and it is at present in an early stage with many crucial problems still unresolved. The process of critique is clearly an essential one, but there is a pressing need to formulate new concepts that are adequate to the object of Marxist feminist inquiry. In the discussion above I have perhaps been concerned more with the possibilities of developing Marxist theory than with developing existing feminist theory. One of the major problems for Marxist feminist theory emerges here. In Marxism we can scrutinize and criticize a body of theory and analysis that already exists as a coherent theoretical perspective, albeit one that has historically neglected the question of gender division in its account of the development of capitalism. I have argued that recent theoretical 'advances' in Marxism, which may appear to facilitate a prioritization of gender division, are in fact no solution to the problem of the relationship between Marxism and feminism. Whilst they appear to rescue sexual politics from their marginality to Marxist analysis, in fact they do so at the expense of any possibility of specifying determinate relations in a real world. Hence, although Althusser's reconceptualization of ideology has been extremely fruitful

39.   Roy Bhaskar, *The Possibility of Naturalism*, Brighton 1979, p.44.

for Marxist feminist theory, in that it has effectively challenged the mechanistic concept used by earlier Marxists and has asserted the importance of gender in the construction of individual subjects, the rejection by some post-Althusserians of all determinate relations is not at all useful, in my view.

Marxist feminist theory encounters rather different problems in its relation to feminism. Feminist theory of the kind proposed by Millett or Delphy might be said to constitute an internally consistent theoretical approach. Yet in posing patriarchy as either completely independent of capitalism, or as the dominant system of power relations, it completely fails to provide an analysis of women's oppression in a society characterized by capitalist relations of production. In rejecting this position, Marxist feminists have to rely on political imperatives stemming from experience of oppression and feminist activity directed against male domination. In the absence of a body of coherent analysis of women's oppression under capitalism, we have to work towards this through insights gained from political work. Undoubtedly much of the impetus towards the development of Marxist feminist theory has come from feminists who are active in the women's liberation movement, and yet concerned to analyse the extent to which women's oppression relates to the specific historical organization of social relations as a whole. Hence although driven by crucially important political motivations, Marxist feminist theory is still at a relatively early stage in formulating a perspective which challenges, but benefits from, the more developed science of Marxism.

In discussing the concepts of patriarchy, reproduction and ideology as they have been used in Marxist feminist work I have tried to make several points. First, that all three have been of central importance in delineating Marxist feminist concerns. Second, that they expose some of the fundamental controversies underlying this work. This is particularly true of patriarchy and reproduction, which present the opposition between Marxism and feminism, and do not easily lend themselves to a reconciliation, although this has been attempted. Third, all three concepts are used with widely differing meanings and some clarification of the various usages is imperative. The discussion has tended so far to be somewhat critical, first of the original sex/class dichotomy, and later of the claims that this has been transcended in developing the theory of ideology. Such a critical exercise is perhaps essential in order to locate the discussion in this book. In the following chapters I shall attempt to cover several areas in which Marxist feminist work has made important advances in our understanding, both historical and contemporary, of women's oppression. In the conclusion I shall return to the central question of the relationship of capitalism to women's oppression and the possibilities for women's liberation in capitalist societies.

The focus of this book, as I have already indicated, is women's oppression in contemporary Britain. However, this emphasis should be seen in terms of the guidelines I shall be following throughout the discussion. Briefly they can be summarized as follows.

The oppression of women in contemporary British capitalism must be seen in the light of the enduring oppression of women throughout the world as we know it. Although the book will be concerned to emphasize the context of this oppression in contemporary capitalism, it must be stressed that male domination, and the struggles of women against it, precede and go beyond that context. As Gayle Rubin so refreshingly puts it, 'no analysis of the reproduction of labour power under capitalism can explain foot-binding, chastity belts, or any of the incredible array of Byzantine, fetishized indignities, let alone the more ordinary ones, which have been inflicted upon women in various times and places'.[40] This point is particularly important in the light of attempts to reduce women's oppression completely to the operations of capitalism. I shall argue later that not only

40. See Gayle Rubin, 'The Traffic in Women', p.163.

is socialist revolution not a sufficient cause of women's liberation, but that certain important changes could be achieved under capitalism.

Second, a major aim of this book will be to address in some detail the relations between the economic and ideological processes of women's oppression. Although I will argue against the view that women's oppression is solely ideological, the role of familial and domestic ideology is considerable. Also it is important to stress that no clear separation can be made between the economic and the ideological. Relations of production, grounded as they are in a deeply ideological division of labour, cannot be investigated through economic categories alone. At this point it is interesting to consider the comparison between women workers and other groups of workers, such as black immigrants, whose position in the division of labour is to some extent constituted in ideological terms. The capitalist division of labour, to which I shall pay considerable attention, is not determined by technical requirements alone.

Third, I shall discuss some of the historical material now accumulated on the changes in women's position during and since the transition to capitalism. It is clear from studies already undertaken that our present assumptions of the male breadwinner and dependent wife are to some extent the outcome of struggle between the different interests of men and women. In this context the changing form of family organization will be significant. An historical approach of this kind, even when concerned with struggles over the reproduction of the working class, need not exclude certain types of functionalist explanation, as I shall argue later.

The substantive material to be dealt with reflects the questions to which the women's liberation movement has paid attention. The oppression of women under capitalism is grounded in a set of relations between several elements. Of these perhaps the most crucial are the economic organization of households and its accompanying familial ideology, the division of labour and relations of production, the educational system and the operations of the state. Yet the continuance and the entrenched nature of this oppression cannot be understood without a consideration of the cultural processes in which men and women are represented differently — created and recreated as gendered human subjects. Nor can it be understood without an analysis of sexuality and gender identity, and the complex question of the relationship between sexuality and biological reproduction as it affects both women and men. These issues have been taken up in various women's liberation campaigns and with good reason, for they are central to the oppression of women today.

2
Femininity, Masculinity and Sexual Practice

Sexuality is a notoriously elusive object of study: it slides under our eyes from biology to poetry and back again. Simone de Beauvoir recalls that 'sometimes, before giving me a book to read, my mother would pin a few pages together; in Wells's *The War of the Worlds* I found a whole chapter had been placed under the ban. I never took the pins out, but I often wondered: what's it all about?[1] Her discovery that the secret so closely guarded by adults contained comical physiological indecencies rather than cosmic radiance was, she reports, instrumental in her disillusionment with the grown-ups — it reduced the universe to a trivial day-to-day level.

For feminists the disillusionment with received ideas about sexuality has not only served to knock men down to size, it has generated a major element of the anger that drives the women's liberation movement on. Co-existing with a persuasive popular ideology of romantic love are the brutal facts of rape, domestic violence, pornography, prostitution, a denial of female sexual autonomy and horrifying practices such as clitoridectomy. It is, perhaps, not surprising that feminism has, at least in the movement's recent history, given a central place to the sexual abuse of women. It has insisted on the political character of sexuality, on the unequal power of those involved in sexual relationships. In this respect the contemporary women's

1. *Memoirs of a Dutiful Daughter*, London 1963, p.82.

movement, insisting at every turn that 'the personal is political' can truly be said to have established 'sexual politics' as a significant area of struggle. This achievement is predicated upon a knowledge that sexual relationships are political because they are socially constructed and therefore could be different. A central element in this argument is recognition of the distinction between the physical characteristics of males and females and the personality and behavioural characteristics deemed 'masculine' and 'feminine' in specific cultural and historical situations.

This distinction has proved crucial for feminist thought. Margaret Mead's revelatory *Sex and Temperament in Three Primitive Societies* demonstrated in 1935 that the qualities we 'naturally' think of as masculine, or feminine, may be turned upside-down in other cultures.[2] Researchers on sexual identity, such as Stoller and Money,[3] drew attention to the fact that in cases of children whose sex had been incorrectly assigned at birth the medical profession commonly decided that it was easier to undertake surgery rather than attempt to eradicate several years of social gender conditioning. Ann Oakley's *Sex, Gender and Society*,[4] presenting these arguments and a wide range of cross-cultural evidence to support them, has been highly influential. The distinction between sex and gender, an important step in the understanding of women's position, is now widely used and accepted both within and beyond the feminist literature.

I

If 'sexual politics' has been established as a significant area of struggle in contemporary life, the credit for this must lie with the major contribution made by early radical feminism. Even the titles of these works — *Sexual Politics, The Dialectic of Sex, The Female Eunuch, Vaginal Politics, The Body Politic* — display a concern with the question of

2. New York 1963.
3. John Money and Patricia Tucker, *Sexual Signatures: On Being a Man or a Woman*, London 1976, p.100.
4. London 1972.

physical sexuality as central to the oppression of women.[5]
The media have trivialized women's liberation, as feminists
rightly complain, by their constant harping on our supposed
obsessions with sex and our alleged inability to distinguish
between sexism and sexuality, but in taking up those issues
they have done no more than reflect a central political
concern of the women's movement. The disruption of the
'Miss World' competition and the plastering of advertisements with 'This Degrades Women' stickers all represent
significant elements of recent feminist political activity.
Indeed these are the issues on which, perhaps, feminists are
least divided. The massive demonstrations in defence of the
1967 Abortion Act have brought more women on to the
streets of Britain than any other demand. The other two
major issues of struggle in the politics of sexuality — rape
and domestic violence against women — have been accepted
as fundamental priorities of all women's liberationists and
have also attracted some support, both moral and financial,
from the liberal community at large.

The radical feminist analysis of sexual politics has
consistently stressed that the sexual abuse of women is
symptomatic of a wider oppression and control of women by
men. One of the major achievements of Kate Millett's *Sexual
Politics* was her demonstration that the representation of
male sexuality in writers such as Lawrence and Mailer
rested on a scornful and manipulative attitude to women
which, she argued, the authors shared with the male
characters they constructed. In general terms the argument
describes sexuality, with variations along a continuum of
masculine aggression (from the celebration of penetration to
the brutality of rape), as the site in which male power and
male supremacy are expressed. Consideration of the
question of rape, to take just one example, cannot but support
this argument. For despite the popular view that rape is the

5. Kate Millett, *Sexual Politics*, London 1972; Shulamith Firestone, *The
Dialectic of Sex*, London 1973; Germaine Greer, *The Female Eunuch*,
London 1971; Ellen Frankfort, *Vaginal Politics*, New York 1973;
Michelene Wandor, ed., *The Body Politic: Writings from the Women's
Liberation Movement in Britain 1969-1972*, London 1972.

consequence of men's inability to control an unbiddable sexual drive, the evidence suggests that in a very large proportion of cases, rape involves forms of brutality and deliberate humiliation of the victim that are not necessarily 'sexual'. Add to this the facts that, in Britain at least, rape within marriage does not legally exist, and that rape trials frequently pivot on an interrogation of the victim's chastity and respectability, and it becomes clear that the issue of rape must be seen in the context of a much broader view of women's oppression. Carol and Barry Smart have, in addition, shown that rape has secondary oppressive consequences for women in that it is often used as a rationale for curtailing women's freedom to go out (at night, unescorted).[6] The logic of this analysis leads to Susan Brownmiller's position that 'all men are potential rapists'.[7] Much as this conclusion has been resisted by men, both liberal and illiberal on the question of feminism, it contains an inescapable grain of truth. For if sexual practice is the area in which systematic inequalities of power between men and women are played out, then all men are in a position to exercise this power (even if only by mild pressure rather than brutal coercion), whether or not they are inclined to do so.

Radical feminist thought on sexuality has tended to argue that the wider context of sexual politics, male supremacy, is grounded in men's attempt to secure control over biological reproduction. Here lies an explanation for the construction of femininity in patriarchy, with its twin images of woman as, on the one hand, the sexual property of men and, on the other, the chaste mothers of their children. The madonna/whore dichotomy runs through western patriarchal culture as the means whereby men have sought to ensure both the sanctity and inheritance of their families and their extra-familial sexual pleasure. Hence at the same time as opposing the sexual abuse of women, their de-personification into objects

6. Carol Smart and Barry Smart, 'Accounting for Rape: Reality and Myth in Press Reporting' in their collection, *Women, Sexuality and Social Control*, London 1978.
7. Susan Brownmiller, *Against Our Will: Men, Women and Rape*, London 1975.

for male satisfaction, feminists have opposed the reduction of women to breeding machines. This argument underlies one of the women's movement's most frequently articulated demands — the right to control our own bodies — and its hostility to the control exercised by the medical profession, the church and the state over women's reproductive functions. This is how feminism locates the struggle over abortion rights and male hostility to lesbianism in particular and non-reproductive sex in general.

It is certainly true that many aspects of sexual relations are simply irreducible to questions of class. Engels, for instance, in arguing a very strong materialist case for the enforced monogamy of bourgeois wives,[8] leaves us with an analysis that is virtually incapable of explaining how or why male control over women's fertility should exist among the proletariat where the inheritance of property is not at issue. Nevertheless, we cannot regard class as a tangential factor and see all women as equally vulnerable to sexual violence from men since, although battering and rape exist in all social classes, material resources may affect a woman's freedom, or lack of it, to remove herself from danger. (A woman whose car breaks down late at night in a rough or isolated area may well realize how much protection it usually gives her.)

Nor is it adequate to point to the oppression of lesbians as an indicator of patriarchy without at the same time providing an explanation of the even greater hostility towards male homosexuality. Homosexual relations between men are still subject to legal restrictions which have never applied to women in this country; sodomy was a capital crime until 1861 and in Ireland it still carries a potential sentence of life imprisonment. Equally, however horrifying it is to discover that clitoridectomy was seen by some nineteenth-century surgeons as an appropriate treatment for a variety of female disorders, it is also the case that castration, hormone injections and aversion therapy have

8. Frederick Engels, *The Origin of the Family, Private Property and the State*, New York 1972.

been inflicted more often on male masturbators, sex offenders and homosexual men.[9] While some definitions of the concept of patriarchy do allow for these oppressive relations between men, as well as between men and women,[10] the radical feminist project of understanding sexuality and biological reproduction solely in terms of male supremacy over women has led to an unwillingness to consider these problems seriously.

It is also worth questioning the implication in such analyses that women are inevitably the passive victims of male power. In considering the ideology of female sexuality that was integral to Italian fascism, Macciocchi has questioned the view that women passively consented to being made the breeding machines of Mussolini's war programme. She argues that women actively colluded in this and that to deny it, absolving women from their responsibilities, is 'just another way of sending women into a vacuum'.[11] An analysis of sexuality in terms of male supremacy, with no real understanding of the construction and meaning of heterosexual femininity as it is experienced by a majority of women today, can lead to a political position of radical lesbian separatism. While this is a possible strategy, it remains a solution which exists *within* a fundamentally gender-divided society, and advances little hope, or even claim, for changes which would affect, let alone liberate, all women. A more satisfactory analysis of the problem of women's 'collusion' in their oppression at the level of sexual politics requires an account of the operations of ideology and the structuring of gendered personality, temperament and subjectivity. I shall be considering attempts to provide this, but first I want briefly to turn to the argument that female sexuality, and the general endorsement of compulsory heterosexual monogamy, can be explained not by reference

9. Vera Bullough and Bonnie Bullough, *Sin, Sickness and Sanity: a History of Sexual Attitudes*, New York 1977, p.69.
10. See Millett, *Sexual Politics*; and Andrew Tolson, *The Limits of Masculinity*, London 1977.
11. Maria-Antonietta Macciocchi, 'Female Sexuality in Fascist Ideology', *Feminist Review*, no.1, 1979.

to patriarchy, or male supremacy, but by the functional
requirements of the capitalist mode of production.

II

The attempt to analyse sexuality with reference to its role in
the organization of capitalist social relations tends to be
conducted in the framework of Engels's *The Origin of the
Family, Private Property and the State*. This work, whatever
its failings, has been highly influential in Marxist thinking
on the family and women's oppression and has provided the
starting point of a materialist analysis of gender relations.
Engels's most important achievement was his perception of
materially different relations between the sexes for members
of different social classes. For the bourgeoisie, he argued, the
need to secure knowledge of paternity, which was a
prerequisite for the inheritance of property through the male
line, led to an insistence on the fidelity of the bourgeois wife.
Coupled with the desire of the rising bourgeoisie in the late
eighteenth and early nineteenth centuries to demonstrate to
the world its ability to sustain a population of non-employed
wives, the premium on female chastity became critical.
Hence the bourgeois family rested on a relationship between
husband and wife in which the former provided the latter's
keep in return for sexual fidelity and the reproduction of
legitimate heirs. Engels regarded this arrangement as a
form of prostitution: 'this marriage of convenience often
enough turns into the crassest prostitution — sometimes on
both sides, but much more generally on the part of the wife,
who differs from the ordinary courtesan only in that she does
not hire out her body, like a wageworker, on piecework, but
sells it into slavery once for all'.[12] Engels argued that the
material basis of the proletarian marriage was different. Not
only was the absence of property significant in removing the
incentive for monogamy, but the employment of proletarian
women in factories and mines led to a basis of equality
between husband and wife which provided the foundations

12. *The Origin of the Family*, p.79.

of true 'sex-love'. In addition to this the proletarian husband had no legal system, such as the bourgeois possessed, to protect his dominance within the family, and Engels concludes that the material foundations of male dominance had ceased to exist (other than in the form of residual brutality) in the proletarian home.

The problems with this account of the proletarian marriage are legion and it has, with some justification, been criticized and to some extent abandoned. Yet Engels's analysis of the material basis of bourgeois sexuality has informed much subsequent work, and has been particularly influential in the attempt to construct a Marxist analysis of features of sexual practice such as 'the double standard' of sexual morality for men and women. It is also likely that his insistence on a materialist analysis, which he couched in terms of the needs of the bourgeoisie to secure the inheritance of its property, has been influential in the recent tendency in Marxist and Marxist feminist work to attribute the present organization of the family and sexuality to a generalized conception of capitalism's requirements for its own social reproduction. This argument starts essentially from the premiss that, as sociologists have argued for a long time, there is a 'functional fit' between industrial capitalism, with its need of a free, mobile labour force, and the nuclear family. If this argument is accepted (which it need not be, since we can conceive of ways in which capitalist social formations might — and do — reproduce themselves without a nuclear family system) then it will follow that stable, heterosexual, pair-bonded, parentally responsible individuals are what capitalism requires of its socialization procedures.

This is the argument put very clearly in David Fernbach's short article 'Toward a Marxist Theory of Gay Liberation'.[13] Fernbach argues that the nuclear family has been created by capitalism and is 'the only way' in which the working class could reproduce itself in capitalism, a way that the working class itself has supported. The nuclear family, and in particular the economic dependence of women on men

13. *Gay Marxist*, no.2, July 1973.

50

'explains' the sexual patterning of our society — girls must grow up repressing clitoral sexuality and seeking satisfaction from vaginal penetration and boys must grow up devaluing women and cultivating an aggressive sexuality. Female homosexuality is repressed as part of the general repression of women's sexual autonomy, and male homosexuality is repressed through the analogy with castration and loss of status. Fernbach relates his analysis of male and female sexuality so closely to the needs of capitalism at given historical periods that he even offers an account, in terms of the conditions under which the working class was reproduced, of the tightening up of the law on homosexuality in 1885 (the Labouchère Amendment) and its liberalization in 1967.

This analysis, which seeks to explain sexuality in terms of the developing needs of capitalism, encounters as many problems as the radical-feminist approach discussed earlier. The problem of functionalism is particularly acute, for the whole analysis rests on the supposed inability of capitalism to reproduce the working class without the nuclear family, and this assertion is highly questionable. Historical work on the family and sexuality, far from demonstrating a connection between the nuclear monogamous family and the rise of capitalism, has generated a major controversy on this issue. Lawrence Stone's study of *The Family, Sex and Marriage in England 1500-1800* indicates a diversity of sexual practice that defies this type of analysis.[14] Finally this analysis is couched in terms of 'repression' of sexuality, and hence encounters a further set of problems.

The notion of the social repression of sexuality occurs in a significant strand of Marxist thought, particularly that of Reich and Marcuse,[15] and also has wide credence in feminist theory. It has seemed a particularly appropriate concept to use in relation to what we know about sexuality in the Victorian period — the denial of women's sexual pleasure

14. London 1977.
15. See for example, Wilhelm Reich, *The Mass Psychology of Fascism*, Harmondsworth 1975.

and the hypocrisy attached to men's publicly avowed marital chastity and proneness to pay clandestine visits to prostitutes. In Reich's work the concept of repression has been extensively used to analyse the character and sexuality of those people raised under fascist ideology (the 'authoritarian personality'). But the notion of repression, especially when used rather loosely in this way, poses the problem of essentialism. It proposes a sexual self, or essence, which is then moulded by the social — for instance by destroying male tenderness or female initiative. There are general arguments to be made against this position[16] and certainly it could not be supported by any comparative (historical or cross-cultural) evidence about sexual practice. At worst it lapses into a biologistic celebration of the liberating potential of physical sexuality — a form of idealism to which Reich succumbed in his later work. Foucault has argued at some length that the notion of repression is highly suspect and that we should understand the discourse of 'repression' in terms of a mechanism by which sexual desire can be harnessed and utilized by the dominant power.[17] A further problem with the notion of repression is outlined by Mary McIntosh, who argues that this approach cannot adequately address the lived experience of sexuality, nor yet our attempts to conceptualize its ambiguities.[18] These difficulties related to the notion of 'repression', and the problem mentioned earlier of a tendency in Marxist work towards unduly functionalist explanations of sexuality, are circumvented by a third approach that locates sexuality, and the construction of gender, primarily at the level of ideology.

III

'Despite appearances, human sex takes place mostly in the head.'[19] Stone is concerned to argue not so much that sex

16. See Reimut Reiche, *Sexuality and Class Struggle*, London 1970.
17. Michel Foucault, *La volonté de savoir* (vol. 1 of *Histoire de la sexualité*), Paris 1976.
18. 'Sexuality', in *Papers from the London Patriarchy Conference*, Lewes 1976.
19. Stone, p.483.

does not take place in the body as that it is governed by *ideas*; he tends to understand changes in sexual practice in terms of shifts in the ideological atmosphere rather than in terms of economic determinations. His emphasis has been shared by a number of writers whose works have been formative for feminist and Marxist feminist thought. Simone de Beauvoir, for instance, predicates her comprehensive account of the construction of femininity on a rejection of what she sees as the 'sexual monism' of Freud and the 'economic monism' of Engels. She sees woman as the product of interaction which systematically constructs her as 'other' in relation to the subject, who is man. In seeking to describe the existential foundation of woman, de Beauvoir accepts some arguments from biology, from psychoanalysis and from historical materialism, but she argues fundamentally for a cultural and ideological perspective: 'the value of muscular strength, of the phallus, of the tool can be defined only in a world of values; it is determined by the basic project through which the existent seeks transcendence'.[20]

De Beauvoir's stress on the shaping of consciousness and gender identity through interaction is echoed in the school of sociological work on sexuality using the interactionist perspective. The pioneering work in this field is that of Simon and Gagnon,[21] who argue that sexual behaviour is learnt rather than biologically given. They take the view that sexual behaviour follows the dramaturgical analogy — one learns, through social interaction, a 'sexual script', which is then acted out where appropriate. It follows from this that the very definition of sexual behaviour is open to question, and that behaviour can legitimately be regarded as 'sexual' only in so far as the actor defines it as such. This perspective has generated some extremely interesting studies on the subjective negotiation of sexuality, a notable example being Plummer's fascinating account of the process by which male homosexual identity and behaviour are

20.   Simone de Beauvoir, *The Second Sex*, Harmondsworth 1974, p.91.
21.   J. H. Gagnon and W. S. Simon, *Sexual Conduct: The Social Sources of Human Sexuality*, Chicago 1973.

learnt.[22] In common with all work derived from an interactionist perspective, however, it tends to suffer from the weakness of this approach in specifying why particular forms of behaviour are learned and not others; it does not adequately address the question of whether social and historical conditions may prescribe the appropriateness of one script rather than another, or make some scripts but not others available.

Attempts to break away from reductionism, and to locate sexuality and gender identity in the specificity of historical ideological processes have culminated in the recent feminist appropriation of psychoanalysis. Juliet Mitchell's extremely influential work of recovery, *Psychoanalysis and Feminism*,[23] has generated an interest in the possibility of using the work of Freud, and subsequent writers in the psychoanalytic tradition (notably Jacques Lacan), to develop a materialist feminist theory of gender and sexuality. The achievement of Mitchell's book lies not only in its intellectual scope and proven relevance to current feminist theory, but also in the courage required to confront a feminist orthodoxy of hostility to Freud which, particularly in American radical feminism, had been pervasive and still retains some force.

Mitchell begins by addressing this hostility and argues that in Freud's work, 'psychoanalysis is not a recommendation *for* a patriarchal society, but an analysis *of* one'.[24] She argues that the libertarian perspective of Reich and Laing involves problems and dangers for feminists, but that Freud's work provides a scientific account of gender and sexuality which may explain, as biology and economics have failed to do, the longevity of women's oppression. Mitchell's reading of Freud stresses that what he is describing is not, as some feminists have thought, a real world (of active men and passive women) but the *mental representation* of social

22. Kenneth Plummer, *Sexual Stigma: An Interactionist Account.* London 1973.
23. Juliet Mitchell, *Psychoanalysis and Feminism*, Harmondsworth 1975.
24. Ibid., p.xv.

reality. The construction of femininity and masculinity, and of sexuality, thus take place at the level of ideology, which, as Mitchell poses ideology in the Althusserian framework, is allowed autonomy — sexuality is not analysed as a mental reflection of social relations necessarily required by a particular mode of production. She sees Freud as having constructed a description of femininity which is of specific concern and value to feminists in that it is grounded in an awareness of patriarchy, which she defines in terms of the law of the father. Hence the analysis given does not concern simply male dominance over women, but explicates this with reference to the mother-father-child triad by which gender identity is developed.

Assessment of Mitchell's work by feminists has tended to revolve around the question of the legitimacy of her 'reading' of Freud. Critics claim that in her desire to present his work as descriptive rather than prescriptive Mitchell has glossed over the more unreflectively sexist aspects of his writings. (The question of pejorative attitudes to women in the traditional clinical practice of psychoanalysis cannot be denied and is not at issue here.) This charge is impossible to assess without a knowledge of the original Freud, and for this reason there is a note at the end of this chapter summarizing his account of the psychosexual development of boys and girls for readers not familiar with his writings.

Perhaps the most controversial aspect of Freud's account, and of the feminist interpretation of it that Juliet Mitchell presents, is the weight Freud attached to 'penis-envy' in the acquisition of femininity. Feminists such as Kate Millett have argued that *if* women are envious of the penis, this is not because of any perceived physical and sexual superiority, but because of the social power and privilege it symbolizes.[25] Mitchell argues precisely this point — that Freud's concern is with ideas rather than anatomy: 'in "penis-envy" we are talking not about an anatomical organ, but about the ideas of it that people hold and live by within the general culture,

25. *Sexual Politics*, p.183.

the order of human society'.[26] The problem here, however, is
that of Freud's ideas about this anatomical organ, for these
inform his observations in significant ways. He writes of
little girls at the moment of discovery of male genitalia:
'They notice the penis of a brother or playmate, strikingly
visible and of large proportions, at once recognize it as the
superior counterpart of their own small and inconspicuous
organ, and from that time forward fall a victim to envy for
the penis. ...A little girl...makes her judgment and her
decision in a flash. She has seen it and knows that she is
without it and wants to have it.'[27] Girls, he comments, 'feel
themselves unfairly treated', but he makes it quite clear that
this unfair treatment is meted out anatomically rather than
ideologically: 'they make attempts to micturate in the
position that is made possible for boys by their possessing a
big penis; and when a girl declares that "she would rather be
a boy", we know what deficiency her wish is intended to put
right'.[28] Freud insisted on the importance of this infantile
experience for later development of femininity: for example
he explicitly opposed Karen Horney's opinion that he had
over-emphasized the girl's primary penis-envy.[29] Indeed,
since he posed it as a central mechanism in the girl's volte-
face in orientation from mother to father, it is impossible to
argue that he could lessen his claims for it. I am not here
particularly concerned with the range of objections which
have been voiced against the notion of penis-envy (although
many of them, even the more polemical arguments advanced
in Kate Millett's attack on Freud,[30] carry some weight with
me), but rather with Mitchell's claim that Freud's discussion
relates to 'mental representation' rather than 'social reality'.
For in this case, and it is clearly a crucial one for the overall

26. *Psychoanalysis and Feminism*, p.xvi.
27. 'Some Psychical Consequences of the Anatomical Distinction Between
    the Sexes', in *On Sexuality*, vol.7, Pelican Freud Library, Harmonds-
    worth 1977, pp.335-6.
28. 'The Sexual Theories of Children', *On Sexuality*, p.196.
29. 'Female Sexuality', *On Sexuality*, p.391. A relevant essay by Karen
    Horney, 'The Flight from Womanhood', is reprinted in Joan Baker
    Miller, ed., *Psychoanalysis and Women*, Harmondsworth 1973.
30. *Sexual Politics*, pp.176-203.

plausibility of his account of female sexuality, his ideas about anatomy lead him to pose the question in exclusively physical rather than mental terms.

My reservations as to the proposed formative influence of penis-envy are no doubt coloured by a refusal to share Freud's view that a desire to carry on an intellectual profession can be explained as one of the many sublimations of this phenomenon to be found in women.[31] The question of 'masculinity' and 'femininity' in Freud's thought also raises the possibility that Juliet Mitchell offers, from a feminist point of view, an unduly charitable reading of his position. Freud throughout his work challenged the notion of an equivalence between maleness and activity, and between femaleness and passivity. In questioning this assumption, as in rejecting the view of sexuality that assumes an instinctive drive towards heterosexual genital union, Freud's work made a radical break with determinism. Juliet Mitchell distinguishes between the position of many post-Freudians — that 'anatomy was the *only* destiny' — and that of Freud himself, for whom 'in the unconscious and preconscious of men and women alike was echoed the great problem of this original duality'.[32] Yet Mitchell's attempt to stress Freud's awareness of this problem does not fully deal with the solution he adopted: the dissociation of the male/ active, female/passive dichotomy in favour of a model which poses *masculinity* as active and *femininity* as passive. For although in one sense Freud takes seriously the distinction between biological sex and socially constructed gender, at another he systematically confuses them. He does this in an obvious sense by choosing to call active female sexuality 'masculine' in character (for instance, he refers to the little girl engaged in clitoral masturbation as 'a little man'). This would appear to be a serious problem for a feminist appropriation of Freud, for if (as Mitchell argues) his theory is not biologistic, but explores the *social* construction of

31. Lecture XXXIII, 'Femininity', in *The Complete Introductory Lectures on Psychoanalysis*. London 1971, p.589.
32. *Psychoanalysis and Feminism*, p.50.

gender in the family, then we expect some considerable discussion of why the active principle should be termed masculine and the passive feminine. Nor is it possible to empty Freud's categories of this culturally specific assumption: to say that in Freudian theory women can be masculine and men feminine hardly meets the case.

One way of approaching this problem is to say that Freud's association of activity with masculinity and of passivity with femininity is an evaluation that can be removed, as a personal or cultural aberration, from his otherwise scientific theoretical schema. One obvious case for this exculpatory activity might be Freud's somewhat unfortunate stance on the moral character of adult women. Freud refers to women in extraordinarily pejorative terms, and furthermore he attempts to generalize his perceptions back over the development of civilization. These remarks occur in the context of substantiating proof for his account of female psychosexual development or, alternatively, as phenomena to be explained by this same account. What is important here is that Freud's perceptions of the female personality are integral to his account of psychosexual development, even in his most speculative moments: 'it seems that women have made few contributions to the discoveries and inventions in the history of civilization; there is, however, one technique which they may have invented — that of plaiting and weaving. If that is so, we should be tempted to guess the unconscious motive for the achievement. Nature herself would seem to have given the model which this achievement imitates by causing the growth at maturity of the pubic hair that conceals the genitals. The step that remained to be taken lay in making the threads adhere to one another, while on the body they stick into the skin and are only matted together. If you reject this idea as fantastic and regard my belief in the influence of lack of a penis on the configuration of femininity as an idée fixe, I am of course defenceless'.[33]

Many feminists have, of course, regarded Freud as defenceless — indeed indefensible — and I remain

33. Lecture XXXIII, 'Femininity', p.596.

unconvinced by Mitchell's attempt to 'recover' for feminism the overall theoretical framework of his writing. The two examples I have discussed (penis-envy and masculinity/ femininity) appear to me to be instances where her interpretation involves some stretching of what Freud actually said. I am not, however, sufficiently convinced of the internal coherence of Freudian psychoanalytic theory to argue that fundamental reservations on crucial stages of his account invalidate his work entirely. On the contrary, I shall be arguing later in this chapter that some of his observations are of great interest and can be useful. Before concluding this section, though, I want to make two brief general points on the compatibility of the psychoanalytic approach and that of Marxist feminism.

The first point concerns historical specificity. The major question asked of psychoanalysis by Marxists and by feminists developing a materialist account of women's oppression must surely be: does it propose the description given as valid only for certain times and places, or as universal? This question is explicitly addressed by Mitchell, who argues that Freud provides an historically bounded description. Yet since Freud himself posed his account in terms of an analysis of the entire history of civilization (see *Totem and Taboo, Civilization and Its Discontents*[34]), we might reasonably be sceptical of claims that Freud's work is historically bounded in any very useful way (it is hard to imagine, for example, its varying application to different modes of production). This discussion is not original to contemporary feminism; it has beset Freud's work from an early date. The position outlined by Laplanche and Pontalis would suggest universalistic claims for psychoanalysis, since they emphasize (as does Lacan) the mythic, 'law'-like agencies at work in psychosexual development and the need to avoid reducing the theory to a discussion of concrete, human, parenting. Hence, they argue, psychoanalysts have responded to the challenge of cultural variation by

34. *Totem and Taboo*, London 1950; *Civilization and its Discontents*, London 1973.

substituting for the child-mother-father mode of analysis the abstract triangular structure of 'the child, the child's natural object and the bearer of the law'.[35]

What perhaps, would be convincing on the question of historical specificity versus universalism would be accounts of psychic structures, psychosexual development and familial relations drawn from comparative studies. Whilst the problems of undertaking such work are obvious, both for the historical and for the cross-cultural possibilities, it would presumably be feasible for some progress to be made towards research that could demarcate the limitations (or otherwise) of the applicability of psychoanalytic theory to other kinship structures. Yet feminists arguing for the compatibility of psychoanalysis with some form of materialism have tended to explore other areas (reworking of Freud's cases, general theoretical discussion of capitalism and patriarchal psychic structures, the application of psychoanalysis to cultural analysis, for example) and hence have left their claims unsubstantiated.[36]

On this question psychoanalytic theory is, perhaps, non-committal; it is relatively open to the interpretation one chooses to put upon it. Timpanaro has argued that it contains an 'intrinsic contradiction' in this respect. 'On the one hand, it eternalizes situations which are historically specific. For example, it abstracts what truth there is in the notion of "hatred of the father" from an authoritarian structure of the family, which remains transient even if it is slow to pass away, and transforms it into a sort of eternal destiny of mankind. ... Yet, in another sense, it remains suspended in a limbo between the "biological" and the "social", rejecting contact with the one no less than with the other.'[37] Timpanaro's remark captures the elusive character

35. J. Laplanche and J. B. Pontalis, *The Language of Psychoanalysis*, London 1973. The entry on 'Oedipus Complex' (pp.282-287) touches on Malinowski's arguments concerning this point.
36. See, for example, the journal *m/f* containing articles on '"Dora" — Fragment of an Analysis' by Jacqueline Rose (no.2), 'Women as Sign' by Elizabeth Cowie (no.1), and 'Representation and Sexuality' by Parveen Adams (no.1).

of psychoanalysis for the materialist who tries to pin it down on the question of history. Yet a central concern of any developing Marxist feminist approach must be with the material, historical structures and processes that delimit sexuality and gender at any given period. On these grounds alone I am sceptical of the claims that psychoanalysis can be adequately reconciled with either Marxism or feminism, and the synthesis of the three is even further distant. We are left, then, with the possibility that some (possibly many) psychoanalytic insights may be extremely useful — in that they do by and large relate to some common features of psychosexual development in capitalism — but that wider theoretical problems remain as yet unresolved.

The second general concluding point I want to make concerns the implications of posing a discussion of gender and sexuality at the level of ideology. In this respect Juliet Mitchell's presentation of Freud, which has been highly influential in recent feminist support for psychoanalysis, can be seen as one of several possible formulations (which would include the existentialist and interactionist perspectives mentioned earlier). Clearly, there are advantages to this approach, when considered in relation to either radical-feminist or traditional Marxist accounts of gender and sexuality. On the one hand it avoids the unsatisfactory reductionism of attempts to explain very diverse sexual behaviour in terms of a rather forced notion of the 'needs' of capitalism; on the other hand it overcomes the monolithic, at times verging on conspiratorial, conception of male aggression offered by some feminist analyses and, perhaps most importantly, provides an explanation of the processes by which women come to 'collude' in their sexual oppression.

I want to argue, however, that there are serious problems in regarding this central area of women's oppression as exclusively 'ideological' in character. First, although the processes described may be attributed great force, the question arises as to the conditions under which a given subject may or may not respond to them and how necessarily

37. Sebastiano Timpanaro, *The Freudian Slip*, London 1976, p.12.

determining they are. In the sociological interactionist approach, for instance, deviant sexual socialization is so well accounted for that one can barely see the overall pressures towards conformity. The case of psychoanalysis is rather different, since although 'normal' and 'abnormal' developments are held to overlap a great deal, the path towards heterosexuality is clearly defined. But psychoanalysis has not adequately related its proposals to the existence of particular family structures, and its relevance to situations other than a publicly monogamous nuclear family is quite unclear.

The central issue here concerns the autonomy of ideology. Attempts to locate gender and sexual practice in an *absolutely* autonomous realm would lead to the relativism and idealism already discussed, and they also lead to a failure to theorize the relations that exist historically between economic and ideological structures. In this respect the criticism levelled against Mitchell, of 'dualism',[38] is pertinent; not only does the separation of the ideological from the economic lead to analytical problems (obscuring, for example, the profoundly ideological character of the sexual division of labour in capitalism), it also leads to a limited political strategy. In particular it tends to the conclusion that class struggle requires economic change, whereas women's liberation requires a 'cultural revolution'.[39] The important truth encapsulated in the feminist slogan 'the personal is political' should not lead us to suppose that the politicization of our personal lives will of itself eradicate women's oppression. The ideology of masculinity and femininity, of heterosexual familialism, is too deeply embedded in the division of labour and capitalist relations of

38. See Steve Burniston, Frank Mort and Christine Weedon, 'Psychoanalysis and the Cultural Acquisition of Sexuality and Subjectivity', in *Women Take Issue*, London 1978, pp.120-3; and Veronica Beechey, 'On Patriarchy', *Feminist Review*, no.3, 1979.
39. *Psychoanalysis and Feminism* p.414, 'a specific struggle against patriarchy — a cultural revolution — is requisite'; and Andrew Tolson, *The Limits to Masculinity*, p.18 ('Women's politics are necessarily cultural politics...').

production to crumble under cultural and ideological offensive alone.

In the second part of this chapter I want to consider gender and sexuality from the point of view set out at the end of Chapter 1. It was insisted there that women's oppression cannot be reduced to the operations of an economic mode of production, and this I believe to be particularly true in the case of sexuality. There are, however, important relations between both the forms in which masculinity and femininity are constructed, and forms of sexual practice, and the overall organization of the capitalist social formation. These relations are an important aspect of the complex arrangement of economic, political and economic structures of contemporary capitalism, and must be seen in the context of their historical development. In approaching the question of the relations between gender, sexuality, and the general features of the capitalist social formation, I am going to consider first two particular problems: whether gender identity and erotic behaviour should be distinguished, and if so how; and whether sexuality and procreation are closely linked, or indeed linked at all. After discussion of these two questions I shall turn to some of the issues raised in the attempt to relate gender and sexuality to the major structures of women's oppression under capitalism — production, the family and the state.

IV

The question of the relationship between gender and eroticism is a complex one. The processes by which gender, and particularly femininity, is socially constructed in capitalist society have been extensively explored. This topic falls within the well-researched area of 'socialization studies' in sociology, and has also been a major focus of feminist accounts.[40] Indeed it would be fair to say that the contemporary women's liberation movement, with its

40. See, for example, Elena Belotti, *Little Girls*, London 1975; and Lee Comer, *Wedlocked Women*, Leeds 1974.

emphasis on the shaping of consciousness as a central dynamic of women's oppression, has taken the processes of gender socialization as among the most important social experiences to be described. Many of these accounts concentrate on the formative childhood years, examining family values and child-rearing practices, the ideology of sexism portrayed in children's reading books, purveyed in schools and so on. Feminists have also looked at the continued process of gender socialization that reproduces femininity in adolescent and adult life.[41] Yet few of these studies systematically engage with the question of sexual practice, or erotic behaviour, and how this does or does not relate to socially acquired gender identity. This absence is perhaps particularly marked in more academic work on socialization, and reflects the marginality of sexuality in the conventional sociological approach. One possible reason for this situation might be that by and large studies of gender socialization tend to argue a strong case on the social and familial pressures towards conformity and the acceptance of heterosexual gender identity; the literature of sexology, on the other hand, since the appearance of the famous Kinsey Reports and before, has tended to demonstrate the enormous diversity of erotic behaviour found in contemporary society.

If it is true that studies of gender do not adequately explore the parameters of erotic behaviour, it is even clearer that studies of eroticism fail to argue their findings back to gender identity. Work in the field of sexology does not constitute this as a central problem, and it might be argued that interactionism (the perspective from which much sociollogical work on sexuality has emerged) tends to conflate gender and sexuality in its accounts of learned behaviour and identity. One notable recent exception to this generalization is Angela Carter's study of eroticism in the writings of de Sade where, among the byzantine details of sexual behaviour, she draws some fascinating inferences

41. See, for example, the essays by Angela McRobbie ('Working Class Girls and the Culture of Femininity') and Janice Winship ('A Woman's World: *Woman* — an Ideology of Femininity') in *Women Take Issue*.

concerning de Sade's perception of the meaning of feminine gender identity in the late eighteenth century.[42]

I want to argue here that an overlap between gender identity, eroticism and sexual orientation may rightly be proposed, but is by no means continuous. At the most obvious level the proposition that gender identity is mechanically played out in sexual behaviour would be challenged by the existence of phenomena such as transvestism or male masochism. More comprehensively, the evidence collected by Kinsey and his associates revealed a diversity of sexual behaviour that cannot be squared either with some biologistic notion of the appropriate behaviour for men and women or with the view that socially constructed gender identity determines acceptable sexual practice. Among Kinsey's findings was that 37% of his male and 13% of his female respondents had experienced homosexual relations to orgasm by the age of 45, and he also reported the widespread currency of various sexual practices which were previously assumed to be very rare.[43] The consternation created by the publication of Kinsey's reports in 1948 and 1953 was no doubt partly caused by their revelation that many 'deviants' were not statistically as deviant as they had imagined.

A consideration of homosexuality throws doubt on the notion that sexual behaviour is closely linked to gender identity. One of the more enduring myths about homosexuality is that it is an almost inevitable outcome of undue masculinity in women or effeminacy in men; given an inverted gender identity the individual's 'normal' sexual orientation will therefore be homosexual (a view encapsulated by the portrait of the lesbian Steven Gordon in Radclyffe Hall's *The Well of Loneliness*[44]). Yet the evidence is that this picture is entirely untrue. The reason why Kinsey

42. *The Sadeian Woman*, London 1979.
43. A. C. Kinsey *et al.*, *Sexual Behaviour in the Human Male* and *Sexual Behaviour in the Human Female*, Philadelphia 1948 and 1953.
44. New York 1929 (the book was published in New York after being banned in Britain).

could elicit high rates of homosexual activity was that he posed his questions in terms of *degrees* of homosexual experience rather than in terms of heterosexual or homosexual identity. Similarly, although we now tend to think of a *choice* between heterosexuality and homosexuality, the notion of an exclusive orientation to one's own sex is a comparatively recent one in Western Europe. Mary McIntosh has pointed to the historical development of 'the homosexual role',[45] and the point is elaborated in Jeffrey Week's history of homosexual politics where he writes: 'as a starting-point we have to distinguish between homosexual behaviour, which is universal, and a homosexual identity, which is historically specific — and a comparatively recent phenomenon in Britain'.[46] A recent report on homosexuality by the (Kinsey) Institute for Sex Research suggests that a notion of homosexuality as a displaced version of normal gender-related sexual behaviour is completely unfounded. The authors report that of their respondents, even those living in stable 'coupled' situations (where we might most expect to see 'straight gay' sex roles in action), 'few described a domestic situation in which one partner took on only "wifely" tasks and the other the "husbandly" ones'. They conclude that 'speculation about sexual "roles" (e.g. active/ passive) may simply be missing the point'.[47] Indeed one might add that what is forcefully expressed in the politics of the contemporary gay liberation movement and lesbian groupings in the women's movement (and to some extent existed in earlier homophile organizations) is, precisely, an outright rejection of these gender-related roles.

Another aspect of discontinuity between gender identity and sexual practice is explored, from a psychoanalytic perspective, in Nancy Chodorow's book *The Reproduction of Mothering*. Chodorow is principally concerned with the

45. 'The Homosexual Role', *Social Problems*, vol.16, no.2, 1968.
46. *Coming Out: Homosexual Politics in Britain from the Nineteenth Century to the Present*, London 1977, p.3.
47. Alan P. Bell and Martin S. Weinberg, *Homosexualities: A Study of Diversity Among Men and Women*, London 1978, pp.101, 111.

question of maternalism, but her argument draws out an interesting implication of the psychoanalytic account: 'most women emerge from their oedipus complex oriented to their father and men as primary *erotic* objects, but it is clear that men tend to remain *emotionally* secondary, or at most emotionally equal, compared to the primacy and exclusivity of an oedipal boy's emotional tie to his mother and women'.[48]

Psychoanalytic theory may also throw some light on another controversial issue in the understanding of female eroticism — the question of vaginal and/or clitoral orgasm. Despite historical recognition of the clitoris as the site of women's sexual pleasure, Freud maintained that a transfer to vaginal sexuality formed an essential part of mature femininity. Controversy on this issue was generated, but the issue itself was apparently resolved, by the publication in 1966 of *Human Sexual Response* by Masters and Johnson, which produced detailed evidence to show that the stages of arousal and orgasm were similar in both men and women, and that the female orgasm takes place through clitoral stimulation, even if this occurs in the course of vaginal penetration.[49] The issue was only partially resolved by these physiological details, however, since the technical insistence that all orgasms in women are essentially clitoral did not tally with many women's lived experience of intercourse. It is at this point that Freud's account may be useful, precisely in demarcating the psychic processes that underlie the pleasure of this experience. What the controversy highlights above all is the need for an understanding of sexuality in terms of meanings, definitions, the discourse of pleasure, in relation to our knowledge of the technical processes involved in sexual activity. In particular, as I shall consider below, it raises the important question of the relationship between sexual pleasure and biological reproduction.

48. *The Reproduction of Mothering: Psychoanalysis and the Sociology of Gender*, Berkeley and Los Angeles 1978, p.193.
49. W. H. Masters and V. E. Johnson, *Human Sexual Response*, Boston 1966.

V

I have suggested that we should try to distinguish between gender identity and sexual practice; that we should reject any direct link between not only maleness and femaleness and a 'natural' orientation to heterosexual genital sexuality, but also between the socially constructed identities of masculinity and femininity and their assumed consequences for sexual behaviour. This is not, however, to propose a radical dissociation of the two. There can be no doubt that the familial and general ideological processes by which the categories of masculine and feminine are established and reproduced in our society lead, at the very least, to a disposition towards 'appropriate' forms of eroticism.[50]

The distinction between gender and eroticism is useful in considering the relationship between sexuality and procreation. It is useful because the idea that sex is, or should be, restricted only to activity which can give rise to biological reproduction reflects the imposition of socially constructed gender responsibilities onto a wide variety of sexual practices of men and women.

At the most general level the ideology of sexuality in our culture has, until comparatively recently, encompassed severe sanctions on the most obvious forms of non-reproductive sexual behaviour. Jeffrey Weeks has pointed out that the death penalty for sodomy applied to heterosexual anal intercourse and to intercourse with animals as well as to homosexual buggery. 'The law against sodomy', he argues, 'was a central aspect of the taboo on all non-procreative sex', and indeed it had considerable flexibility since the 'crime against nature' that it sought to

---

50. Jeffrey Weeks, in a forthcoming paper, suggests the usefulness of a reinterpretation of Freud by Campioni and Gross. He argues that the possibilities of heterosexuality and homosexuality are developed in the familial, emotional structuring of psychological masculinity and femininity: what is created 'is not an identity but a propensity'. See 'Discourse, Desire and Sexual Deviance: Some Problems in the History of Homosexuality' in K. Plummer, ed., *The Making of the Modern Homosexual*, London 1980.

punish was *inter Christianos non nominandum* (not to be named among Christians).[51] Similar sanctions have been applied to the woman who attempted to dissociate sexual activity from procreation: abortion has in most Western European countries been illegal except under medically authorized procedures and has even carried a death penalty in some places.

There is considerable evidence that the prohibition on non-procreative sexual activity has come to play a large part in the history of sexuality that we have inherited. Lawrence Stone cites several phenomena that clearly illustrate the strength of this proscription and its importance to the sexual practice that Christianity sought to enforce. Religious authorities in early modern Europe even argued that sexual passion *within* marriage was no better than adultery. Stone quotes one cleric of 1584: 'the husband who, transported by immoderate love, has intercourse with his wife so *ardently* in order to satisfy his passion that, even had she not been his wife he would have wished to have commerce with her, is committing a sin'.[52] The ideology of 'matrimonial chastity' is found also in extraordinary beliefs about the efficacy of various sexual practices for conception. Stone describes the ways in which theologians tried to interfere with sexual intercourse, proscribing any position other than the 'missionary', with the male partner uppermost, since conception was less likely if the semen had to struggle against gravity.[53] Curiously enough the theologians and the medical professions did not prohibit clitoral stimulation for women: they believed that both male and female fluids were necessary for conception, and even that female sexual pleasure made the mouth of the womb more receptive to male sperm, and hence endorsed masturbation to orgasm as a legitimate part of intercourse.[54]

I say 'curiously enough' since our knowledge of sexual

51. *Coming Out*, pp.12-14.
52. Stone, p.483.
53. Ibid., p.500.
54. Ibid, pp.489-90.

morality, particularly that of the Victorian period, tends to assume a denial or a 'repression' of female sexual pleasure. To some extent this view is borne out historically. The often-quoted remark of William Acton, that 'the majority of women (happily for them) are not very much troubled with sexual feeling of any kind',[55] was not necessarily representative of the period but did have some resonance in an era where the only recognized physical desire women were to indulge was a passion for maternity. Here lies an important aspect of the relationship between sexuality and procreation — that it has been posed as much closer for women than for men. The most obvious example of this is the 'double standard' of sexual morality, according to which the crime of adultery was a much more serious one for the married woman than for the married man. Consideration of the double standard has tended to emphasize its importance to the nineteenth century's flourishing prostitution, and the way in which this widespread practice preserved the sanctity of the bourgeois family and the legitimate inheritance of its property. Yet it seems that the discrepancy between the freedom of men and that of women goes further back. Boswell, writing in 1776, records a conversation with a woman who was considering committing adultery: 'I argued that the chastity of women was of much more consequence than that of men, as the property and rights of families depend upon it. "Surely," said she, "that is easily answered, for the objection is removed if a woman does not intrigue but when she is with child." I really could not answer her. Yet I thought she was wrong, and I was uneasy.'[56]

Boswell's 'unease' is significant. It is impossible to analyse the double standard in terms of solely economic criteria such as the inheritance of property, important as these may be for the bourgeoisie; the constraints on women's extra-marital sexual activity are rooted in an ideology of gender division which to some extent must be seen as historically prior to and

55. William Acton, *The Function and Disorders of the Reproductive Organs*, London 1857.
56. Stone, pp.506-7.

independent of strictly capitalist social organization. Indeed the Victorian attitude to sexuality tended if anything to exert pressure against a formerly accepted double standard: in the seventeenth and eighteenth centuries the conventions on bastard children made illegitimacy considerably more open and acceptable.

The question of the double standard is frequently perceived in terms of a link between sexuality and procreation that is more forcibly maintained in the case of women than of men. Yet this view would encounter serious problems in trying to explain why it should be the case that, in Britain at least, lesbianism has never figured in the criminal law. From the point of view of biological reproduction, there is clearly not much to choose between male and female homosexuality, and the relatively tolerant attitude towards lesbianism requires further historical analysis.[57]

It would seem, then, that the link between sexuality and procreation is a very complex one. Although sexual activity has never, throughout our recent history, been restricted to procreative ends the ideology that it should be restricted in this way has tended to vary. During this century major changes have taken place in the direction of freeing women from the reproductive consequences of sexual intercourse. The development and increasing acceptability of contraception is obviously the most important of these, although the resistance to this of religious and other forces should not be overlooked. Also it is clear that the liberalization of the law on homosexuality, and greater acknowledgment of non-procreative female sexual pleasure have been important features of the last two decades. These changes have not, however, totally dissociated sexuality from procreation and to talk about their 'liberating' character would be premature. The extent to which sexual practice is circumscribed by the ideology of gender and women's responsibilities for

57. Annabel Faraday's 'Liberating Lesbian Research' deals incisively with the shortcomings of existing sociological and historical work on lesbianism. See *The Making of the Modern Homosexual*.

procreation can be seen quite clearly.

Sally MacIntyre, in a study of single pregnant women, analysed the assumptions underlying the treatment they received from doctors, nurses and social workers.[58] She found that although these professionals articulated a belief in a 'maternal instinct' they did not hold this to apply to unmarried women — they 'bracketed together' sex, marriage and biological reproduction and did not perceive single motherhood as medically or socially desirable. Although MacIntyre's study concerned the 'vocabularies of motive' of the professionals and the women concerned, drawing out important differences in their perceptions of the situation, it is clear that these assumptions must be considered as part of a wider ideology linking pregnancy (and sexual intercourse) to the social institution of marriage. Hence the disapproval of unmarried motherhood relates precisely to a socially constructed category of femininity and maternal responsibility.

Similarly Mary McIntosh has pointed out that neither sociologists nor sexologists have questioned the assumption that the institution of prostitution exists to service the 'imperious' male sexual urge. 'Innately, it seems, women have sexual attractiveness while men have sexual urges. Prostitution is there for the needs of the male hunchback — no one asks how the female hunchback manages.'[59] For women, it seems, even if sexual activity cannot be linked directly to procreation, it can nevertheless be linked to a stable emotional relationship; for men many forms of casual experience are not only tolerated but expected and encouraged. So, although it may be true to argue that the prohibition on non-reproductive sexuality has weakened considerably in recent times, it remains a powerful component of the ideology of sexuality and affects men and women differently.

58. '"Who Wants Babies?", The Social Construction of "Instincts"', *in* *Sexual Divisions and Society: Process and Change*, Diana Leonard Barker and Sheila Allen, eds., London 1976.
59. 'Who Needs Prostitutes? The Ideology of Male Sexual Needs', in *Women, Sexuality and Social Control*.

It should be clear that I have been discussing an assumed rather than a necessary link between sexuality and procreation. Clearly a connection exists at the level of biology between heterosexual intercourse and procreation. Yet the widespread practices of contraception and abortion, and the high incidence of non-procreative sexual activity render this initial equation totally unsatisfactory as an account of sexual practice and ideology. What is more useful to consider is the variation in beliefs about the relationship between sexuality and procreation. Such beliefs are not necessarily rational in terms of our knowledge of biology in any case. The view frequently expressed, by feminists and more generally, that sexuality and procreation are more closely linked for women than men is a case in point. In one sense this view is correct, in that heterosexual intercourse may, and frequently does, leave the woman with a pregnancy to consider while the man may even remain ignorant of his impending paternity. Yet, if we look at it another way, the connection for *men* between sexuality and procreation is much closer than it is for women. For men (except in rare cases of 'multiple orgasm') the ejaculation of sperm is absolutely coterminous with orgastic pleasure; for women (notwithstanding the opinion of the theologians) there is no relationship between orgasm and conception. This separation, in fact, may provide a physiological basis on which the denial of women's autonomous sexual pleasure has been built.[60]

The foregoing discussion may lead to a more useful way of considering the thorny question of the relationship of biology to the social divisions of gender. In the previous chapter I referred to 'biologistic' accounts of gender division as unsatisfactory; a further reason for their inadequacy is that they fail to separate the different elements — gender identity, sexual practices, procreation — that have been distinguished here. In fact, accounts couched in biologistic terms tend inevitably to collapse these elements of sexuality together, seeing procreative heterosexuality as the

60. I am indebted to Mary McIntosh for this point.

'naturally' given basis of all sexual behaviour. The emphasis on procreation tends to present women in terms of a naturally given responsibility for children and dissociates them from sexual pleasure. The emphasis on heterosexuality tends to stress the act of penetration, of male activity and aggression, and to dissociate men from procreation. This 'reading' of biology is not without its contradictions. The appeal to biological imperatives is supposed on the one hand to justify the inevitability of procreation and its necessary structuring of sexual practice, and on the other it allegedly underlies male pleasure and male promiscuity.

Acceptance of this biologistic 'common sense' is fraught with dangers for feminism. It can lead to fatalism and impotence, or to a destructively hostile separatism. Furthermore, it leads to a celebration of 'natural' differences which are supposed to underlie women's pacifism, nurturance, tenderness, maternalism. To argue in this way is to take on board the social definitions of biological difference which have developed historically: it is to accept that the entire gamut of femininity and masculinity is necessarily grounded in biological difference.

Yet feminist arguments against biological determination have not been notably strong. Feminists, and notably socialist feminists, tend to point to historical variation as the proof that gender is culturally constructed rather than biologically given. We cling desperately to that wonderful discovery of Margaret Mead — the Tchambuli, where the women manage and the men are coquettish. We point with relief to the ways in which capitalism has constructed a form of dependence for women simply not characteristic of the medieval period. This line of analysis is I think the right one, and indeed the bulk of this book is concerned to explicate it. But we run the risk, if as feminists we ignore arguments from the level of biology, of leaving the forces of anti-feminism comfortably encamped on this ground with their persuasive and popular arguments unanswered. Consider Lesley Stern's description of a particular socialist feminist approach that sees sexual difference as a social construction: 'this tendency argues that sexual difference is not natural or based on biology but that individuals are produced, on the level of the ideological, as sexed subjects, inserted within categories of women/men'.[61]

Now, if this read 'gender difference is not...based on biology' it would be correct. But 'sexual' difference precisely *is* biological difference. Just as biologism reduces gender to what it sees as the 'facts' of sexual differences, so this form of idealism absorbs sexual differences into an account of the social construction of gender. Timpanaro, at a more general level, has launched a polemic against such forms of idealism in Marxist argument. He insists that a materialist analysis must take account of the relationship between the natural and the social.[62] In this approach sex differences, along with other biological characteristics of human beings, would form part of the raw material on which social relations are constructed and which they transform in the course of history. He sees biology, the realm of the naturally given, as the infrastructure on which human social relations must necessarily be built, and he attempts to identify the characteristics which mark humans off from other animals inhabiting the natural world. This position is very unfashionable today, since it positively, indeed necessarily, reeks of 'humanism' in its attempt to specify the qualities of purposiveness, of reflection and planning, that separate human social behaviour from the behaviour of animals. Yet it is I think a salutary one, and worth exploring.

One difficulty, and a very serious one, in examining this question is the prevalence of social assumptions in the relevant spheres of scientific research. The findings of primatology, of evolutionary anthropology and of socio-biology are riddled with the most blatantly sexist inferences, making them an extremely unreliable source of information.[63] The roles of men and women in the reproduction of the species clearly constitute the most decisive difference

61. *m/f*, no.4, 1980, p.23.
62. Sebastiano Timpanaro, *On Materialism*, London 1975 (my thanks to Perry Anderson for drawing my attention to this argument).

between them. Childbirth itself, as a biological event, is incontrovertibly painful, tiring and dangerous. Lactation imposes restrictions on a feeding mother for a period of time. Menstruation and menopausal changes may cause physical problems, although we know that their social inconvenience varies strikingly between different cultures. So how do we assess the importance of these biological facts?

If we choose to regard these events as 'biological liabilities' of the female condition, we then have to ask how we weigh up their social implications. This, however, is partly a question of the meaning attached to them. We can see this by looking at them in comparison with diseases from which men are more prone to suffer than women in Britain at present. Is a planned pregnancy for a thirty-five-year-old woman more or less disruptive to her working life than an unplanned heart attack for a man of the same age? Is eighteen months of lactation more or less restrictive than a bout of chronic ulcerative colitis? These questions are not as banal as they might look. Even in the present situation, where the ascription of family responsibilities to women leads to considerable strain in maintaining the 'double shift', some surprising facts emerge. Anti-feminists often argue that women are not 'worth' training, since child-rearing is likely to assume prominence later in their lives. Yet in the medical profession, where this argument has been most strongly put in the past because of the length and expense of the training required, research has shown that the rate at which women cease to practice is no greater than the rate at which men leave the profession through emigration or involuntary removal from the medical register.[64]

The most important point raised by a consideration of

63. See the excellent discussion of this problem in Dorothy Griffiths and Esther Saraga, 'Sex Differences and Cognitive Abilities: a Sterile Field of Inquiry?' in O. Hartnett *et al.*, eds., *Sex-Role Stereotyping*, London 1979; see also the article by Sayers in the same volume; and Ruth Herschberger, *Adam's Rib*, New York 1970.
64. B. R. Bewley and T. H. Bewley, 'The Hospital Doctor's Career: Structure and Misuse of Medical Womanpower', *The Lancet*, August 9, 1975.

biological difference is the constant slippage from women's role in procreation to women's supposed responsibility for childcare. There is no biological reason why women should be particularly or exclusively concerned with child-rearing yet in many cultures and many periods of history this has been seen as a logical extension of the physiological division of labour. Although it is understandable that this has been seen as in some ways suggested by the process of human reproduction, it is not in any precise sense determined by it. We must insist, in fact, that biological difference simply cannot explain the social arrangements of gender. The 'requirements', even by the grossest extension, of reproductive biology could never explain the degradation of women in contemporary society. The widespread availability of contraception, small family size, the absence of a need to increase the population, the technology of childbirth, all render this factor relatively much less important than it might be under other conditions. Furthermore, the way in which the biology of human reproduction is integrated into social relations is not a biological question: it is a political issue.[65] Human history constitutes a struggle to transcend the constraints imposed upon us by the natural world and, as Timpanaro stresses, the level of social and economic relations is constructed from that raw material (distinguishing, according to Marx, the worst of architects from the best of bees). So, in so far as the social oppression of women rests — in however small a way — on biological difference our task is to challenge and change the socially wrought meaning of that difference. The pattern of gender relations in our society is overwhelmingly a social rather than a natural one, but it is a social construction that caricatures biological difference in the most grotesque way and then appeals to this misrepresented natural world for its own justification.

Returning, then, to the relationship between sexual behaviour and procreation, we can see that the diversity of the former is not explicable in terms of the dictates of the

65. See Linda Gordon, *Woman's Body, Woman's Right: A Social History of Birth Control in America* New York 1976.

latter. The link between biological reproduction and eroticism is one which operates to a considerable extent in social and ideological terms. It is situated within an ideology of femininity and masculinity which reproduces socially gendered subjects, and it should be considered in a broader analysis of the social context of sexual practice.

VI

A central concern of such a broader analysis would, of course, be the historical development of the family. For it is within the family that masculine and feminine people are constructed and it is through the family that the categories of gender are reproduced. Although erotic behaviour is not directly constrained by socially created gender identity, there can be no doubt that the dominant patterns of sexual activity bear a close relationship to the organization of the family and its role in the social formation generally. I shall be discussing the family, and its central place in any analysis of women's oppression, in Chapter 6, but some essential features must be noted here.

First, due weight must be attached to the sweeping changes wrought in the family during the development of capitalism. Some of these changes, the separation of home and workplace for example, are closely related to the developing wage-labour relations of capitalist production. Other historical changes in the form of the family are less plausibly attributed directly to any specific forms of capitalist production and reproduction. Among these changes we might note the increased possibilities of divorce this century and the development in the nineteenth century, if not before, of a 'romantic' free choice of partner, with its tendency to erode the longevity and indissolubility of marriage. The increasing number of years of children's dependence has also been significant. Most importantly, perhaps, the foundations were laid, in the nineteenth century, for a family form which attempted to approximate the 'ideal' of the wage-earning husband and the dependent, caring wife and mother.

The significance of this model cannot be over-estimated. For although few families have in fact depended only upon the male wage, the belief that they do underlies our present sexual division of labour in a fundamental way and has, furthermore, been influential in determining the attitude of the labour movement to women's wage-work. The struggles of both bourgeois philanthropists and male trade unionists succeeded, in the protective legislation of the 1830s and 40s, in setting a model of the working-class family which has been a powerful one ever since. It is in the context of woman's role in the home, financially dependent upon her husband, unpaid for domestic labour except in her upkeep and badly paid outside the home, that we must consider the dominant features of female sexuality — passivity, maternalism and so on — as they have been developed in the ideology of contemporary capitalism.

Family forms have changed in such a way as not only to incorporate, but to actively exacerbate, the gender division of pre-capitalist society. The separation of home and workplace has entrenched women more squarely in domestic and familial responsibilities, and detached and disadvantaged them in the sphere of wage labour. The role of the state, as I suggest in Chapter 7, has been particularly important in this process, constructing women's dependence on men through its statutory provisions on social security, income tax and so on. In addition to this, the state has played an important part in regulating sexual behaviour: marriage, divorce, domestic violence, rape, prostitution, pornography, incest, homo-sexuality, adolescent female promiscuity and so on all fall, to a greater or lesser extent, within the operations of the state. Although the state is formally only interested in such 'private' matters as sexuality only in so far as they affect the 'public' good, it is clear that the degree of state involvement in sexuality and procreation renders the public/private distinction untenable. These two worlds are, as Virginia Woolf put it, 'inseparably connected' — 'the tyrannies and servilities of the one are the tyrannies and servilities of the other'.[66]

The women's liberation movement has laid great stress on the experiential aspects of oppression in marriage, in sexual relationships and in the ideology of femininity and male dominance. In the establishment of 'sexual politics' as a central area of struggle it has succeeded in drawing back the veil on privatized relationships. This politicization of personal life, needless to say a source of great irritation to the unconverted, is a major achievement of feminist activity and one from which Marxism has learnt a great deal. It does not, however, provide an adequate account of women's oppression under capitalism, since it has tended to ignore the ways in which private oppression is related to broader questions of relations of production and the class structure. I shall be considering these problems later in the book, and arguing that the ideology of masculinity and femininity has a crucial role in the division of labour as it has developed historically. First, however, I want to turn to another area which Marxism has until recently relegated to the status of a 'reflection' of material conditions — that of culture and ideology.

66. Virginia Woolf, *Three Guineas*, London 1938, p.258.

NOTE: *Freud's Account of Psychosexual Development*

Juliet Mitchell argues, in my view correctly, that no understanding of Freud's description of psychosexual development can take place without a prior understanding of the two central postulates of psychoanalytic theory in general: the unconscious and the meaning of sexuality.

Laplanche and Pontalis comment that 'if Freud's discovery had to be summed up in a single word, that word would without doubt have to be "unconscious".'[67] Freud posed the unconscious as the area of the psyche that is not accessible to consciousness unless or until, through psychoanalytic treatment, resistances are overcome and its contents can be revealed. These contents are constituted by a process of repression of desire, phantasy, pleasure, in the face of repeated non-satisfaction: it results from the conflict between what Freud termed the 'pleasure principle' and the 'reality principle'. The unconscious drives are contained by vigilant censorship of the socially acquired conscious mind, but can break through in dreams and parapraxes (the celebrated 'Freudian slip') which Freud saw as having a 'wish-fulfilment' function.

Freud's theorization of the unconscious led him to his 'discovery' of infantile sexuality. Infantile sexual pleasure is gained from activities (sucking, excretion and so on) that are not specifically genital and are auto-erotic rather than directed to an object outside the young child. Hence, Freud sought to argue, the conventional view of sexuality (still held today to a large extent), of an instinctive drive towards coitus with a partner of the opposite sex, was wrong. Genital heterosexuality was rather the end product of a tortuous progress of development from an initial perverse bisexuality in which 'normal' and 'abnormal' sexuality frequently overlapped. The radical implications of this view should not be overlooked.

These two tenets — the mental unconscious and the theory of sexuality — underlie Freud's account of psychosexual development. The baby is seen as having a diverse sexual drive that is both active and passive. These urges can be

67. *The Language of Psychoanalysis.*

satisfied by auto-eroticism, or from the mother's body, which the child sees as an extension of its own. The continuity between the child's body and that of its mother is broken as the infant constructs an imaginary notion of itself paralleling its bodily schema and this elementary psychic unit forms the basis of the ego (or conscious structure of personality). In Freud this process is seen as 'primary narcissism'; in Lacan's work it is characterized as the 'mirror stage' since it is exemplified concretely in the experience in which the child first sees its reflection in a mirror. This infant is still bisexual, however, with both active (for Freud 'masculine') and passive ('feminine') sexuality. Its poly-morphously perverse drives are never grown out of, but repressed through cultural constraints.

This process takes place through the oedipal stage, a notion central to Freud's account and which unfolds differently for boys and girls. The paradigmatic case is that of the boy, and Freud only later considered how female psychosexual development differed from male. The boy's first love object (or object of cathexis) is his mother, the source of his pleasure. He begins to perceive his father as a rival and wishes to murder his father and take his place in his mother's affections. This is represented in the myth of Oedipus, who inadvertently murdered his father, assumed sexual relations with his mother and, on discovering his crime, punished himself with blindness (which is seen as symbolic castration). Laplanche and Pontalis stress that this has a *'founding character'* for Freud: in *Totem and Taboo* he proposes that the genesis of mankind lies in the murder of the primal father. This should be understood not as an actual, concrete, event or experience but as a myth which prohibits incest and carries the proscriptive weight of 'law'.[68] Juliet Mitchell emphasizes that Freud's acceptance of the importance of this myth leads him to define civilization as, precisely, *patriarchal.*[69] She explores at some length a fact noted by Laplanche and Pontalis, that Freud's account conforms with Lévi-Strauss's notion of the incest prohibition as a universal law of human culture.[70]

68. See footnote 35 above.
69. *Psychoanalysis and Feminism*, p.366.
70. Ibid., p.286.

The oedipus complex is resolved for boys through the castration complex. The little boy becomes aware that girls have no penis and fears that this is a punishment by his father. He learns to reject his rivalry and to identify with his father in the hope of obtaining another woman to substitute for his mother later in life. This resolution has a double orientation, since the boy also wishes to take his mother's place as a love-object of his father.

For girls the oedipal situation is more difficult to resolve, because it involves the complete abandonment of the original love-object (the mother) without the symbolic retention heterosexuality provides for boys. The sight of the male penis by the little girl causes an instant reaction of inferiority and is a wound to her narcissism. She sees her lack of a penis as common to all women and begins to share men's contempt for women. Freud held that penis-envy continued to exist for adult women, displaced onto female jealousy. The girl blames her mother for this and becomes detached from her. She abandons masturbation of her inferior genitalia and hence abandons her active ('masculine') sexuality. This process is crucial for the construction of femininity — the little girl relinquishes her wish for a penis and replaces it with a wish for a child, and therefore takes her father as her love-object. The ensuing rivalry with her mother is therefore very different from the oedipal stage for boys: it is a secondary formation *arising from* the castration complex, whereas for boys the castration complex is the means by which the prior oedipus complex is resolved.

Freud argues that the wave of repression which smooths the path towards femininity may throw up abnormalities (such as female homosexuality, which he saw as a regression into early masculinity). For the purposes of this book, however, it is worth noting his conclusions in the essays on female sexuality and the adult feminine personality.[71] He stresses that the acquisition of femininity involves the

71. The best sources here are (a) Freud's Lecture XXXIII, 'Femininity'; (b) 'Some Psychical Consequences of the Anatomical Distinction Between the Sexes' and 'Female Sexuality'; and (c) Laplanche and Pontalis (an invaluable reference work), entries on Masculinity/ Femininity, Oedipus Complex, Sexuality.

crucial transfer from the clitoris to the vagina of the site of female sexual pleasure, with an accompanying ascendancy of passive over active sexuality. Secondly, since the oedipal situation is never clearly resolved ('it may be slowly abandoned or dealt with by repression') in women, their full acceptance of the 'law of the father', of cultural and ethical constraints, does not reach that of men. Hence, for Freud, women's super-ego (moral conscience) is never as well developed as that of men, and he concludes: 'Character traits which critics of every epoch have brought up against women — that they show less sense of justice than men, that they are less ready to submit to the great exigencies of life, that they are more often influenced in their judgments by feelings of affection or hostility — all these would be amply accounted for by the modification in the formation of their super-ego which we have inferred above.'[72] Finally we should note that Freud was highly conscious of the problem of gender, as distinct from biological sex. It was an issue he never satisfactorily resolved. In 1905 he wrote: 'if we were able to give a more definite connotation to the concepts of "masculine" and "feminine", it would even be possible to maintain that libido is invariably and necessarily of a masculine nature, whether it occurs in men or in women and irrespectively of whether its object is a man or a woman'.[73] By 1915 he was suggesting that the concepts of 'masculine' and 'feminine' are 'among the most confused that occur in science', and that '[sociological] observation shows that in human beings pure masculinity or femininity is not to be found either in a psychological or a biological sense'.[74] By 1930 he was complaining that 'we far too readily identify activity with maleness and passivity with femaleness, a view which is by no means universally confirmed in the animal kingdom'.[75] Critics may well feel Freud did right to include himself in this observation.

72. 'Some Psychical Consequences', p.342.
73. 'Three Essays on the Theory of Sexuality', in *On Sexuality*, p.141.
74. Ibid., p.142.
75. *Civilization and Its Discontents*, p.43.

3
Ideology and
the Cultural Production
of Gender

The concept of ideology is an intractable one for Marxist feminism, not least because it remains inadequately theorized in both Marxist and feminist theory. Although feminists have frequently posed ideology as central to women's oppression this very centrality is presented as self-evident rather than argued for. This can be seen in an obvious way by considering one of the major fields of 'women's studies' — the analysis of literature. Much excellent work has been done on many aspects of this subject by feminists, and I shall be considering some of it later, but among it all I can find no sustained argument as to *why* feminists should be so interested in literature or what theoretical or political ends such a study might serve. Nor is it easy to find systematic accounts of any relationship between analysis of women's oppression in, say, literature and in, say, the family. Many women's studies courses are explicitly inter-disciplinary in perspective and yet the traditional disciplinary divisions between the 'arts' and the 'social sciences' have been difficult to transcend, other than by the juxtaposition of their respective subject-matters.

Related to this is the inadequacy of feminist attempts to explore the ways in which material conditions have historically structured the mental aspects of oppression. Some earlier feminist writers, Simone de Beauvoir and Virginia Woolf, for example, paid more attention to this question than it has received in recent years. Approaches taken by contemporary feminism seem in comparison notably unsatisfactory. One solution has been to ground the ideology of oppression irrevocably in biology, to take procreation and its different consequences for men and women as the root cause. Another has been to present it as completely self-sustaining and in need of no further explanation; Cora Kaplan has suggested that this view of ideology — the 'energy source' of patriarchal domination — underlies Kate Millett's work.[1] Yet another solution has been found in the application of a particular Marxist perspective that sees ideology (in this case sexist ideology) as the reflection of material conditions of male power and dominance. Hence the ideology of women's inferiority is seen as a manipulation of reality that serves men's interests, and women's own collusion in oppression is explained as a variety of false consciousness. These solutions are all unsatisfactory, and the latter is particularly so in that it simply transposes an already inadequate theory of ideology on to different ground. For if a theory that sees ideology as the unproblematic reflection of class relations is inadequate, the difficulties are compounded if it is merely transferred to the question of gender.

Feminism has, however, played an important part in challenging the validity of the mechanical conception that sees ideology as the playing out of economic contradictions at the mental level. As I have already suggested, there has been a fruitful alignment of interests between those who seek to raise the question of gender and its place in Marxist theory, and those who seek to challenge economism in Marxism, insisting on the importance of ideological processes. It is clear that a conception of capitalism in which all forms of ideology are perceived as a reflection of the exploitation of labour by capital, in which gender plays no part, can be of little use to feminist analysis. It should be noted, perhaps, that the strong form of economism indicated above has never gained the hold on Western European Marxism that it has elsewhere. Indeed Perry Anderson has

1. Cora Kaplan, 'Radical Feminism and Literature: Rethinking Millett's *Sexual Politics*', *Red Letters*, no.9, 1979, p.7.

argued that the political context of the twentieth-century development of Western Marxism has encouraged an exploration of culture and ideology at the expense of an insistence on the primacy of economic or political considerations.[2]

I

It is in this context that we should consider the argument that post-Althusserian developments in the theory of ideology offer an opportunity for feminist analysis which earlier versions of Marxism have denied. This claim can be identified with a particular tendency in contemporary feminist work, the appropriation of the theory developed by Barry Hindess and Paul Hirst, and is found most systematically in articles published by the journal *m/f*. It is not relevant here to enter into a sustained engagement with the ideas of Hindess and Hirst, which I will discuss only insofar as is necessary for an assessment of the claims made by feminists who have taken them over.[3]

As a basis for discussion I want to quote a passage of argument which expresses clearly the logic and assumptions of this theoretical position. 'My argument is that as long as feminist theories of ideology work with a theory of representation within which representation is always a representation of reality, however attenuated a relation that may be, the analysis of sexual difference cannot be advanced because reality is always already apparently structured by

2. Perry Anderson, *Considerations on Western Marxism*, London 1976.
3. The individual and collaborative works of Barry Hindess and Paul Q. Hirst, and their collective work with Anthony Cutler and Athar Hussain, are known colloquially as 'Hindess and Hirst', 'post-Althusserianism' and 'discourse theory'. There now exist several general critical responses to their arguments, such as Andrew Collier, 'In Defence of Epistemology', in vol.3 of *Issues in Marxist Philosophy*, John Mepham and David-Hillel-Ruben, eds., Brighton 1979; Laurence Harris, 'The Science of the Economy', *Economy and Society*, vol.7, no.3, 1978 (and see the subsequent debate in vol.8, no.3, 1979); Philip Corrigan and Derek Sayer, 'Hindess and Hirst: A Critical Review', *The Socialist Register*, 1978.

sexual division, by an already antagonistic relation between two social groups. And thus the complicated and contradictory ways in which sexual difference is generated in various discursive and social practices is always reduced to an effect of that always existent sexual division. In terms of sexual division what has to be explained is how reality functions to effect the continuation of *its* already given divisions. (The different ways in which sexual differences are produced is actually denied as a political fact in this position.) In terms of sexual *differences*, on the other hand, what has to be grasped is, precisely, the *production* of differences through systems of representation; the work of representation produces differences that cannot be known in advance.'[4] I will come back later to the political implications of this argument. For the moment, consider the rather startling statement that sexual differences 'cannot be known in advance'. Let us not sink to the vulgarity of pointing out that biological differences can be known in advance, since we know that this level of reality is uncongenial to exponents of this approach. More seriously, this analysis of 'social and discursive practices' appears also to deny that *gender* differences, as a set of historically constructed and systematic categories, can be predicted with any confidence within a given historical conjuncture. Underlying this argument are a series of principles which need to be examined. These can be identified (rather negatively perhaps) as (i) a rejection of theories of ideology; (ii) a denial that there is any knowable relationship between representation and that which is represented; (iii) an insistence that functionalist formulations are always and necessarily incorrect.

Ideology

It is clear that a position resting on a rejection of epistemological theories must inevitably reject any elements of determination in its approach to ideology. Paul Hirst, in a

4. Parveen Adams, 'A Note on the Distinction Between Sexual Division and Sexual Differences', *m/f*, no.3, 1979, p.52.

critique of Althusser, points to the 'fragile' character of the thesis that ideology is 'relatively autonomous' of its supposed economic determinants. He argues that the notion of relative autonomy 'attempts to overcome economism without facing the theoretical consequences of doing so'. On the face of it, such a criticism might point to an espousal of the view that ideology is 'absolutely' autonomous. But this turns out to be a naive or wilful misreading of the text. 'Autonomy from what?', asks Hirst rhetorically, insisting that even to pose questions of causality is to assume a social totality in which particular instances are governed by their place in the whole.[5] This enlightenment induces distaste for the concept of ideology itself, and a preference for that of 'discursive practices'. As the editors of *m/f* emphasize: 'it is indeed *theories of ideology* that present the categories of men and women as exclusive and exhaustive'.[6] This is certainly a stylish way of dealing with the problem. But I think we have to ask whether in following it we really have shaken the mundane dust of ideology off our feet. We have, after all, been led through a series of increasingly radical breaks with the Marxism of Marx and Althusser, and the final transcendence of the epistemological problematic of 'ideology' is built on the earlier advances made within this framework. In particular, the way in which the concept of discursive practice is deployed owes much to previous attempts to demonstrate the autonomy and materiality of ideology. To put this another way: they have shifted the discourse of ideology onto the terrain of the discourse of discourse and while in their terms this may be as real an advance as any other, to the critic of discursive imperialism it may seem a nominal rather than a conceptual gain. For this reason I want to take issue with a tenet which (although an epistemological one and therefore rejected by discourse theory) has provided for many people the stepping stone to

5. See Paul Q. Hirst, 'Althusser and the Theory of Ideology', *Economy and Society*, vol.5, no.4, p.395; *On Law and Ideology*, London 1979, p.18.
6. *m/f*, no.4, 1980, p.23.

support for the more radical position: the 'materiality of ideology'.

This tenet is now so much *de rigeur* in the British Marxist avant-garde that to be caught artlessly counterposing 'material conditions' and 'ideology' is an embarassing error — 'but surely ideology *is* material' will be the inevitable reproof. Yet this assumption will not withstand closer investigation. The insistence that ideology *is material* arises, I suspect, from an unsuccessful attempt to resolve a classic paradox in Marxism: that being may determine consciousness but revolutionary transformation of the conditions of being will depend upon raising the level of class-consciousness. Virginia Woolf once said 'a republic might be brought into being by a poem' and indeed it is possible, if unlikely, that a powerfully-wrought poem could goad an exploited proletariat into successful seizure of the means of production. Yet however colossal the material *effects* of this poem, they would have no bearing on the question of whether the poem itself had a material existence.

To reject the view that ideology is material does not imply a retreat to the view that the economic and the ideological are related in a one-way system of determination of the latter by the former. On the contrary, it is important to stress a degree of reciprocity here. It is impossible to understand the division of labour, for instance, with its differential definitions of 'skill', without taking into account the material effects of gender ideology. The belief that a (white) man has a 'right' to work over and above any rights of married women or immigrants has had significant effects in the organization of the labour force. Such a belief has therefore to be taken into account when analysing the division of labour, but its location in material practices does not render it material in the same way.

The argument turns on what might be seen as an extension of Althusser's approach to ideology. For while Althusser argues, in my view correctly, that ideology exists *in* (material) apparatuses and their practices it requires a considerable leap of faith to translate this as meaning that ideology *is* material. Stuart Hall and Richard Johnson have made this point very clearly: Johnson suggests that a 'genuine insight' here becomes 'reckless hyperbole' and Hall argues that the *'slide'* from one meaning to the other enables 'the magical qualifier, "materialist"' to serve as an undeserved emblem of legitimation.[7]

The notion of the materiality of ideology has been influential and has reinforced the claim that ideology should be regarded as absolutely autonomous. For why, if ideology is as material as the economic relations we used to think of as 'material conditions', should it not be assigned an equal place in our analysis? The crucial questions concerning the relationship of ideological processes to historical conditions of the production and reproduction of material life are left unexamined in this attempt to colonize the world for a newly privileged concept of ideology in which everything is material. Yet in drawing the net of ideology so wide we are left with no means, no tools, for distinguishing anything. As Terry Eagleton trenchantly remarks, 'there is no possible sense in which meanings and values can be said to be "material", other than in the most sloppily metaphorical use of the term... If meanings *are* material, then the term "materialism" naturally ceases to be intelligible. Since there is nothing which the concept excludes, it ceases to have value'.[8]

Representation

Parveen Adams argues that 'the classical theory of representation' must be rejected. What would such a rejection entail? This classical theory, central to Marxist aesthetics, poses representation (usually seen as ideological,

7. Richard Johnson, 'Histories of Culture/Theories of Ideology', in *Ideology and Cultural Production*, Michèle Barrett, Philip Corrigan, Annette Kuhn and Janet Wolff, eds., London 1979, p.59; Stuart Hall, 'Some Problems with the Ideology/Subject Couplet', *Ideology and Consciousness*, no.3, 1978, p.116.
8. Terry Eagleton 'Ideology, Fiction, Narrative', *Social Text*, forthcoming 1980.

and often explored through the analysis of cultural products) as to some degree a reflection of specific historical conditions. Debate has raged over whether literary texts, for instance, can be understood as direct reflections, or even distortions, of reality or should be seen as mediated in complex ways. Such texts are held, however, always to bear *some* relation to the social relations in which they were produced. It is this relationship that is being challenged here. Paul Hirst, in the critique of Althusser already mentioned, has argued that representation must necessarily entail *means of* representation and that once these are allowed it must follow that they 'determine' that which is represented. It is but a step from this to argue that *nothing other* than the means of representation determine what is represented — that 'the real' can never exist prior to its representation. This short step, however, constitutes an important break in the argument. For while it is true, as Hirst argues, that the signified does not exist (in semiotic theory) prior to its signification, this does not rule out the existence of a material referent of the sign as a whole. So Hirst's preference for the conceptual framework of signification over that of representation, and his claim that the former facilitates a break with the constraints of the classic theory of ideology, remain unjustified.

Certainly it is true that the means of representation are important. In the area of cultural production, for example, it is easy to see how forms of representation are governed by genres, conventions, the presence of established modes of communication and so on. Yet these are not determining in the absolute sense being argued for here. They do not in themselves account for what is represented. We can approach this problem by way of an example, by looking at the imagery of gender. Suppose I am an enterprising motor-car manufacturer, and it occurs to me that I can tap a market of independent salaried women for my product. I advertise my car with a seductive, scantily-clad male model draped over its bonnet and an admiring, yet slightly ser~ snappily-dressed man politely opening the car door fo

putative client. Will my efforts be crowned with success? It is
unlikely — and the reason why it is unlikely is, precisely, that
representation *does* bear a relation to something which we
can know previously existed.

This point is explored in two interesting articles on the
imagery, and cultural stereotyping, of gender. Griselda
Pollock argues that we should not be content to view the
cultural representation of gender as 'images of women'. She
rejects this approach because it cannot explain why it should
be that the inversion or reversal of accepted imagery simply
does not succeed.[9] This is so not only because the representation of women is linked to a broader chain, or system,
of signification. It also occurs because representation is
linked to historically constituted real relations. To put the
matter simply, we can understand why female models may
be more persuasive to male customers than *vice versa* only if
we take account of a prior commoditization of women's
bodies. Why this should have been so, and how, are clearly
questions for historical analysis, but the fact remains that a
connection has been established in which not only have
women's bodies become commodities themselves (for
instance in prostitution) but the association between them
and consumerism has more generally taken hold. A related
case is made by T. E. Perkins in a discussion of
stereotyping.[10] Perkins argues that however irrational or
erroneous a particular stereotype may be thought, we do not
have the option of eradicating it by the voluntary
substitution of a different one. Stereotypes are tied to
historical social relations, and indeed, Perkins argues, the
chances of success in challenging a stereotype will depend
upon the social location of the group in question.

To argue in this way does not imply any pre-given, or
ahistorical, content of representation. Parveen Adams
appears to be arguing that *either* we talk of 'sexual division'

9. Griselda Pollock, 'What's Wrong With Images of Women?', *Screen
    Education*, no.24, 1977.
10. T. E. Perkins, 'Rethinking Stereotypes', in *Ideology and Cultural
    Production*.

as 'an always already antagonistic relation between two social groups who are frozen into a mutually exclusive and jointly exhaustive division',[11] *or* we talk of 'sexual differences' as the apparently spontaneous production of something that we cannot know in advance. These, however, do not constitute our only options. We do not need to talk of sexual division as 'always already' there; we can explore the historical construction of the categories of masculinity and femininity without being obliged to deny that, historically specific as they are, they nevertheless exist today in systematic and even predictable terms. Without denying that representation plays an important constitutive role in this process we can still insist that at any given time we can have a knowledge of these categories prior to any particular representation in which they may be reproduced or subverted.

Functionalism

It is clearly true that the problem of functionalism has been a serious one for Marxist feminism. Both feminist and Marxist accounts of women's oppression have tended to slide uncritically into a mode of explanation which is undeniably functionalist; many feminist accounts explain various forms of oppression in terms of their supposedly self-evident functions of perpetuating patriarchal dominance, and many Marxist accounts centre on the supposed benefits, or functions, for capital of women's subordinate position. These forms of functionalism, and arguments derived from functionalist sociology, have undoubtedly been influential in many Marxist feminist explanations too.[12] Clearly any account of women's oppression that is organized around its importance for the smooth reproduction of capitalist social relations must run the risk of over-emphasizing this

11. *m/f*, no.3, p.57.
12. The problem is addressed explicitly by Mary McIntosh in 'The State and the Oppression of Women' (in Annette Kuhn and AnnMarie Wolpe, eds., *Feminism and Materialism*, London 1978).

supposedly functional relationship at the expense of a proper consideration of contradiction, conflict and political struggle.

Dissatisfaction with these accounts must lie behind the appeal of the alternative approach now being discussed. Criticism of the notion of function is a central point of their attack. Adams castigates the uncritical use of the term 'sexual division' for enabling merely a description of pre-given functions.[13] Coward suggests that the entire debate as to the profitability or otherwise of the family for capitalism can be 'cleared away' by posing the problem in terms of particular conjunctures in which specific conditions of existence of the relations of production are secured.[14] This approach draws on the rejection (by Hindess and Hirst) of general entities such as 'the capitalist mode of production' and the equally firm rejection of any 'necessary correspondence' between economic and ideological relations. It relies, in fact, on the assumption of a 'non-correspondence' — on the pre-given impossibility of establishing such relations or correspondences. This case is not however proven, even in its own terms, for if the notion of 'necessary correspondence' is invalid so also must any notion of 'necessary non-correspondence' lapse into dogmatism. The notion of 'difference' merely assumes the role of that which is 'always already' there, and is equally unjustified.

More importantly, the argument is predicated upon a caricature of the position it seeks to reject. Analyses couched in terms of modes of production, even in terms of proposed functional relations within these modes, need not *necessarily* fail to grasp the centrality of contradiction and struggle. Richard Johnson has argued that we may usefully return to Gramsci's conception of capitalist reproduction: 'a hard and constantly resisted labour, a political and ideological work for capital and for the dominant classes, on very obstinate materials indeed'.[15] Such a view is not only

13. *m/f*, no.3, p.52.
14. *m/f*, no.4, p.92.
15. 'Histories of Culture/Theories of Ideology', p.74.

analytically sounder than the one I have been discussing, it is grounded in a more fruitful political context. Here it may be useful to consider briefly the political implications of the feminist application of discourse theory. This is particularly important since although these writers do spell out quite openly the political consequences of their position, the language in which the debate is cast is so impenetrable that relatively few critics have so far engaged with it.

First, insofar as a knowledge of real social relations is denied, it must follow that discourse itself must be the site of struggle. We do not even seek a cultural revolution; we seek a revolution in discourse. I do not want to deny either the importance of ideological struggle or the role of discourse within it (indeed it would be hard to see why I was writing this book if I did). However, there is a world of difference between assigning some weight to ideological struggle and concluding that no other struggle is relevant or important. The relief with which the intellectual left has seized upon these ideas as a justification and political legitimation of any form of academic work is in itself suspicious and alarming. For although I would not dispute the political significance of such activity, a distinction must be retained between this form of struggle and the more terrestrial kind. Are we really to see the Peterloo massacre, the storming of the Winter Palace in Petrograd, the Long March, the Grunwick picket — as the struggle of discourses?

The exclusive emphasis placed on discursive practice has led to a critical consideration of the discourse of feminism itself. In some respects this is both proper and valuable, since the language in which feminist demands are expressed must be constructed with care and integrity. Political slogans, for instance, inevitably aim at popular mobilization and may do so at a cost of oversimplification or compromise. Yet the critique of feminist slogans elaborated in successive articles in *m/f* is surely politically inappropriate to the point of being destructive. One by one the campaigning slogans of women's liberation — *the personal is political, a woman's right to choose, control of our bodies* — are found to rest on errors of epistemology. They rely on humanism, essentialism, inadequate theories of the subject and so on.[16] This critical exercise is in my view misplaced, in that it rests on a failure to appreciate the grounding of such slogans in particular historical struggles. More importantly, perhaps, it leads us to ask what alternative political strategy is being offered if we take seriously the post-Althusserian critique of traditional ways of perceiving women's oppression.

I find the political purchase of this approach particularly negative here. If we take, for instance, the question of whether feminist demands are reformist or not we find Rosalind Coward asserting that 'there can no longer be any distinction between reformist and revolutionary activity....'.[17] It may very well be that received socialist truth on this question needs to be challenged, but this cannot be done by dismissing the problem in such a cavalier way. At the least, to do so manifests a refusal to engage with a salient area of current political debate. Fundamentally, it is unclear that the project to deconstruct the category of woman could ever provide a basis for a feminist politics. If there are no 'women' to be oppressed then on what criteria do we struggle, and against what? The difficulty here is to see the connection between the theoretical project and its stated designation as 'feminist'. The feminism enters as an act of ethical goodwill rather than a political practice tied to an analysis of the world; it remains a 'self-evident' and unexplained goal which in fact the theoretical consequences of discourse theory must systematically undermine.

II

I have discussed these arguments at some length, since they are proposed as a solution to the crucial question faced by

16. See Parveen Adams and Jeff Minson, 'The "Subject" of Feminism', *m/f*, no.2, 1978; Beverley Brown and Parveen Adams, 'The Feminine Body and Feminist Politics', *m/f*, no.3, 1979.
17. *m/f*, no.2, p.94. Although I have cited this article more than once as an admirably clear exposition of the feminist appropriation of discourse theory I am not implying that Coward's work as a whole is limited to the parameters defining this project. On the contrary.

Marxist feminist analysis — what is the relationship between women's oppression and the general features of a mode of production? I am unconvinced that the post-Althusserian development of discourse theory has rendered this question obsolete. These writers have, however, usefully alerted us once again to the underdeveloped nature of the theory of ideology, and in the following section I will attempt to sketch out a more useful way of deploying this concept.

I want to suggest first that for a concept of ideology to have any analytic use it must be bounded. We must retrench from a position where ideology is claimed to be as determining, as material, as the relations of production. The concept of 'relative autonomy' must, whatever its apparent fragility, be further explored and defined. This need not necessarily involve intellectual acrobatics of the kind which would be required to prove that ideology is at one and the same time autonomous and not. To perceive this problem in terms of abstract logic is to misunderstand it. What it does involve is the specification, for a given social historical context, of the limits to the autonomous operation of ideology. Hence we should be able to specify what range of possibilities exist for the ideological processes of a particular social formation, without necessarily being able to predict the specific form they may take.

Second, I want to restrict the term to phenomena which are mental rather than material. Hence the concept of ideology refers to those processes which have to do with consciousness, motive, emotionality; it can best be located in the category of *meaning*. Ideology is a generic term for the processes by which meaning is produced, challenged, reproduced, transformed. Since meaning is negotiated primarily through means of communication and significa-tion, it is possible to suggest that cultural production provides an important site for the construction of ideological processes. Thus, it is not inappropriate to claim, as Eagleton and others have, that literature (for instance) can usefully be analysed as a paradigm case of ideology in particular social formations.[18] Ideology is embedded historically in material practice but it does not follow *either* that ideology is theoretically indistinguishable from material practices *or* that it bears any direct relationship to them. We may learn much, from an analysis of novels, about the ways in which meaning was constructed in a particular historical period, but our knowledge will not add up to a general knowledge of that social formation. For if literature does constitute a primary site of ideological negotiation, nonetheless it cannot provide the historian with an adequate knowledge of other, equally important aspects of a social formation. The mediation of social reality operating in any fictional work will ensure that the historian will face many dangers in pillaging literature for its 'social content'. One reason why this should be so is that literary texts operate, as Pierre Macherey has argued, through their absences as well as through what is present in them.[19] Following Althusser's method of 'symptomatic reading', in which the analyst can supposedly detect the gaps and weaknesses of the author's original problematic, Macherey suggests that we should concentrate not on what the text overtly presents to us, but on what is *not said* in it. There are clearly problems with this model, which I shall come back to later, but Macherey points to an important danger here.

Third, lest it should be thought this represents a return to an economistic base/superstructure model of society, I should emphasize the integral connection between ideology and the relations of production. This is particularly important and easily demonstrated, in the case of the ideology of gender. As I shall argue later, this ideology has played an important part in the historical construction of the capitalist division of labour and in the reproduction of labour power. A sexual division of labour, and accompanying ideologies of the appropriate meaning of labour for men and women, have been embedded in the capitalist division of labour from its beginnings. It is impossible to over-emphasize here the importance of an historical analysis. I

18. Terry Eagleton, 'Ideology, Fiction, Narrative'.
19. Pierre Macherey, *A Theory of Literary Production*, London 1978.

make no claim for the inevitability of this particular ideology as a functional requisite for capitalist production — it is one of several possible options. Nevertheless there are grounds to accept a point made by Colin Sumner in his fascinating and controversial book: that once such an ideology *is* historically embedded it may *become* essential for the maintenance of the system.[20]

In stressing the role of ideology in the relations of production it is perhaps necessary, to avoid misunderstanding, to stress the fact that the term 'relations of production' does not refer simply to class relations. It must comprise the divisions of gender, of race, definitions of different forms of labour (mental, manual and so on), of who should work and at what. Relations of production reflect and embody the outcome of struggles: over the division of labour, the length of the working day, the costs of reproduction. Marx's allusion to the 'historical and moral element' in the value of labour-power requires further exploration and elaboration. It is, perhaps, useful here to distinguish between the 'relations of production', in which the ideology of gender plays a very important part, and the means and forces of production. For while it is true that the ideology of gender plays a very significant role in the *relations* of production, it is far more difficult to argue that it plays a crucial part in the essential reproduction of raw materials, installations and machinery; and although domestic labour is vital to the present form in which labour power is reproduced, this need not necessarily be the case. Indeed it can plausibly be argued that the wage-labour relation and the contradiction between labour and capital — the defining characteristics of the capitalist mode of production — are 'sex-blind' and operate quite independently of gender.

III

I want now to discuss the ways in which the ideology of gender is produced and reproduced in cultural practice. Much

20. Colin Sumner, *Reading Ideologies: An Investigation into the Marxist Theory of Ideology and Law*, London 1979.

of the discussion will relate to the question of literature, since this is a practice which has generated considerable work in this area, and is the practice most familiar to me, but parallels with other forms will be drawn where possible. I shall look first of all at the question of what we need to consider if we want to arrive at a systematic analysis of gender ideology. This is important, since much of the work so far undertaken has concentrated disproportionally on describing *how* gender is presented — 'what images of women are portrayed?' is the commonest question — and has not sought to locate this in a broader theoretical framework. So it will only be after considering the *context* of this imagery that I shall attempt to draw out the dominant themes of gender imagery in contemporary cultural practice. Finally, I shall consider the political potential of cultural production, returning to the question of whether a revolution at the level of culture is possible or adequate.

The first point to make in considering the necessary elements of an analysis of gender ideology in cultural production cannot be stressed too strongly: we must avoid making the text itself our only basis for analysis. In rejecting this approach, we should be clear that we are not only rejecting the tradition of literary criticism which has constantly insisted that the text 'speaks for itself': we are also rejecting the apparently more sophisticated 'structuralist' analyses that have tended to replace conventional literary and other criticisms. To restrict our analysis solely to the text itself is to turn the *object* of analysis into its own means of explanation; by definition this cannot provide an adequate account. To reduce the problem solely to the text is a form of reductionism as unprofitable as reducing it to the mechanical expression of economic relations. As I and others have argued elsewhere, this reduction to the text 'simply privileges the artefact itself, divorced from its conditions of production and existence, and claims that it alone provides the means of its own analysis'.[21]

21. 'Representation and Cultural Production', in *Ideology and Cultural Production*, p.11.

To avoid this form of reduction we have to move away from a dependence upon our 'reading' of the text. This is far more difficult than it might appear. The history of both bourgeois and materialist criticism is rooted in the struggle for a 'correct' reading. In bourgeois criticism this takes the form of posing moral and aesthetic questions to which the critic, depending on his or her own sensitivity, will produce more or less satisfactory answers. The text has sometimes here been seen as potentially providing answers not only about its own construction (characterization, narrative and so on) but to larger questions about 'human nature' or 'beauty'. This approach is criticized by Marxist and feminist critics. They tend to ask instead, 'what does my reading of this text tell me about' class consciousness, or responses to industrialization, or sexism, or whatever. But the argument is still posed in terms of a subjective reading: *you* may read this text as 'about' human nature, *I* read it as 'about' capitalism or patriarchy. Nor is this debate really resolved by trying to look for what the text does not say, as a means for reading what it is 'about'. As Colin Sumner has argued, this (neo-structuralist) technique relies heavily on introspection.[22]

If we are to get beyond basing our analysis on a reading of the text we need to construct a theoretical framework in which these broader questions are built into the method. This project is at a very early stage as yet, and perhaps the most systematic attempt to develop the constituent elements of such an approach is that provided by Terry Eagleton's 'categories for a materialist criticism'.[23] Eagleton suggests that the text should be understood as the product of the 'complex historical articulations' of various structures, and proposes the following schema:—

(i)   General mode of production
(ii) Literary mode of production
(iii) General ideology
(iv) Authorial ideology

22. Sumner, p.172-3.
23. Terry Eagleton, *Criticism and Ideology*, London 1976.

(v) Aesthetic ideology

(vi) Text

These categories, although somewhat unwieldy, are a major advance on the unformulated methods of materialist criticism that Eagleton has attempted to synthesize. They constitute a useful set of related structures which can profitably be used as a general framework in which to develop specific analyses. I do not want to discuss them in detail here, but will comment briefly on only one of these categories: the 'literary mode of production'.

I am not convinced that it is necessary or profitable to elevate the forces and relations of literary production to the status of a 'mode of production'. Nonetheless, in adopting this term Eagleton creates an opportunity to explore in very fruitful ways the specifically literary constraints in which a text is historically produced. Although Eagleton does not totally displace the centrality of the text, his account does by definition constitute an attack on the idealist view that 'art' can transcend its conditions of production. Eagleton's literary mode of production is constituted by forces and relations of production, distribution, exchange and consumption. Any given period may have residual features of earlier literary modes of production, or may contain forms prefiguring later modes, but will be characterized by a dominant mode which exerts specific determinations on the text to be produced. Analysis of these processes would take into account the stage of the development of the forces of literary production (an obvious example being the effects of the invention of printing) and the relations in which work was produced (different forms of patronage and so on). In addition to this Eagleton argues that such an analysis would be essential to grasp the meaning of the text. The material conditions of its production are internalized: 'every literary text intimates by its very conventions the way it is to be consumed, encodes within itself its own ideology of how, by whom and for whom it was produced'.[24] We can conclude

24. Ibid., p.48.

from this that if women are situated differently from men in respect of the forces and relations of literary production, we might expect to see this internalized in texts — and we do.

IV

In arguing for a more systematic approach to the ideology of gender, we can isolate three specific elements in the process. These I shall refer to by the shorthand terms of production, consumption and representation, and I shall deal first with the question of *production*.

It is immediately clear that the conditions under which men and women produce literature are materially different. This important question has been curiously neglected by recent feminist work, and the most systematic exploration of this issue is still, fifty years after its publication, Virginia Woolf's *A Room of One's Own*.[25] Naive as this essay undoubtedly is in some respects, it nonetheless provides us with a very useful starting-point. Woolf bases her arguments in this book and in related essays on materialist propositions.[26] Writing, she argues, is not 'spun in mid-air by incorporeal creatures': it is based on material things (health, money, the houses we live in). These material conditions must govern the writer's 'angle of vision', his or her perception of society. They must influence the art-form chosen, the genre chosen within the form, the style, the tone, the implied reader, the representation of character.

Woolf argues that a crucial difference between men and women has lain historically in the restricted access of the latter to the means of literary production. Their education was frequently sacrificed to that of their brothers; they lacked access to publishers and the distribution of their work; they could not earn a living by writing as men did, since (before the Married Women's Property Acts) they could

25. Harmondsworth 1970 (first published in 1929).
26. A selection of these may be found in Virginia Woolf, *Women and Writing*, London 1979.

not even retain their earnings if they were married. Relative poverty and lack of access to an artistic training meant that the bourgeois woman encountered specific constraints on her creative work: Woolf suggests that one reason why women have been so prolific in literary production and almost absent from forms such as musical composition and visual art is that the latter require greater financial resources than 'the scratching of a pen' ('For ten and sixpence one can buy paper enough to write all the plays of Shakespeare. . .'). Less plausibly and more controversially, she argues that even the choice of literary form was affected by women's social position: they opted for the new form of the novel rather than for poetry or drama, since it required less concentration and was therefore more compatible with the inevitable interruptions of household obligations.

A strength of Woolf's analysis is that her discussion of representation is located in an analysis of both the historical production and distribution of literature and its social consumption and reception. She argues that accepted social and literary-critical attitudes that denigrated women's writing played an important part in influencing the production of literature by women. They did this not only by forcing women writers to adopt male pseudonyms in order to get their work published and neutrally assessed, but by engendering an over-aggressive or over-defensive tone in women's writing. She refers here to what the Marxist-Feminist Literature Collective now call 'gender criticism': the approach that 'subsumes the text into the sexually-defined personality of its author, and thereby obliterates its literarity'.[27]

Although Woolf's account is more systematic than most, we still await a substantial account of *consumption* and reception of texts from the point of view of the ideology of gender (or from any other point of view, one could add). There has been a failure to develop a theory of reading. This is

27. 'Women's Writing: *Jane Eyre, Shirley, Villette, Aurora Leigh*', *Ideology and Consciousness*, no.3, 1978, p.31.

largely, I suspect, because any such analysis would have to confront directly one of the most difficult problems of a materialist aesthetics: the problem of value. Virginia Woolf, it might be noted, simply ignored this problem. Although challenging much of what constituted 'the canon' of great literature of her period, she slides quite unremorsefully into the worst kind of aesthetic league-tabling in much of her criticism. Preoccupation with the question of value ('quality', 'standards') has been detrimental for feminist criticism and appears to have been posed as a choice between two limited options. On the one hand, we have the view exemplified by Virginia Woolf: that women have not reached the achievements of male writers, but that this is to be attributed to the constraints historically inherent in the conditions in which their work was produced and consumed. On the other hand, there is the view that women *have* achieved equally in respect of aesthetic value and we only think otherwise because of the warped and prejudiced response of a predominantly male, and sexist, critical and academic establishment.

This debate is fruitless (although admittedly seductive) in that it reproduces the assumption that aesthetic judgment is independent of social and historical context. Simply to pose the question at this level is to deny what we do already know: that not only are refined details of aesthetic ranking highly culturally specific, but that there is not even any consensus across classes, let alone across cultures, as to which cultural products can legitimately be subjected to such judgments. I am not contending that these observations obviate the problem of aesthetic value, since I believe it to be an urgent task of feminist criticism to take it on in the context of the female literary tradition, but merely that it should not be posed in simplistic terms.

In respect of literary production and distribution, consumption and reception, we should attend to the different ways in which men and women have historically been situated as authors. I am not so sure that this difference is equally relevant to the *representation* of gender in cultural products. For, while I do not wish to exculpate any particular male author from responsibility for irredeemably sexist work, it remains true that the imagery of gender affects both men and women profoundly, if differently. Problems arise when we try to distinguish, at the level of our reading of novels, between the images presented by male authors and those presented by female. The question of representation is beset by the problem of interpretation, and this is why I have been arguing that we cannot rely on subjective readings. If, for instance, a novel is published by a feminist publishing house and it carries on its jacket a blurb telling us it is 'a telling indictment of patriarchy' we are likely to read the contents (the story of a woman's humiliation at the hands of her brutal male lover) as precisely that. If, as is conceivable, a similar story is published by another firm with a blurb referring to 'sex and violence' and a cover picture of a supine woman wearing only a torn negligée, we shall read it rather differently (if we read it at all). Yet these readings will be determined not by any differences in the text itself but by the inferences about it we have drawn from its presentation.

This simple example illustrates two problems. The first is that we cannot assume that a particular meaning is intrinsic to the text, since it must depend on how it is read. Put another way: ideology is not 'transparent', and this, as I shall emphasize later, has implications for overtly politicized art. Second, it raises the question of authorial intention, which leads down many disastrous alley-ways. There has been a general tendency for feminist criticism to approach male and female authors very differently. Female authors are 'credited' with trying to pose the question of gender, or women's oppression, in their work, and male authors are 'discredited' by means of an assumption that any sexism they portray is necessarily their own. It seems extraordinary that these tendencies, both of which in their rampant moralism deny precisely the fictional, the *literary*, structure of the texts, should have taken such hold in the field of 'women and literature'. The attempt to present women writers as 'trying to solve' problems of gender is particularly fraught with problems. For although women writers frequently do, quite understandably, structure their work around the issues which their experience has provided them with, we ignore the *fictional* nature of their work at our peril. To construe a novelist as a sociologist manqué is to lead to the position adopted by Rachel Harrison, who makes the singularly misplaced comment that 'in *Shirley*, Charlotte Brontë is working with a necessarily descriptive account of the changing forces and relations of production' and then goes on to specify the 'later theoretical developments' that might have improved her analysis.[28]

If this identification of text and female author is unsatisfactory, so too is the parallel treatment of male authors. Cora Kaplan, in her very interesting assessment of *Sexual Politics*, suggests that Millett's refusal to see the ambivalence in her authors' work, her intransigent criticism of their sexism, is based on 'the unproblematic identification of author, protagonist and point of view, and the unspoken assumption that literature is always a conscious rendering of authorial ideology'.[29]

It is neither plausible nor profitable to study literature for the purpose of berating morally reprehensible authors. Nor is it possible to take literary texts, or any other cultural products, as necessary reflections of the social reality of any particular period. They cannot even provide us with a reliable knowledge of directly inferrable ideology. What they can offer, I suggest, is an indication of the bounds within which particular meanings are constructed and negotiated in a given social formation; but this would depend upon considering a fairly wide range of such products. Imagery is a notoriously misleading indicator: think of the impression created by studying, for example, the iconography of royalty in contemporary Britain. The proverbial Martian might be forgiven for concluding, from all those pictures of the

28. Rachel Harrison, '*Shirley*: Relations of Reproduction and the Ideology of Romance', *Women Take Issue*, London 1978, pp.185-6, 187.
29. Cora Kaplan, p.10.

Queen reviewing regiments, opening Parliament, enthron-
ing archbishops and so on, that she controlled all the
repressive and ideological state apparatuses. It would take a
more systematic study to dispel this illusion.

In spite of all these reservations we can usefully isolate
some of the processes by which the work of reproducing
gender ideology is done. In a rough and preliminary way we
can identify processes of stereotyping, compensation,
collusion and recuperation, across a range of cultural
practices.

The notion of a 'stereotype' has become so over-used that it
may be thought to lack sufficient clarity, but it is I think of
use in looking at the way gender difference is rigidly
represented in, for instance, the mass media. Recent work
has shown the pervasive operation of gender stereotypes in
advertising and in children's books. Trevor Millum has
described the extremely limited images of women presented
in a sample of advertisements: they relate almost exclusively
to women's role in the home, oscillating between the
glamorous and efficient hostess and the dutiful, caring
mother.[30] With regard to children's books, Nightingale and
others have commented on the extent to which they
represent a sexual division of labour far more rigid than even
the sharp differentiation we know to exist.[31] Many children
whose mothers are in regular employment must be surprised
to find that the mothers in their early school reading books
are invariably and exclusively engaged in housework. This
process of stereotyping is probably the one best-documented
documented in feminist studies, and the existence of such
rigid formulations in many different cultural practices
clearly indicates a degree of hard work being put into their
maintenance. We could, perhaps, be forgiven for regarding
this imagery as the 'wish-fulfilment of patriarchy'.

30. Trevor Millum, *Images of Women: Advertising in Women's Magazines*,
     London 1975.
31. Camilla Nightingale, 'Boys Will Be Boys But What Will Girls Be?' in
     Martin Hoyles, ed., *The Politics of Literacy*, London 1977. See also Bob
     Dixon, *Catching Them Young 1: Sex, Race and Class in Children's
     Fiction*, London 1977.

The category of 'compensation' refers to the presentation of imagery and ideas that tend to elevate the 'moral value' of femininity. One could take examples from the plethora of practices which, in the context of systematic denial of opportunities for women, attempt to 'compensate' for this by a corresponding ideology of moral worth. The dichotomous view of woman embodied in the ideology of the Catholic Church, Rosemary Ruether argues, does precisely this: juxtaposing madonna and whore, mariolatry and an oppressive and contemptuous attitude to its female members.[32] An important element of such compensatory work is the romanticism of woman that it generates. This romanticism may well be 'genuinely' felt by both men and women and I do not use the term 'compensation' to imply that these processes are necessarily conscious or intentional. An interesting example of this process is given in a study by Hilary Graham of the literature handed out to pregnant women.[33] Graham's analysis of the romantic photography of this genre (softly focused shots of idyllic mother-and-child scenes) compares rather ill with the patronizing and curt clinical treatment they get when they leave the waiting room and enter the examination cubicle. Finally we should note the importance of an historical account of this process. As Catherine Hall's and Leonore Davidoff's work in different ways demonstrates,[34] the 'ideology of domesticity', with its

32. Rosemary Radford Ruether, ed., *Religion and Sexism*, New York 1974. See the editor's own paper ('Misogynism and Virginal Feminism in the Fathers of the Church') for this argument.
33. Hilary Graham, 'Images of Pregnancy in Ante-Natal Literature', in R. Dingwall *et al.*, ed., *Health Care and Health Knowledge*, London 1977.
34. Leonore Davidoff, 'The Rationalization of Housework', in D. Leonard Barker and S. Allen, eds., *Dependence and Exploitation in Work and Marriage*, London 1976; Leonore Davidoff *et al.*, 'Landscape with Figures: Home and Community in English Society', in Juliet Mitchell and Ann Oakley, eds., *The Rights and Wrongs of Women*, Harmondsworth 1976; Catherine Hall, 'The Early Formation of Victorian Domestic Ideology', in S. Burman, ed., *Fit Work for Women*, London 1979; Catherine Hall, 'Married Women at Home in Birmingham in the 1920s and 1930s', in *Oral History* (Women's History Issue), vol.5, no.2, Autumn 1977.

intense moral and sentimental elevation of the family home was developed in the stultifying ethos of Victorian restrictions on female activity.

The notion of 'collusion' may be taken to refer to two processes that it is useful to distinguish. On the one hand, we can note the attempts made to manipulate and parade women's 'consent' to their subordination and objectification. The classic example here is provided in John Berger's discussion of the female-nude painting tradition. Having stressed the blatant voyeurism of much of this genre he comments on the practice of portraying a female nude surveying herself in a mirror: 'you painted a naked woman because you enjoyed looking at her, you put a mirror in her hand and you called the painting *Vanity*, thus morally condemning the woman whose nakedness you had depicted for your own pleasure. The real function of the mirror was otherwise. It was to make the woman connive in treating herself as, first and foremost, a sight'.[35] This connivance, or collusion, does not always take the form Berger outlines. The second process to which the notion of collusion refers is crucially important: that of women's willing consent and their internalization of oppression. This point has already been touched on in connection with the question of sexuality, and indeed one reason why psychoanalytic theory has acquired its present credence among feminists is precisely that it does offer an explanation of consent and collusion. An analysis of gender ideology in which women are always innocent, always passive victims of patriarchal power, is patently not satisfactory. Simone de Beauvoir's solution to the problem was to suggest a general inclination towards 'bad faith': if women are offered the chance of relinquishing the existential burden of subjective responsibility, men may expect them to show 'complicity'.[36]

Acceptance of the importance of collusion need not necessarily lead either to a crude formulation of women's consciousness as simply 'false consciousness', or to a denial of objective conditions of oppression. It is important to

35. John Berger, *Ways of Seeing*, Harmondsworth 1977, p.51.

remember the extent to which our consciousness is formed in conditions of subordination and oppression. We cannot, by the simple act of will, wish away politically 'incorrect' elements of our consciousness or 'reactionary' sources of pleasure. I am not suggesting that collusion should be regarded with complacency, for clearly it should be contested, but we need to develop further our understanding of the means by which it is constructed and of what the conditions of its amelioration would be.

Finally I want to mention the process of 'recuperation'. I refer here to the ideological effort that goes into negating and defusing challenges to the historically dominant meaning of gender in particular periods. Anyone disputing the work involved in ideological reproduction could profitably consider the 'hard labour' that has been put into accommodating women's liberation in the media. It is, of course, particularly apparent in advertising. Although I cited Trevor Millum's account of stereotyping in advertisements, this picture should be modified by looking at the ways in which the advertising media have sought to recapture lost ground on the question of women's independence. Although clearly some advertisements that play with the notion of an independent woman are aimed at a market of female purchasers (such as the ambiguous 'Every Woman Needs Her Daily Mail'), many others are explicitly addressed to redressing the effects of women's liberation. An obvious example of this might be the advertisement of tights 'for women who don't want to wear the trousers'.

The question of recuperation is perhaps one of the most interesting in the study of ideology. Elizabeth Cowie's detailed interpretation of the film *Coma* provides a suggestive discussion of this phenomenon.[37] The film, although ostensibly constructed around a female character

36.   Simone de Beauvoir, *The Second Sex*, Harmondsworth 1974, p.21. I am not suggesting that de Beauvoir sees collusion as anything other than a *response*: she also argues that 'woman is shut up in a kitchen or boudoir, and astonishment is expressed that her horizon is limited. Her wings are clipped, and it is found deplorable that she cannot fly'. (p.616).

who plays an intelligent and courageous role of detection, takes away with one hand what it has given with the other: our heroine cracks the riddle but finally has to be saved by her boyfriend. This type of scenario is not solely a response to the activity of the present women's liberation movement, although clearly we may look forward to more of it as the movement gains ground. It is a response, to changes in the position of women, which may be generated at other times. Helen Roberts, for example, has outlined parallel processes.[38] Taking both popular fiction and the work of novelists such as Winifred Holtby and Dorothy Sayers, Roberts describes the presentation of women whose independence is initially convincingly depicted (particularly by Sayers), but eventually denied by the action of the narrative.

What implications does the approach outlined in this chapter have for 'cultural revolution' and for political art? I want to recapitulate two significant points: the first, that ideology — as the work of constructing meaning — cannot be divorced from its material conditions in a given historical period. Hence we cannot look to culture alone to liberate us — it cannot plausibly be assigned such transcendental powers. Second, since there is no one-to-one relationship between an author's intentions and the way in which a text will be received, the feminist artist cannot predict or control in any ultimate sense the effects of her work. These two points constitute an important limitation for the practice of politicized art, and in addition we have to consider the material resources (of production and distribution) which limit, often cruelly, the effectiveness of such work.

Nonetheless the struggle over the *meaning* of gender is crucial. It is vital for our purposes to establish its meaning in

37. 'The Popular Film as a Progressive Text — a Discussion of *Coma*', *m/f*, nos. 3 and 4, 1979 and 1980.
38. Helen Roberts, 'Propaganda and Ideology in Women's Fiction' in D. Laurenson, ed., *The Sociology of Literature: Applied Studies* (Sociological Review Monograph no.26, Keele 1978).

contemporary capitalism as *not* simply 'difference', but as division, oppression, inequality, internalized inferiority for women. Cultural practice is an essential site of this struggle. It can play an incalculable role in the raising of consciousness and the transformation of our subjectivity.[39]

39. Some of the ideas touched on in this chapter are explored at greater length in two fascinating books not published at the time of writing. Both take up feminist issues in the context of an incisive reconsideration of a materialist analysis of art. See Janet Wolff, *The Social Production of Art*, and Terry Lovell, *Pictures of Reality: Aesthetics, Politics, Pleasure*, both forthcoming, London 1980.

4
The Educational System: Gender and Class

Sociological and Marxist accounts of the educational system have, until recently, focused on the question of class to the exclusion of any systematic consideration of gender. The dominant tradition in Britain has sought to document empirically the ways in which educational opportunity, and hence social mobility, has depended upon social class. The progressive character of this work should not be overlooked, since it has provided successive Labour governments in this country with evidence and arguments on which to base their programme of reforms, notably in the democratization of secondary education. Yet this tradition of work is vulnerable to criticism on two major grounds. First, it offers no analysis of the role of the educational system in the creation of a sharply sex-segregated labour force. This question is not addressed theoretically and, indeed, it is hard to see how it could be, given that many of the now classic studies in this field are, literally, studies of the education of boys.[1] A parallel case may be made on the question of racial division. Second, from a Marxist point of view, such studies operate within a descriptive sociological framework of ideas about stratification and, as AnnMarie Wolpe has argued,[2] cannot provide a satisfactory explanation of the processes involved.

1. See, for example, Brian Jackson and Dennis Marsden's *Education and the Working Class*, Harmondsworth 1972, or David Hargreaves's *Social Relations in a Secondary School*, London 1966.
2. AnnMarie Wolpe, 'Education and the Sexual Division of Labour', in *Feminism and Materialism*.

Feminist response to this problem has taken three forms. There has been an important drive towards describing and analysing the processes and elements in the educational system that have been neglected in previous work. This research has been extremely valuable and I shall discuss it later in this chapter. Second, some feminists have argued that approaches such as the one developed by Michael F. D. Young (known in the profession as the 'new' sociology of education) provide, through their emphasis on the social and political definition of legitimate knowledge, useful insights into the problem of a male-defined curriculum. I will return to these arguments, on which I have general reservations, later. The third response, which I consider to be the most important in the context of developing a Marxist feminist theoretical perspective, has been the attempt to consider systematically the place of gender in an analysis of the educational system as a principal agent in the reproduction of capitalism. These arguments have not only been dominated by the influence of Louis Althusser, but have historically been constructed as a debate with the analysis of education provided in his 'Ideology and Ideological State Apparatuses'.[3]

This chapter returns, in a specific context, to the problems of debates of Chapter 1. In the first section I discuss attempts by Marxist feminists to explore the educational system from the point of view of an Althusserian conception of social reproduction. The most serious difficulty with this approach is the problem of transposing onto the divisions of gender a theoretical framework conceived and elaborated in terms of class relations. Feminists attempting this analysis are brought back necessarily to the 'sex and class' debate, which needs to be resolved in one way or another for us to move on. For this reason the second section of the chapter is centred on a detailed consideration of the different ways in which this question has been addressed, and some conclusions are suggested. In the light of these the third and final section of the chapter explores some specific aspects of the con-

---

3. In *Lenin and Philosophy and Other Essays*, pp.123-73.

temporary British educational system and its relation to the division of labour.

I

Althusser's main points as regards education may be summarized as follows. Capitalist production ultimately depends on the continued reproduction not only of the means (such as raw materials, buildings, machinery) and forces (such as labour power) but also the relations of production (dominance and subordinacy). Labour power must be reproduced in a form where differentiation exists according to definitions of 'skill' and this provision is met through ideological processes. In Althusser's view, consideration of these problems requires a reformulation of the Marxist theory of the state.

He argues that some apparatuses of the state function primarily by repression (the army, the police), others primarily by ideology (the educational system, the family, the law, the political system, trade-union institutions, communications and cultural institutions). In contemporary capitalism, the dominant ideological state apparatus is the educational system (Althusser here suggests, but does not explore, the possibility that the 'School-Family couple' is dominant). Schools take children and drill them in the ruling ideology. Around the age of sixteen a huge mass are ejected, as workers or peasants; others continue to become the petty bourgeoisie; others proceed further to emerge as agents of exploitation, agents of repression or professional ideologists. Each group is provided with the ideology to suit its role, yet the mechanisms whereby this occurs are disguised by the apparently neutral character of the school.

These theses, and the debate surrounding them, have been enormously influential; in particular, Althusser has placed the question of the *reproduction* of the relations of production firmly on the agenda of Marxist concerns. It is not difficult to see that posing the analysis in terms of relations of production and the division of labour provides a more hospitable ground for the insertion of feminist questions about gender than do analyses which pose the problem strictly in terms of the labour-capital contradiction and conventional Marxist definitions of social classes. The concepts of 'dominance' and 'subordinacy' are flexible ones; they may perhaps provide a useful framework for the analysis of women's subordination in capitalism.

I want now to examine, in the context of this general concern with education as a dominant agent of capitalist reproduction, attempts to develop a Marxist feminist perspective on the processes by which a gender-divided workforce is trained and reproduced. Such attempts are indebted to the theoretical groundwork recently undertaken by AnnMarie Wolpe and it is necessary to consider her arguments in some detail. Wolpe's article 'Education: the Road to Dependency', published in 1977, has been particularly influential in Britain.[4] It begins with a concise statement of how we should understand the educational system in relation to the sexual division of labour. She argues that there is a division of labour within the family whereby women (through their domestic labour) reproduce not only the future generation of labour power, but also current members of the employed labour force. This division within the family is paralleled by the sexual division of labour in employment, where women habitually occupy the 'secondary' sector of the labour market with its characteristic features of low pay, little training and ease of dispensability. These two systems are closely linked, and the educational system 'functions to satisfy the requirements' of both. The dominance of men and the dependence of women, both within and outside the family, are here posed mainly in terms of the ideological system by which they are secured. Wolpe argues that 'the educational system is a key means of the production and reproduction of the ideological structure' and that it embodies the dominant ideology in its organization.[5]

4. Published in *Some Processes in Sexist Education*, by AnnMarie Wolpe, Women's Research and Resources Centre, 1977.
5. Ibid., pp.2-3.

Within the system two processes can be isolated: basic
training in the skills and qualifications appropriate to the
concrete division of labour, and the transmission of
ideologies. Wolpe concentrates her subsequent discussion on
the latter, documenting from empirical research the ways in
which the curriculum, school organization, the teachers as
agents, and state policy reports all contribute to the
reproduction of the ideology of women's role. She concludes
that change will not be secured by, for instance, changing the
curriculum: 'the education system is too closely linked with
the division of labour in society, as are the ideologies which
legitimate this structure'.[6]

Wolpe's formulation here is in many ways very useful. She
rightly insists on the relations between the educational
system and the division of labour, and she rightly examines
the ideological processes by which a gender-differentiated
workforce is produced and sustained. This analysis is a
creative and stimulating attempt to apply the perspective
developed in (the first part of) Althusser's essay to the
question of gender. It remains the case, however, that this
line of argument poses important theoretical questions
which need to be resolved. These can be summarized as (i) the
'problem' of functionalism, (ii) the conceptualization of the
state and its relation to ideology, and (iii) the question of
gender and class.

In the summary given above Wolpe's argument appears to
be functionalist to a high degree. The educational system is
posed as an instrument by which an existing division of
labour is somewhat mechanistically reproduced. Even the
particular constituent elements identified (occupationally
related skills and the transmission of ideologies) are
reminiscent of the 'functions' of the educational system
('allocation' and 'socialization') identified by the functionalist sociologist Talcott Parsons.[7] Several points can be made

6. Ibid., p.18.
7. Talcott Parsons, 'The School Class as a Social System', in *Harvard
Educational Review*, 29, 1959, pp.297-318.

here. First, programmatic theoretical statements frequently give rise to this problem: what the reader gains from concise, lucid statements is inevitably counter-balanced by over-simplification. In the discussion which follows the theoretical introduction I have referred to, Wolpe examines in some detail the precise processes through which the ideology of gender is constructed. Second, she has in her subsequent work developed an alternative (non-functionalist) approach to these questions and it perhaps tells us more about the readership than about the author that the most functionalist formulation is invariably seized on as having, apparently, the greater explanatory value.

In 'Education and the Sexual Division of Labour', Wolpe argues that the specificity of the educational system is defined by a process of struggle and is not directly functional for production. The educational system is hence ascribed a 'relative autonomy' in relation to the capitalist mode of production; it is presented as an agency of 'mediation' between pupils and their allocation to places in the division of labour. Wolpe points to a series of contradictions within official British educational discourse and she emphasizes that the educational system is the product of historical struggle. 'At any one time,' she argues, 'there is ... a necessary disjunction between the "requirements" of the economy and the range of skills the educational system can produce'.[8] These points are important qualifications of Wolpe's earlier position. The reproduction of technically and ideologically equipped agents becomes dependent upon the outcome of struggle, and the allocation of these agents to places in the division of labour is a *mediated* rather than a direct process.

In these respects Wolpe's later arguments are not unlike those put forward by Bourdieu and Passeron in their analysis of *Reproduction in Education, Society and Culture*. A central point of this recondite text on the subject of pedagogic mystification is that the educational system makes a 'relatively autonomous' contribution to the

8. 'Education and the Sexual Division of Labour', p.314.

reproduction of class relations and that its operations should not be reduced mechanistically to the expression of class interests.[9] Bourdieu and Passeron argue that the ideology of democracy insists that class privilege be legitimated by certification from an apparently neutral educational system. Legitimation *by* the school rests on social recognition of the legitimacy and neutrality *of* the school. The relative autonomy of the educational system resides in its ability to conceal the truth of its functions and mask its relationship to the class structure.

There is not space here to go into these arguments in detail. They are relevant, however, to the question of gender division in the educational and training processes of capitalism in that the position taken on these general theoretical issues will affect the analysis produced. My own view is that the attempt to move away from a functionalist perspective on education is somewhat misplaced. Education systems are generically, in capitalism, instruments of state policy in a sense that is simply not true of, say, systems of cultural production. We should not let a general hostility to 'functionalist' forms of explanation blind us to the fact that some institutions of capitalism are the product of explicit state policy and that therefore *any* account of them must inevitably be a 'functionalist' one. I am not convinced that the argument of Bourdieu and Passeron, that the strength of the school's legitimating power lies in social recognition of its neutrality and legitimacy, could ever establish the autonomy of the school in the way they imply. A distinction should be made between the ideology and *appearance* of autonomy (which will have important effects) and the analytic ascription of autonomy. In this case, I would argue, the legitimating force of the school could be achieved

9. Pierre Bourdieu and Jean-Claude Passeron, *Reproduction in Educa-tion, Society and Culture*, trans. R. Nice, London 1977. These authors argue that academic discourse and practices are mystificatory, inflict-ing 'symbolic violence' on those whose class background does not equip them with the necessary cultural and linguistic capital to benefit from them. On every page the impenetrable and pretentious prose illustrates the truth of this thesis.

through successful social representation of its autonomy and neutrality; we do not need to assume from this that it *is* therefore autonomous. (It is, perhaps, useful at this point to repeat what should be understood by the term 'relative autonomy'. It does not mean 'somewhat autonomous' but indicates autonomy *in relation to* something else — hence the usage in these contexts of the notion of 'articulation', where x and y may be autonomous but nevertheless operate in some respects in relation to each other.) Nor am I convinced by AnnMarie Wolpe's argument that there is a 'necessary disjunction' between the requirements of the economy and the skills the educational system can provide. A disjunction there may be but I am unclear as to why it should be necessary. It is more fruitful, surely, to approach this disjunction by asking why the state fails in its intentions with regard to the training of the labour force, rather than by attempting to establish theoretically the relative autonomy of the educational system. We can then ask, as Richard Johnson does in his discussion of the expansion of schooling in the nineteenth century, why state policy on education may have 'effects ... which were not those that were intended'.[10] Undoubtedly the answer will be framed in terms of struggle, the 'obstinacy' of the working class and the inefficiency or failure of the state in securing its ends.

I am arguing, therefore, that analysis of gender division in education would benefit from the analytic separation of two elements: the relationship of the educational system to the state (where a functionalist argument is inevitable), and the relationship of gender division to the state (where a functionalist argument would be much more contentious). These two elements are considered below.

To a large extent we can endorse Althusser's conceptualization of the educational system as an institution which

10. Richard Johnson, 'Notes on the Schooling of the English Working Class, 1780-1850', in R. Dale *et al.*, eds., *Schooling and Capitalism*, London 1976.

functions to reproduce a divided workforce. There are, however, significant problems in his characterization of this system as the 'dominant ideological state apparatus' of mature capitalist social formations. First, we may question the extent to which education is an ideological process. Althusser argues that the ideological apparatuses of the state function secondarily by repression but he does not explore this point. In fact the educational system does not merely have a repressive aspect which lurks in the wings — it is circumscribed by state repression and has its operation within these boundaries. Parents who resist state provision for their children's education may find their children in council care or themselves in prison. Students who appropriate the administrative machinery of their institutions may find the police, or even the army, restraining their actions. In addition to this it may be argued that the educational system is determined by economic considerations, not merely in 'the lonely hour' of the last instance, but for most of the time. The changes made in the British educational system subsequent to entry into the European Economic Community cannot be said to have been determined by ideological rather than economic requirements. This is not to suggest the reverse, but simply to note the difficulties which attend the separation by Althusser of the economic from the ideological 'level'.

More importantly, perhaps, we should question Althusser's overall conception of 'the state' to which these ideological apparatuses belong. In this essay Althusser acknowledges his indebtedness to the work of Antonio Gramsci, and it is worth considering the ways in which his analysis differs from that of Gramsci. With regard to the educational system their positions are strikingly similar. Gramsci argues that schools are related to the historical needs of classes, that each social class has its own appropriate type of school, that education does not transcend class, that the democracy of the educational system is an illusion. One task of the school, for Gramsci, is the production of 'intellectuals', or, more accurately, the production of people who have the social function of intellectuals: 'intellectuals are the dominant group's "deputies" exercising the ... functions of social hegemony and political government'.[11] The concept of 'hegemony' refers to the organization of popular consent to the ideology of the dominant group and for 'hegemony' to be secured everyone must accept, at the level of 'common-sense' knowledge, the view of the dominant class.

Althusser and Gramsci share a functionalist perspective on the educational system in the process of the production and reproduction of 'consent'. Gramsci refers to intellectuals explicitly as the 'functionaries' of classes. They differ in that Althusser has collapsed Gramsci's notion of 'civil society', originally posed in opposition to 'the state', into the various ideological state apparatuses. Hence, the family, the media, the trade unions, and so on, which figure in Gramsci's conception of civil society are absorbed under the umbrella of the state in Althusser's account. Of the two, I find Gramsci's approach the more useful. In broadening the definition of 'the state' to include these institutions Althusser renders this concept so general that it loses much of its analytic potential.[12] Equally important, it is simply not established that an institution such as the family can properly be regarded as a state apparatus *tout court*. I shall discuss in Chapter 7 the extent to which the form of the family in contemporary capitalism may be attributed to the operations of the state. For the moment, however, it must be emphasized that Althusser's categorization is not self-evident and would need to be argued through in some detail.

In the two sections above I have touched on some general implications of Althusser's account of the educational system. The problems of functionalism, and of how we should conceptualize the state, would be common to any uses

11. Antonio Gramsci, *Prison Notebooks*, Selections edited and translated by Quintin Hoare and Geoffrey Nowell-Smith, London 1971, pp.40-41,12.
12. This argument is put by Paul Hirst in 'Problems and Advances in the Theory of Ideology', in his *On Law and Ideology*, pp.22-39.

of Althusser's work. For feminists, however, there is a much more serious obstacle to any appropriation of these arguments. For although a functionalist perspective on the educational system is to some extent not only inevitable but correct, such a perspective on the relationship between gender division and the state would be far more contentious. To argue, from an Althusserian point of view, that gender division in the educational system may be understood in terms of the reproduction of the sexual division of labour and of relations of dominance and subordinacy between men and women, would beg some fundamental questions. Althusser's conceptual framework has been developed in the context of the reproduction of class relations, not the reproduction of gender. In this respect his work is no different from that of most Marxists. This means, however, that his concepts cannot be transposed unproblematically on to the question of gender. For *either* we must argue that gender divisions are separate from class divisions, but that Althusser's *method* in relation to the latter is applicable to analysis of the reproduction of the former, *or* we must argue that gender division can be integrated analytically into the class structure and that we may therefore retain the *substance* of his analysis. Feminist use of Althusser's work must, therefore, depend upon a resolution of the question of the relationship of women and of men (*qua* women and men) to the class structure.

II

In order to discuss this question it is necessary to outline schematically the alternative ways of posing the relation between gender and class which are currently on offer.

1. First there is the view that gender is not a separable element of class relations, but is completely absorbed within them. This perspective depends upon seeing the family, rather than the individual, as the basic unit of which classes are composed: it aggregates the members of the family into an internally unified entity which can then be located in the

class structure. This assumption has undoubtedly characterized sociological approaches to stratification, the class
position of all members of a family being allocated on the
basis of the occupation of the (normally male) head of
household. It has, quite rightly, been criticized by numerous
recent feminist studies.[13] Feminists have argued that this
assumption rules out of court some important considerations: conflict of interest within the family, women's own
occupational position, the extent to which women's employment is related to their work in the household, for example.
These critiques, although principally directed towards
sociological analysis of class, are in fact equally applicable
to Marx's own work. Marx defines class with reference to
relationship to ownership of the means of production. As
Geoffrey Kay explains in his clear presentation of Marx's
theory of the working class, the proletariat is defined by its
complete dependence on the wage.[14] Yet it is evident that for
Marx the typical wage-labourer is male. In his discussion of
the introduction of machinery, Marx refers to 'women and
children' as 'that mighty substitute for labour and
labourers'. He states that 'the value of labour power was
determined, not only by the labour-time necessary to
maintain the individual adult labourer, but also by that
necessary to maintain his family'.[15] Furthermore, Marx goes
on to argue that capital's expansion into the employment of
women and children had the consequences of usurping the
labour necessary in the home, of depreciating the value of
labour power and raising the degree of exploitation. It is
currently a matter of dispute as to whether Marx is correct in
this argument,[16] and I shall discuss below some alternative
formulations offered within the broader Marxist tradition.

13. See, for example, J. Acker, 'Women and Social Stratification: A Case of
   Intellectual Sexism', in *American Journal of Sociology*, vol.78, no.4,
   1973.
14. Geoffrey Kay, *The Economic Theory of the Working Class*, London
   1979.
15. *Capital*, vol.1, London 1980, p.395.
16. See Michèle Barrett and Mary McIntosh, 'The "Family Wage": Some
   Problems for Socialists and Feminists', *Capital and Class*, no.11, 1980.

Insofar as Marx's own position occupies a privileged and influential role within Marxist thought as a whole, it is important to emphasize the inadequacy of his assumptions on this question. In regarding both women and children simply as 'substitutes' for the male labourer, Marx is clearly guilty of the naturalistic aggregation of individuals into the family unit which feminists have criticized in sociological theory.

2. In radical opposition to this perspective, various arguments have been put forward to the effect that gender division constitutes a system of oppression which is utterly independent of class division. Such arguments are commonly posed in terms of the concept of patriarchy, which I discussed in Chapter 1. My reservations there are applicable here. Perhaps the strongest formulation of this position is that which argues that gender division is analytically prior to class division, as in Firestone's conception of struggle between men and women as the prime motor of history or in Millett's view that 'women tend to transcend the usual class stratifications in patriarchy'. These claims, although politically significant for feminism, are difficult to substantiate and have been convincingly criticized.[17] A more plausible argument has been developed in the view that patriarchy can be seen as independent of class structure but as operating through analogous mechanisms. Different formulations are possible here. One involves posing patriarchy and capitalism as two identifiably separate structures, historically coexisting in particular societies. This, as I understand it, is the sense in which the term 'capitalist patriarchy' has been used (particularly in the United States) to describe contemporary societies such as are found in Western Europe and the USA.[18] A second formulation would be constituted by posing a 'domestic mode of production', with its own mechanisms of exploitation,

17. C. Middleton, 'Sexual Inequality and Stratification Theory', in F. Parkin, ed., *The Social Analysis of Class Structure*, London 1974.
18. See the collection edited by Z. Eisenstein, *Capitalist Patriarchy and the Case for Socialist Feminism*, New York 1978.

which may be held to coexist alongside a capitalist mode of production.[19] Third, the analogy with social class can be extended to the point of arguing that women do in fact constitute, themselves, an identifiable social class.[20] These formulations are not necessarily, in this work, mutually exclusive and some writers draw on more than one of them in their analysis.[21] All of them, in my view, are difficult to reconcile with a Marxist analysis, and I should stress that this comment applies to the self-consciously 'Marxist feminist' analyses of 'capitalist patriarchy' just as it does to the non-Marxist arguments put forward by some feminists.

The reasons for this difficulty are complex. I am not suggesting that Marxism is a rigid explanatory framework which cannot be modified, and I shall discuss below some possible avenues for a more satisfactory reconceptualization of a Marxist theory of class and gender. I am simply suggesting here that there is no unproblematic way in which Marxist categories of class can be juxtaposed with, or transposed on to, feminist categories of gender. To do so would be to strip from Marxism precisely its ability to analyse the mechanisms underlying the appearance of social reality, reducing it to a set of descriptive, empirical categories. This danger is particularly acute in the argument that women can be said to constitute a social class. In purely descriptive terms it is plausible to argue that certain categories of women, most obviously full-time housewives, occupy a unique occupational role which we might want to designate as a social class. In terms of a sociological definition of class, based on occupational status, this would be acceptable. Marxist categories of class, however, are not descriptive of occupation in this way; they operate according

19. See J. Harrison, 'The Political Economy of Housework', in *Bulletin of the Conference of Socialist Economists*, Winter 1973.
20. See (for a sociological treatment of this argument) D. H. J. Morgan, *Social Theory and the Family*, London 1975 (Chapter 5, 'Women as a Social Class').
21. Some of the difficulties encountered here are discussed by Maxine Molyneux in 'Beyond the Domestic Labour Debate', *New Left Review*, no.116, 1979.

to specified *relations* within a mode of production.

The two perspectives mentioned so far represent the binary opposition between Marxist and feminist theory with which this book began. I want now to consider briefly the possible ways in which a *relation* between the two, in terms of the gender and class debate, has been posed.

3. One way of approaching this question is to deal with it empirically, as do John Westergaard and Harriet Resler in their study of contemporary Britain. Looking at the differentials between men's pay and women's, they observe that the gap widens as one goes down the occupational scale. In 1971, for instance, women school teachers earned about one fifth less than men, clerical workers earned about a third less than men, while women manual workers got little more than half the comparable male wage. They remark that 'sex inequality in pay ... reinforces class inequality: it strikes hardest at the lowest levels of the occupational hierarchy'. Westergaard and Resler consider that other features of the labour market corroborate this conclusion (discrimination, women's position relative to men's at each level, and so on). They note that the deterioration in women's position at work has also followed class lines, being more marked for manual work. They conclude that class divisions are 'accentuated' by sex discrimination in the labour market: 'there is no neutralization or contradiction here of one form of inequality by another: the two are linked'.[22] This argument poses class and gender as cumulative factors in the determination of occupational inequality. In deducing this from the empirical correlation of these two factors the method employed is characteristically empiricist. The drawbacks of drawing theoretical conclusions from empirical data in this way are demonstrated yet more clearly in a fascinating passage from *Schooling in Capitalist America* by Samuel Bowles and Herbert Gintis.

Bowles and Gintis draw on a study by Bluestone which

22.   J. Westergaard and H. Resler, *Class in a Capitalist Society*, Harmonds-
      worth 1976, pp.101-106.

attempted to isolate statistically the weight of different factors affecting pay differences. They 'construct' a hypothetical white, male, unionized, 'primary sector' worker and a black, female, non-unionized, 'secondary sector' worker. Statistical returns allow the prediction that the male worker's hourly wage is likely to be more than three times greater than the female's. Of this difference, regression analysis informs us that 36% is due to sexual differences, 17% to racial differences, 22% to labour market segmentation, and 25% to differences in education and job experience.[23] These certainly add up to 100, and it is perhaps interesting to know that 36% of the gap can be attributed to sexual differences alone. What these figures cannot tell us about, however, is the relationships between any of these variables. Indeed they cannot throw any light on the theoretical problems of analysing class, race and gender in terms of reproducing a divided labour force. One reason why they cannot is that they can provide no information or discussion about contradictions between any of the variables. The difficulty of drawing theoretical conclusions from empirical data of this kind is, in fact, neatly illustrated by a comparison between the arguments of Bowles and Gintis and those of Westergaard and Resler. The former conclude that race and gender are independent factors that must be considered as a separable element of income inequality (if ultimately functional for the capitalist system); whereas the latter conclude that gender inequality reinforces and accentuates the inequality of class.

The problem of gender and class is impossible to resolve in the quantification of occupational and income inequality. This is because the categories themselves constitute an unsatisfactory definition of class. One way of illustrating this point is by looking at the work that has been undertaken to demonstrate the limitations of the view discussed earlier, that a woman's class position is that of her husband. Sociologists arguing against this view have produced evi-

23. S. Bowles and H. Gintis, *Schooling in Capitalist America*, London 1976, p.91.

dence to show that where a married woman's *own* occupation is taken into account the picture changes substantially. If we rank a married woman with reference to her own occupation and then compare this with the position she would have been ascribed on the basis of her husband's, we find major discrepancies. Unfortunately most official statistics do not provide the information necessary for this exercise, but it has been attempted with the data collected in the 1971 British Census. Both Elizabeth Garnsey and Richard Brown draw attention to the fact that when a wife's own occupation is considered, many households have husbands and wives in different social classes. As Garnsey puts it: 'for no category did the majority of husbands have wives in the same social class as themselves, and a significant proportion of wives were on the other side of the manual/non-manual divide'.[24]

The problem here is that the categories used by official statisticians, and by sociologists, are simply inadequate. Although it might be predicted, on the basis of women's financial dependence on men, that women's occupational class assignment will usually be lower than that of their husband, the historical construction of the sexual division of labour has resulted in many women occupying 'non-manual' positions which are always ranked higher (although usually lower paid) than comparable 'manual' positions. To this extent, occupational classification uncritically reproduces the ideology of a mental-manual hierarchy of labour that has characterized the capitalist division of labour. Acceptance of this hierarchy is a significant barrier to an adequate analysis of women's work and to understanding of women's class position. In particular, there is now considerable evidence to suggest that many of the non-manual forms of work in which the bulk of female wage labourers are engaged have become routinized to the point of rendering invalid any distinction between these so-called 'mental' tasks and so-called 'manual' ones.

24. Elizabeth Garnsey, 'Women's Work and Theories of Class Stratification', in *Sociology* vol.12, no.2, May 1978, p.229; and Richard Brown, 'Work', in P. Abrams, ed., *Work, Urbanism and Inequality*, London 1978.

The important point to note here is that the empirical classification of social class by occupation is unsatisfactory. It does not advance us very far to discover that according to these categories many households cut across social class divisions, indeed it points to the inadequacy of the existing categories. It is of course the case that occupational classification is not in any sense a Marxist approach to the question of class. It hardly needs to be repeated here that a Marxist definition of class rests on relationship to ownership of the means of production and not on the occupational and skill differentials which have emerged in the construction of a divided working class. These sociological approaches have been introduced here for specific reasons. First, many Marxist analyses of contemporary capitalism do in practice rest on these sociologistic categories rather than on a Marxist definition of class and it is important to be aware of this. Second, insofar as Marx himself assumed that the family rather than the individual was the basic unit for the reproduction of the working class under the capitalist wage-system, he shared the sociological assumptions which are implicitly and explicitly challenged by empirical evidence about occupational differences within family units. Third, the new evidence demonstrating the inadequacy of the mental/manual distinction has a useful bearing on a Marxist analysis of the sexual division of labour, and I shall return to this point below.

4. I want now to consider the attempts made from a Marxist feminist position to reconcile theoretically the arguments about gender division and class structure.

One way of approaching this is to argue that the oppression of women differs significantly from class to class. Engels stressed this point, asserting that the proletarian home in which both husband and wife were engaged in wage-labour was in broad material terms an egalitarian one. Certainly he argued that the situation of the bourgeois wife, where upkeep was provided in return for the production of legitimate heirs, was tantamount to prostitution. This was the basis of his view that the entrance of all women into social production was the precondition for their emancipation. Although Engels's work has been extensively criticized by Marxist feminists, his central insistence on the material factors distinguishing proletarian from bourgeois women has been influential. McDonough and Harrison, for instance, argue that 'patriarchal' control of woman's procreative capacity and sexuality takes different forms for different social classes. For the bourgeoisie this arises from the requirement to produce legitimate heirs, for the proletariat, with the need to reproduce efficiently the next generation of labour-power.

It should be noted that this formulation, although apparently making a useful distinction between the forms of oppression suffered by women of different social classes, results in a collapse of both bourgeois and proletarian patriarchal mechanisms into a model in which both, ultimately, are simply 'functional' for capital. The difference is that the capitalist as posed here is gendered: McDonough and Harrison refer to 'the interests of the male capitalist, ... his need for legitimate heirs and for fresh labour-power'.[25] This is unsatisfactory, for several reasons. First, although it apparently concedes autonomy to patriarchal control, it implicitly withdraws this by posing these mechanisms as functional for the typical capitalist. Second, the entire question of class and gender is evaded by posing the capitalist as male. Some capitalists are female. Third, it incorporates the unmediated functionalism of much work on domestic labour, which has tended to see women's work in the home exclusively in terms of its functions for capital — hence failing to explain why it must be women who undertake such work. Finally, if we can doubt the validity of a functionalist explanation of women's oppression in the proletariat, how much more dubious is this view in relation to the bourgeoisie. The reproduction of capital does not necessarily *require* legitimate heirs or, for that matter, many

25. Roisin McDonough and Rachel Harrison, 'Patriarchy and Relations of Production', *Feminism and Materialism*, pp.36-7.

other of the elements of the ideological baggage which has historically accompanied the growth of the bourgeoisie. Unlike the reproduction of labour-power, which *depends* upon the reproduction of the living, human labourer, the reproduction of capital does not depend on individual ownership in the same way. Hence, to incorporate gender division into the structure and definition of 'the capitalist' is a particularly fraught exercise. As Hilary Wainwright notes: 'there is little to be said about sex inequalities as far as ownership of capital is concerned. Primarily for reasons of tax and inheritance women have an almost equal share in the ownership of wealth: they owned about 40 per cent of all private wealth in 1970'.[26]

It is not, in fact, adequate to address the question of class and gender by posing a unity of interest between capitalists and men, since the capitalist class is composed of both men and women. This problem is to some extent avoided by the argument that gender division, and hence women's oppression, is historically constituted as outside the labour/capital relation with which a Marxist analysis of capitalist society is fundamentally concerned. Much of the discussion of the sexual division of labour is directed, ultimately, at the question of women and class. For if women's position in the relations of production in capitalism could be established then clarification of their class position would follow. Lucy Bland and her co-authors have argued that women's subordination cannot be understood through the categories of capital alone. They argue that 'outside' these economic relations, and historically prior to their emergence, lie the patriarchal relations between men and women which capital has 'taken over' or 'colonized'.[27] A rather similar position is taken by Heidi Hartmann, who

26. Hilary Wainwright, 'Women and the Division of Labour', in P. Abrams, ed., *Work, Urbanism and Inequality*, p.163. Wainwright correctly adds that ownership is not to be equated with *control* of capital: 'it is family property, invested by the husband'.
27. Lucy Bland, Charlotte Brunsdon, Dorothy Hobson and Janice Winship, 'Women "Inside and Outside" the Relations of Production', in *Women Take Issue*.

argues that the sex-blind categories of Marxism can never in themselves explain why women occupy the situation they do, and must be supplemented by an independent analysis of gender relations as they have developed historically.[28] The most obvious drawback of these arguments is that they run the risk of characterizing Marxism simply as a method for identifying the essential component parts of the capitalist class structure, and stripping it of any ability to explain these in concrete rather than abstract terms. The argument leads to the conclusion that Marxist theory can specify the 'places' which need to be filled, but that feminist theory must be invoked to explain who fills them.[29] This problem of 'dualism', as Veronica Beechey has argued, also arises in attempts to bring Marxist analysis to bear on the question of capitalist *production*, and feminist analysis to bear on the question of the *reproduction* of these relations of production.[30]

The problem can be posed more fruitfully, perhaps, by looking at the nature of women's relationship to the wage in capitalism. This is the focus of an article by Margaret Coulson, Branka Magaš and Hilary Wainwright, who argue that the oppression of women in capitalism resides in the contradiction between their roles as wage labourers and as domestic labourers. This contradiction has important implications for militancy, organized forms of resistance and consciousness.[31] Jean Gardiner, meanwhile, has drawn attention to the failure of Marxism to address, theoretically or politically, the implications of this dual relationship that women have to the class structure. She argues for a definition of the working class as not simply those who

28. 'The Unhappy Marriage of Marxism and Feminism: Towards a More Progressive Union', in *Capital and Class*, no.8, 1979; and 'Capitalism, Patriarchy and Job-Segregation by Sex', in Eisenstein, ed., *Capitalist Patriarchy and the Case for Socialist Feminism*.
29. I am indebted to Anne Phillips for this succinct way of expressing the problem.
30. 'On Patriarchy', *Feminist Review*, no.3, 1979.
31. Margaret Coulson, Branka Magaš and Hilary Wainwright, '"The Housewife and her Labour under Capitalism" — a Critique', in *New Left Review*, no.89, 1975.

create surplus value, nor even those who sell their labour power, but as all those who are dependent upon the sale of labour power, albeit vicariously. Hence the old, the sick, the unemployed, children and housewives are all 'of the working class', but their indirect relationship to the sale of labour power, and hence the wage, affects their position 'materially and ideologically'.[32]

Gardiner suggests that it is useful to distinguish between the direct involvement in wage labour which most women now have, and the indirect relationship to the wage experienced by those women who are dependent upon a male wage. An aspect of women's relationship to the class structure is that it is mediated, to some extent at least, by the configuration of the family, dependence on men, and domestic labour. This duality is an important determinant of women's consciousness of class; it may, for instance, lead to militancy in support of childcare facilities and shorter hours, and against social services cuts, rather than to militancy in support of higher wages. These points are politically significant. The notion of women's dependence on the male wage has bolstered arguments for a family wage system in which a male breadwinner earns a wage adequate to support a wife and family. Controversial though such arguments undoubtedly are, there can be no doubt that they have led the trade union movement to support a demand for a family wage which now conflicts, as Campbell and Charlton have argued, with support for equal pay for women.[33] It is clear that an understanding of women's position in the class structure, and of the forms taken by class struggle involving women, depend upon a more adequate analysis of the wage relation and the processes by which the wage is distributed within the working class. Such an analysis would need to take into account the mystificatory appearance of the wage form, and the ideology which defines mediated dependence

32. Jean Gardiner, 'Women in the Labour Process and Class Structure', in Alan Hunt, ed., *Class and Class Structure*, London 1977.
33. Beatrix Campbell and Valerie Charlton, 'Work to Rule — Wages and the Family', *Red Rag*, 1978.

on the wage as subordinate to the direct wage-dependence of the 'male breadwinner'.

Many of the difficulties encountered in considering the position of women in the class structure are related to a general confusion in contemporary Marxist analysis of class. The terms in which Marx himself posed the issue, as an increasing polarization between those who owned the means of production and those who depended for their subsistence on the sale of their labour power, have been to some extent overtaken by subsequent developments of capitalist production in the twentieth century. The economy has increasingly had to be analysed not only in terms of capitalist production but also in terms of state production and domestic production, and the implications of this for a Marxist analysis of class structure are as yet far from clear. The twentieth century has seen the exponential expansion of 'service' or 'non-productive' industries, in relation to manufacturing industry. The distinction between 'mental' and 'manual' labour was useful to Marx as an element of an account of the processes whereby the wage labourer was degraded and alienated in the division of labour which emerged in the course of capital accumulation; it is now a rather different object of Marxist analysis. As Braverman has convincingly argued, the degradation of work in the twentieth century has stripped the 'mental' labourer of the illusions of control previously suggested by this definition.[34] Insofar as the expansion of wage labour among women has been primarily located in the clerical and service sectors, analysis of women's position in the class structure has encountered many of these general difficulties.[35] We can see that none of the existing formulations of the class and gender relation is entirely satisfactory, although this situation reflects a general difficulty with the

34. Harry Braverman, *Labor and Monopoly Capital*, New York 1974; see especially Chapter 15.
35. See Jackie West, 'Women, Sex, and Class', in *Feminism and Materialism*.

contemporary Marxist theory of class as well as a particular difficulty in dealing with the class positions of women. Of the several approaches mentioned here, my own view is that the positions argued by Coulson, Magăs and Wainwright, and by Jean Gardiner, are potentially very useful, since they point to the specific factors which distinguish women's relation to the class structure from that of men, yet do not do so at the cost of abandoning the corpus of a Marxist approach to the analysis of the capitalist class structure in general; this is an important consideration, not for doctrinal reasons but because the general relations of production by which capitalism is defined in Marxism constitute the historical context in which gender relations are now played out.

It is important to stress here the importance of an historical approach to the question of gender and class. Consideration of the effect of the transition to capitalism on the sexual division of labour is essential. It is clear that on the one hand the wage relation characteristic of capitalism, and the accompanying separation of home and workplace, have historically made a substantial contribution to the formation of the present sexual division of labour in which women's position is located principally in relation to responsibility for domestic labour and financial dependence on a male wage-earner. On the other hand, some elements of this sexual division undoubtedly existed prior to the development of capitalism; they have not been totally constructed by capitalism.[36] In addition to this historically prior sexual division of labour, upon which capitalism has built a more rigidly segregated division, we can isolate many points of struggle in which the eventual outcome is not pre-given in terms of requirements of capital. The classic case in point here is the protective legislation on women's working conditions passed in the mid-nineteenth century. Although interpretations of this vary,[37] I would argue that this

36. See Christopher Middleton, 'The Sexual Division of Labour in Feudal England', *New Left Review*, nos. 113-114, 1979.

represented a material defeat of the interests of working women and, furthermore, a defeat that is not simply explicable in terms of a proposed logic of capitalist development. It involved an assumption, shared by the labour movement among others, that the relegation of women to domesticity and childcare was natural and desirable. In this respect the eventual outcome was a product of an ideology of gender division that was incorporated into the capitalist division of labour rather than spontaneously generated by it. If this argument is correct, it would suggest that although we may usefully argue that gender division has been built into the capitalist division of labour and is an important element of capitalist relations of production, it is more difficult to argue that gender division *necessarily* occupies a particular place in the class structure of capitalism. It has not, at least as yet, been demonstrated that the sexual division of labour forms not simply a *historically constituted* but a *logically pre-given* element of the class structure that would *automatically* be reproduced by the reproduction of this class structure.

III

This lengthy discussion of gender and class has been necessary in order to re-consider the question of whether an Althusserian approach to the reproduction of capitalism can provide an analysis of the reproduction of gender division in capitalism. I suggested that our ability to integrate gender and class would have implications for the validity of this analysis. If it were true that the sexual division of labour was so functional for capitalism that reproduction of the latter depended upon reproduction of the former, the Althusserian approach would prove relatively unproblematic. If, however, it is seen as more autonomous then we would encounter

37. See Jane Humphries, 'Class Struggle and the Persistence of the Work-
     ing Class Family', in *Cambridge Journal of Economics*, vol.1, no.3,
     1977; Barrett and McIntosh. 'The Family Wage'; and Barbara Taylor
     'Socialism, Feminism and Sexual Antagonism in the London Tailoring
     Trade in the Early 1830s', *Feminist Studies*, vol.5, no.1, 1979.

serious difficulties, and my view is that this is in fact the case. Hence the *substance* of Althusser's argument would need to be modified in profound ways for it to be of use to feminists. Nor am I convinced that the *method* which seeks to understand education and training processes in terms of the reproduction of relations of dominance and subordinacy can be transposed on to the question of gender. To do this would be to argue that just as the capitalist class is reproduced in a relationship of total dominance over the working class, so men are reproduced as totally dominant over women. Without denying the general pattern of male dominance, we can still see particular drawbacks in this argument. It would be difficult to argue, for instance, that the qualifications and skills imparted to a girl at a major independent school would in any sense 'equip' her for a place in the division of labour that was subordinate to that of a woorking class boy who left school at the minimum age with no formal qualifications.

The notion that women have a *dual* relationship to the class structure is pertinent here. The education and training that a woman receives by virtue of her class background provide a highly significant contribution to the position she will occupy in the labour force. Yet it is equally clear that the relationship she has to the class structure by virtue of her wage labour (or her ownership of the means of production) will be substantially influenced by the mediation of this direct relationship through dependence on men and responsibility for domestic labour and childcare. For working-class women this may result in simultaneous direct exploitation by capital via their own wage-labour and indirect exploitation via vicarious dependence on the wage of a male breadwinner. For bourgeois women this may result in simultaneous ownership of, yet lack of control over, capital.

The dual character of women's class positions can be seen in the processes of educating and training a workforce which is divided by both class and gender. In the discussion that follows I shall concentrate on the aspects of these systems which reproduce gender division and a mediated relationship to the wage, and am to some extent taking as read the importance of the educational system in the processes by which class differentiation is secured. It will be convenient to break down the discussion into some broad headings under which these processes can be located: 1. strictly ideological aspects, according to the definition of ideology put forward in the previous chapter; 2. the structure and organization of the institutions that comprise the system of education and training; 3. the mechanisms by which, in the educational system, pupils are channelled into a sexual division of labour; 4. definitions of the curriculum and of legitimate knowledge. These will be discussed in turn, and drawn together in conclusion.

1. It is clear that within the culture of the school, as outside it, there exist processes by which femininity and masculinity are defined and constructed. I have already mentioned the growing concern with the rigidly stereotyped imagery of gender presented to children in the books used in schools. Anna Davin, in her fascinating account of the parallel imagery used in late-nineteenth-century school books,[38] rightly points to the difficulty of assessing the impact of these stereotypes on the reader, but it is nevertheless likely that they do have some effect on the children who are daily exposed to them. There is considerable continuity between the ideal of conformity to domesticity expressed for girls in such books and the findings of recent studies on the behaviour of girls and boys in the classroom. Elena Belotti, for instance, has described the ways in which the assumption that girls should perform domestic services for boys is acted out in the classroom at a very early age in the various tasks of clearing up and so on that little girls are enjoined to perform.[39]

Similarly, Rosemary Deem has pointed to the various studies of classroom interaction which have suggested that

38. Anna Davin, '"Mind that You Do as You Are Told": Reading Books for Board School Girls, 1870-1902', *Feminist Review*, no.3, 1979.
39. Elena G. Belotti, *Little Girls*, London, 1975.

girls are encouraged to be more conformist in school than boys.[40] AnnMarie Wolpe's observation of girls in a secondary school led to a description of various incidents where adolescent girls were implicitly and even explicitly 'coached' by their teachers into appropriately feminine behaviour, and she comments that social relations in the school situation were more overtly sexualized than she had anticipated.[41] As many writers have noted, children are in school for much of the period when they are maturing sexually, becoming aware of the importance of sexual relationships, and learning the definitions of adult masculinity and femininity. The perceptions of self consolidated in this period tend to reflect the perceptions of teachers, which in turn frequently reflect the ideology of gender in society at large. Michelle Stanworth has uncovered, in observation of a Further Education college, some of the ways in which male teachers tended to marginalize or simply ignore the female students and the extent to which this contributed to the passive and self-deprecating perceptions the girls had of themselves.[42] In this context it is worth recalling Mirra Komarovsky's classic study of gender interaction in higher education, where she found that the odium attaching to academically successful women was such that a substantial proportion of them lied about their qualifications and achievements in order to appear more acceptable to men they dated.[43]

It seems reasonable to suppose that these processes, although taking place within the educational system, are not necessarily constructed by and for that system but are essentially located in the general ideology of gender in the society of which educational institutions are part. If we consider, however, the structure and organization of the school system we can see that in fundamental ways it has

40. Rosemary Deem, *Women and Schooling*, London 1978, pp.39-40.
41. AnnMarie Wolpe, *Some Processes in Sexist Education*, p.36.
42. Michelle Stanworth, M. A. Dissertation, University of Essex. Forth-coming pamphlet, Women's Research and Resources Centre, 1980.
43. Mirra Komarovsky, 'Cultural Contradictions and Sex Roles', *American Journal of Sociology*, vol.52, 1946.

incorporated a division between the sexes to a degree that is inexplicable in any strictly educational terms.

2. Gender is a salient organizing category in the educational system. In some respects it constitutes an apparently arbitrary division which relates solely to administrative convenience: children have to be marshalled in some way, so why not into boys and girls? During roll-call, when children are sent out for milk or in to dinners,[44] the distinction between boys and girls presents itself as an obvious organizational aid. Yet this arbitrary appearance is deceptive, since these administrative classifications are symptomatic of significant gender divisions engrained in the structure of the institutions themselves. This can be seen by considering the sexual division of labour in schools from the point of view of its similarity with the sexual division of labour in the family. In many schools at the secondary level there is a headmaster, with whom executive and disciplinary powers reside, and a senior mistress, whose role is conceived of as primarily 'pastoral'. Indeed it is virtually a requirement in British co-educational schools that the second most senior staff member be of the opposite sex from the head. Similarly, pastoral and welfare work is in general more readily assigned to female members of staff, often on the assumption that they will prove more conscientious in their 'care'. This pattern clearly mirrors the norm of the nuclear family, and is refracted in many other aspects of school structure.

The teaching profession is divided by gender in several ways, and these, I would argue, are closely connected with the sexual division of labour generally. The profession is divided hierarchically by gender: as you move to more senior posts the proportion of women falls. This is particularly true of primary schools, where 90.4% of the most junior grade is female, but only 42.8% of head teachers are women. In secondary schools 19.9% of head teachers are female, but again in the junior grade (Scale 1) the proportion rises to

---

44. The effect of current public expenditure cuts may make these particular exercises redundant.

58.6%.[45] This division has two important aspects. As far as promotion and a career are concerned, men are distinctly advantaged over women: they tend to occupy the senior posts, particularly in primary education, in a proportion far greater than their numbers in the profession as a whole would indicate. Hence, on average, their salaries are substantially higher. Second, and this is particularly important for the effect it will have on children, the ratio of male to female teachers rises dramatically as the child gets older. A child of five is almost certain to be taught by a woman, since 99.1% of teachers for this age group are women;[46] a graduate of twenty-one will be almost as certain to find that the head of his or her department is not a woman, since less than 2% of professors in British universities are women.[47] It hardly needs pointing out that the higher one goes up the educational hierarchy, the larger the salary and the greater the prestige attached to the job.

The profession is also divided by subject area. I shall discuss below the processes by which boys and girls are 'channelled' into different subjects, principally in secondary and tertiary education, and it is clear that the existing segregation by subject of the teaching staff may have something to do with this. Eileen Byrne has approached this question by proposing that there should be an equal number of men and women teaching the 'common core' of the curriculum. She points out that this is roughly true of secondary-level teachers of English, but that less than a third of the comparable group of mathematics teachers are women, and this proportion is lower still for subjects such as physics and chemistry.[48] Furthermore, the girl who does decide to proceed to university in, say, an engineering subject, will find herself in a department dominated by men

45. Equal Opportunities Commission, *Third Annual Report, 1978*, HMSO, London 1979, p.83.
46. Eileen Byrne, *Women and Education*, London 1978, p.217.
47. Tessa Blackstone and Oliver Fulton, 'Sex Discrimination Among University Teachers: a British-American Comparison', in *British Journal of Sociology*, vol.26, 1975.
48. Byrne, p.143.

and an ethos of masculinity.[49] Much of the pattern of subject-stereotyping by sex, which results in girls going into arts and social science subjects and boys into science and technology, is established very firmly in terms of the teaching staff. Indeed, most institutions reproduce the contemporary sexual division of labour in the staffing of both academic and non-academic posts. In most British universities, colleges and polytechnics, for instance, the principal, senior staff and technical and portering staff are male, with female employees located in junior teaching and research positions and in secretarial, catering and cleaning work.

It has been suggested in the past that the extension of co-educational schooling would have advantages over sex-segregated education in this respect. But research on this question indicates that the reverse may be true: girls in single-sex schools are more likely than girls in co-educational schools to pursue further and higher education generally, and in particular, are more likely to take advanced courses in science subjects.[50] The only explanation for this is that the processes of stereotyping are more marked in schools where the divisions between girls and boys are daily confronted and the pupils are constantly exposed to differentiation by gender.

3. There is now a considerable amount of data relating to the processes of subject 'channelling' in the educational system, and I shall simply mention some basic points here. First, we have to contend with the tradition in British schools that girls should take subjects related to their future domestic role: needlework, cookery, domestic science and 'housecraft', and that boys should take woodwork, metalwork and technical drawing. Under the Sex Discrimination Act, 1975, it is now illegal to ban either sex from such classes, but legal

49. In the institution where I work one of the lecturers in an engineering department emphasizes this by having a full-colour blown-up nude from the London *Sun*'s notorious 'page 3' on the wall of his office.
50. See Jenny Shaw, 'Finishing School: Some Implications of Sex-Segregated Education', in D. Leonard Barker and S. Allen, eds., *Sexual Divisions and Society*, London 1976; and Byrne, p.135.

action in such cases has not been very successful. Certainly it remains the case that in 1976 over 26,000 boys but only 400 girls passed 'O'-level technical drawing, whereas nearly 29,000 girls but only 400 boys passed in cookery.[51] This obviously constitutes an extreme example of a vocationally oriented, gender-divided curriculum, which it has in the past been official policy to encourage.[52]

An occupational choice must also be influenced by the availability of certain subjects. One argument in favour of co-educational schools points out that these would offer more girls the opportunity to take science subjects, since specialist staff would be available to teach them. Byrne quotes Department of Education statistics that demonstrate this. If we take physics, for instance, this was offered to only 62% of girls in single-sex schools but to 75% of girls in mixed schools. However — and here lies the importance of stereotyping — the proportion of girls who actually studied the physics on offer was in fact lower (11%) in the mixed schools than in the girls' schools (14%).[53] Factors such as these play an important part in determining employment opportunities open to boys and girls and I want to consider briefly the destinations of school leavers.

The Equal Opportunities Commission points out that far more boys than girls go on to take degree courses (in universities and polytechnics): in 1976 it was 8.8% of boys and 5.4% of girls. Boys are massively outnumbered by girls on teacher-training courses, as well as on nursing, catering and secretarial courses. In addition to this the EOC's compilation of figures shows clearly that women are concentrated in non-advanced further education courses and outnumbered by men on more advanced courses. For those women who go to university, an interesting pattern can be detected. At undergraduate level, women students constitute roughly just over a third of the student population as a whole,

51. Equal Opportunities Commission, *Third Report*, p.60.
52. AnnMarie Wolpe, 'The Official Ideology of Education for Girls', in M. Flude and J. Ahier, eds., *Educability, Schools and Society*, London 1974.
53. Byrne, p.136.

but because of the channelling they outnumber men in the area of language and literature studies. At postgraduate level men outnumber women in a ratio of nearly 3 to 1 and although this imbalance is most marked in the scientific and technological areas, there are larger numbers of men graduate students than women *even* in the previously 'feminine' subjects.[54] This constitutes an important break, since postgraduate study is not only mandatory for academic posts, but is also useful for promotion in other occupations. Hence the point at which large numbers of women drop out or are excluded is the point which distinguishes a certain type of career from the kind of employment open to any graduate.

This raises questions about the training of women generally and about the social definitions of levels of skill. Evidence collected by the Manpower Services Commission in 1975 demonstrates that *any* training is generically more common for men than for women. At all levels of the occupational structure, more men than women have been trained for four years or more, and more women than men have been trained for less than one month.[55] This situation is reflected in the proportion of women involved in apprentice-ships and day-release schemes.[56] The one area where women outnumber men is adult education, and it is clear that the opportunities denied women at an earlier stage in their lives play a part in this. The implications of present government policy for this field of educational provision are not clear at present. On the one hand it seems unlikely that this precarious, apparently non-essential educational area can survive public expenditure cuts, let alone be funded for expansion. On the other hand, the EOC has attached some weight to it as a measure for equalizing educational provision between men and women, and the British government is also under some pressure from the EEC to

54. Equal Opportunities Commission, *Third Report*, pp.62-7.
55. *Social Trends 9*, Government Statistical Service, HMSO, London, 1979, p.93.
56. Equal Opportunities Commission, *Third Report*, pp.68-9.

increase its involvement in line with the greater provision of recurrent education in other European countries.

These aspects of the role of education and training in the construction of a gender-divided workforce should be seen in relation to major aspects of the general division of labour. When we consider the destination of school leavers, for example, it is relevant to look at the overall determination of class in the processes under discussion. Although I have expressed reservations about the theoretical interpretation of empirical data (and particularly, one might add, of official statistics), it is worth pausing briefly to note that this data does demonstrate that the link between education and employment for women cannot be detached from a class analysis. For instance, if we take girls who went to university, the figures for 1975-6 show that only 2.9% of girls from comprehensive schools went, as against 16.9% from grammar schools, 30.1% from direct grant schools and 15.5% from recognized independent schools.[57] I shall return to the relationship between gender and class in the conclusion, but I want first to consider a rather different aspect of the situation — the question of definitions of knowledge and of the curriculum in terms of gender division and gender ideology.

4. The question of 'legitimate knowledge' has recently been taken up vigorously in both Marxist and feminist work. Weberian sociology, with its claims to present a 'value-free' knowledge of society, has been particularly vulnerable to this attack, which has also been launched in disciplines as far apart as statistics, literature, natural science and anthropology. The notion underlying many of these analyses is frequently the view articulated by Marx that the knowledge validated by a particular society is not neutral but is constructed in the interests of the dominant class. Recognition that knowledge is not neutral, but must in itself be an object of our analysis, carries with it the parallel recognition that our own analysis must be grounded in a

57. *Social Trends 9*, p.78.

particular historical conjuncture. Hence a radical critique of 'legitimate' knowledge must accept that the conditions of its own existence lie in the economic, political and ideological context in which it is produced. This point can be made very simply in relation to the development of 'women's studies' or 'black studies': they have not arisen spontaneously through a rational awareness of sexism and racism in existing bodies of knowledge, but have been brought into existence by political movements which continue to struggle for legitimacy.

Feminist critiques of legitimate knowledge have addressed the problem at various levels. It has been easy to point to instances where the curriculum, for example in school courses, blatantly incorporates sexist assumptions. The sexual division of labour is built into the context and objectives of the curriculum; many feminists have commented on the assumptions explicit in the various home economics and housecraft courses that girls have been encouraged to take.[58] Feminists have argued also that sexism is not only a part of the school curriculum but a salient factor in the theory and methods employed by specific academic disciplines. In sociology feminists have suggested that the sub-divisions within the discipline, and the weight attached to industrial sociology compared with the sociology of the family, for instance, reflect the absence of any systematic consideration of gender.[59] Feminist anthropologists have likewise commented on an 'androcentric' bias in the subject.[60] In the area of literary studies feminists have argued that the establishment of 'the canon' of reputedly excellent writers is equally dominated by male prejudice.

At a more general level it is also important to point to the alleged congruence between rationality, knowledge and masculinity. This is obviously somewhat intangible but it is

58. See AnnMarie Wolpe, 'The Official Ideology of Education for Girls', and Rosemary Deem, *Women and Schooling*, p.45.
59. See Ann Oakley, *The Sociology of Housework*, London, 1974 (Chapter 1).
60. See Maxine Molyneux, 'Androcentrism in Marxist Anthropology', in *Critique of Anthropology*, no.9/10, 1977.

possible to discern a general ideological polarization between the logical, scientific, rational, technological, numerate and 'masculine', and the literate, sensitive, insightful, unfalsifiable and 'feminine'. Such a polarity is encouraged by a situation where it is precisely in the arts and 'qualitative' subjects that women are most frequently found, whereas in the scientific and technological subjects they are most notably absent. It is at least arguable that the cultural imagery of gender in our society has been incorporated into the very framework in which we receive and assess all forms of knowledge.

This is the context in which we should locate the emergence of feminist critiques of existing academic disciplines and the development of 'women's studies' as a field of inquiry. Recent trends in the sociology of knowledge have provided legitimation for developments of this sort and it is therefore relevant to discuss here the general problems involved in attempting to specify the 'objective' character of knowledge, or, conversely, its necessarily relative character. This debate has been dominated by the influence of Michael F. D. Young's work, which has pioneered the attempt to retrieve the study of education from the grasp of sociological empiricism and locate it in a discussion of definitions of knowledge. Young's position rests to some extent on phenomenological arguments, notably those of Alfred Shütz, that knowledge is real if it is *believed* to be real and that all knowledge is socially derived. Young argues that we should treat as problematic the way in which educators pose their problems: their assumptions must be an object of our analysis. Pushed to its limit, this argument implies that all definitions of 'right' and 'wrong', all claims to 'objective' knowledge, are phenomena to be explained. Young in fact does endorse these totally relativistic arguments, and rejects the notion that any 'realist' form of knowledge is possible.[61]

61. Michael F. D. Young, ed., *Knowledge and Control*, London 1971 (see editor's introduction); and idem, 'Curriculum Change: Limits and Possibilities', in Young and Geoff Whitty, eds., *Society, State and Schooling*, Falmer 1977.

In the light of my earlier comments about Marxism as a 'realist' science, it will be clear that I do not accept these arguments. There are dangers attached to such a wholesale rejection of the possibility of objective knowledge: it is a high price to pay for the demystification of existing bodies of knowledge.

This type of relativism is, however, a significant element in the expansion of the field of 'women's studies'. Although I would argue that a systematic consideration of gender is a fundamental condition of any adequate analysis or knowledge of contemporary society, there are dangers in assuming that this will be secured by simply exploring a new area (women) at a descriptive level. This is far from being an argument against women's studies, which has historically proved a useful vehicle for placing questions about the oppression of women on the agenda in institutions of education; I am merely pointing to the possibility that an unduly relativistic attitude to knowledge may underly the tolerance with which this field is sometimes viewed by otherwise unsympathetic parties. The consequence of accepting any such tolerance is undoubtedly that of 'ghetto-ization': women's studies take on the role of a marginal, descriptive, addition to a curriculum which remains essentially unchallenged by it.

A further difficulty to which women's studies is vulnerable is that of recuperation by the ideological categories it seeks to subvert. In particular, although most of us, as feminists, are well aware of the danger of recuperation, it is possible to see ways in which women's studies has reproduced some elements of the ideological configuration I discussed earlier. The necessary process of revaluing the characteristics ideologically attributed to 'femininity' (such as 'sensitivity') may lead to an unreflective assertion of these as the pre-given characteristics of women. Women's studies must necessarily exist at present in the context of these pervasive assumptions about gender, and the task of protecting it from recuperation in this way is a difficult one. It is not, in my view, materially assisted by the relativization of all forms of knowledge. A more fruitful perspective is to argue that a 'realist' knowledge of the social formation is possible, and to insist that any adequate knowledge of contemporary capitalism must pay attention to the profound gender division within it.

The latter part of this chapter has concentrated on the aspects of the educational system that relate to the reproduction of a workforce divided by gender. I have to a large extent assumed the processes by which the system reproduces class division, and I am not convinced that these two processes can in any unproblematic way be integrated. It is clear, however, that the educational system does function to reproduce both of these fundamental divisions in the workforce, and that the relation between class and gender must be examined further. I have suggested that one useful way of posing this complex relation would be to argue that, as Jean Gardiner has put it, women have a dual relationship to the class structure. This duality consists in a direct relation of exploitation by capital insofar as the majority of women are wage labourers, and an indirect one insofar as many women depend upon the mediated wage of a male breadwinner. Such a duality must necessarily pose in some detail the relation between production and the family, and it is to this question that I turn in the following two chapters.

5
Gender and the Division of Labour

The division of labour in contemporary capitalism involves a sharp differentiation between male and female workers. Women are concentrated in particular industries at particular levels, and are systematically subjected to poorer pay and working conditions than men. The characteristic features of women's work are by now well documented and in this chapter I shall describe briefly some essential points only, and then discuss the implications of this situation. The divisions between men and women in the sphere of wage work constitute a central element of the 'sexual division of labour' generally but I shall argue that these divisions cannot be taken as any explanation of women's oppression. As Edholm, Harris and Young have argued,[1] the sexual division of labour is an object to be explained by further analysis and not in itself a key to the understanding of gender division. It follows that throughout this chapter we shall encounter situations which cannot be grasped without an analysis of family forms and indeed it is written in such a way as to highlight this point. The discussion here of the division of labour refers back to the ideological construction of masculine and feminine categories, and looks forward to the consideration of the family (in my view the central locus of women's oppression) and to an analysis of the role of the state in organizing a particular relationship between domestic life and the labour force.

1. Felicity Edholm, Olivia Harris and Kate Young, 'Conceptualizing Women', *Critique of Anthropology*, vol.3, no.9/10, 1977.

Obviously there are connections between all the aspects of women's oppression in capitalism raised under the different chapter-headings of this book; I shall argue, however, that this oppression is inexplicable without an understanding of the connections between the division of labour at work and in the home. This chapter and the next must therefore constitute a major testing ground for the exploration of the possibilities of a 'Marxist feminist' approach. The present chapter first considers the characteristics of women's wage labour in contemporary capitalism, and the explanations offered of them; then, the role of gender ideology in structuring a divided working class; and finally, the extent to which these divisions, and particularly the division by which domestic labour is assigned to women, can be explained in terms of the supposed needs of capitalism.

I

Evidence of the intractable nature of women's subordination as wage labourers has been provided by a consideration of the effects of the British legislation on equal pay. This legislation made provision against sex discrimination and made it illegal for employers to differentiate in pay between women and men undertaking 'like work'. The easiest way to consider its effectiveness is to take the figures showing women's pay as a percentage of men's over the relevant time period.[2] The calculation on which the gap between male and female earnings is narrowest is for average hourly pay, where in 1974 women earned 67.4% of what men earned and in 1976 earned 75.1%. This relative rise in women's pay has, however, not been maintained and appears to be to some extent a temporary effect of the legislation. The latest figures available show that in 1978 the proportion had slipped back to 73.9%. The gap is broader (for reasons outlined below) if we consider gross weekly rather than hourly earnings. In the public sector these rose for women from 65.4% of men's pay in

2. The following figures are drawn from the digest printed in the Equal Opportunities Commission *Third Report*, p.81f.

1974 to 72.1% in 1976, and back to 70.3% in 1978. The discrepancies are much greater in the private sector, where women's weekly rates have never yet reached 60% of male earnings — in 1978 the figure was 57.6% The situation is posed most starkly by comparing the hourly and weekly figures of rates of pay in 1978: taking all men and women into account, we see that the figure for women's earnings as a percentage of men's is 73.9% for hourly rates but only 64.8% for weekly earnings.

These figures are of course an appalling indictment of the failure of the equal-pay legislation. Several particular points should be made before we attempt to isolate the most significant factors at work in a situation where women's average weekly pay is less than two thirds that of men's. First, as Mandy Snell has documented,[3] many employers have successfully undertaken 'regrading' exercises to remove the possibility of comparison between male and female work on which implementation of the legislation depends. Second, it might well be noted that the figures would be still worse were it not for the large numbers of women employed in the public sector, which has a better record than the private sector in this respect. Third, a large proportion of the difference between hourly and weekly rates can be attributed to overtime, and bonuses, and here there are major differences between the hours worked by men and women. Overtime, shift work and premiums attached to certain kinds of work all raise the question of the protective legislation which governs women's working conditions. It is at present a controversial issue whether these restrictions are ultimately in women's interests, and I shall return to it in the discussion of trade-union strategy in a later section of this chapter. For the moment I want to concentrate on describing the processes that may be said to constitute the character of female wage labour in general terms. It is useful to think of these in terms of the divisions referred to in the last chapter: the vertical division of labour through which

3. Mandy Snell, 'The Equal Pay and Sex Discrimination Acts: Their Impact in the Workplace', *Feminist Review*, no.1, 1979.

women are disadvantaged relative to men in pay and conditions of work, and the horizontal division of labour by which women are concentrated in particular types of work. Connections between the two will be made, but it is useful to separate them for purposes of description.

Female wage labour is not only characterized by low pay. Assembly work on piece-rate contract in the home, arguably the most exploited work of all, is mainly undertaken by women because of their domestic and childcare responsibilities.[4] The pay and security of part-time work are widely accepted as disadvantaged in comparison with full-time work, but a staggering 41% of all women with jobs in this country work part-time.[5] Many employers set the part-time hours just under the minimum specified in the employment protection legislation and legal actions to claim an equal-pay ratio by part-time workers have been remarkably unsuccessful. It is incontrovertibly the case that women workers are more vulnerable than men to redundancy in times of recession. The Department of Employment's figures show that the recession since 1974 has resulted in women being made unemployed at roughly three times the rate of men. Since married women are frequently not eligible for state benefits it is unclear at any one time what proportion of unemployed women are registered as such, and evidence from the General Household Survey demonstrates some fluctuation.[6] A further aspect of this situation is the question of promotion and seniority. Many women workers (particularly if they have returned to employment after raising a family) will be very vulnerable where the 'last-in-first-out' principle is applied. In addition to this the low representation of women in senior grades, and in the 'higher professional' occupations in general, reflects

4. See Emily Hope *et al.*, 'Homeworkers in North London', in *Dependence and Exploitation in Work and Marriage.*
5. *Social Trends 9*, HMSO, London 1979, p.86.
6. The GHS elicits information on those seeking work but not registered as unemployed. Irene Bruegel has calculated that this category increased between 1974 and 1976 by 10% for men and 28% for women ('Women as a Reserve Army of Labour' in *Feminist Review*, no.3, 1979).

the educational and training divisions discussed in the
last chapter and suggests a process of systematic
discrimination.[7]

It is clear from existing writing on the subject that the
vertical division of labour is pronounced in respect of gender.
Women occupy jobs which are lower paid, more insecure, less
likely to bring promotion than men. This generalization
holds within particular trades, industries and professions,
and across the range of them, and constitutes an important
dimension of the segmentation of the labour market.[8] These
processes are separate from, but exacerbated by, a horizontal
division of labour in which women are concentrated in
particular, often low-paid, industries. This phenomenon of
job segregation renders equal pay legislation based on a
comparison of 'like work' peculiarly impotent. As the Equal
Opportunities Commission drily notes: 'one of the major
causes of the low level of women's pay is that they work in
low-paid occupations, though it is unclear which factor is the
cause of the other.[9] Women have traditionally constituted a
high proportion of the workforce in industries such as
textiles and today they make up 74% of the workforce in the
clothing and footwear industry. The distribution of women
across particular occupations is extremely uneven: women
comprise 64.8% of the education, health and welfare labour
force, 73.4% of the clerical, 58.6% of selling, 75.5% of personal
services (catering, hairdressing and so on). Furthermore,
over 60% of the entire female workforce is concentrated in
only ten occupations. These 'top ten' jobs for women are
headed by clerical work, which takes 17.5% of women
workers, followed by shop assistants, typists and secretaries,
maids, cleaners, nurses, teachers, canteen assistants, shop
managers, sewing and textile workers. It is obvious that

7. For detailed figures on women in the professions see Lindsay Mackie
    and Polly Pattullo, *Women at Work*, London 1977, Chapter 4.
8. The classic British study of labour market segmentation in this respect
    is R. D. Barron and G. M. Norris, 'Sexual Divisions and the Dual
    Labour Market', in *Dependence and Exploitation in Work and
    Marriage*.
9. EOC, *Third Report*, p.81.

most of these jobs can broadly be described as service work, the 'caring' professions and socialized forms of domestic service, and many feminists have pointed out that the distribution of women in the employed workforce bears a striking resemblance to the division of labour in the family. Although twentieth-century developments have absorbed a huge proportion of the female workforce into clerical and retail work, there are parallels between the present distribution of female labour and that which obtained in the nineteenth century. Sally Alexander's study of women's work in mid-nineteenth-century London leads her to conclude that the sexual division of labour in capitalism reflects an intensification and rigidification of the division of labour in the pre-capitalist household, which was then transferred from the family on to social production.[10]

In assessing the factors which might account for the position of women as wage labourers it is impossible to escape the conclusion that family structure and the ideology of domestic responsibility play an important part. It is clear, for instance, that women's involvement in the highly exploited areas of part-time work and home-work is the direct consequence of their responsibility for childcare. This type of work is not only most convenient for a worker with responsibility for children, it is often (in the absence of nursery or after-school provision) literally the only work available. In addition to this, the categories of work primarily undertaken by women have clearly been constructed along the lines of an ideology of gender which poses servicing and caring work as pre-eminently 'feminine'. Furthermore, the construction of a family form in which the male head of household is supposedly responsible for the financial support of a dependent wife and children has militated against demands for equal pay and an equal 'right to work' for women. The 'right' of married women to take jobs at the expense of male workers has frequently been explicitly challenged. I shall discuss below some of these aspects of the

10. 'Women's Work in Nineteenth-Century London; a Study of the Years 1820-50', in *The Rights and Wrongs of Women*.

division of labour in more detail but it can clearly be argued that family responsibilities play a direct role in the structure of women's wage labour and in setting limits on women's participation.

Household structure and familial ideology also play an indirect part in the limitation of women's participation in wage labour, insofar as they inform and influence other relevant structures. These processes are undoubtedly reciprocal, leading to a reinforcing cycle which is difficult to break, both analytically and politically. Education and training systems operate in such a way as to reproduce systematically a division of labour between men and women in wage work; as such they not only reflect, but also reinforce, the division of labour between men and women at home. If this is true of education, how much more true is it of institutions that can far less readily be viewed as instruments of state policy. I am thinking here particularly of the mass media, in which rigid meanings of gender division are daily reproduced and endorsed. More problematically for the left, it is equally the case that gender division, and a particular conception of family life, has played an important role in the strategy and objectives of the trade-union movement.

It is in this context that I want to consider the argument that the characteristics of women's wage work can best be understood by analysing the problem in terms of capitalism's need for a 'reserve army' of labour. Many feminists have observed that women workers have historically constituted a 'pool' of labour to be drawn on in times of need, notably, in this country, during major wars. Marxist feminists have developed an analysis of women's wage labour, particularly that of married women, in terms of Marx's concept of an 'industrial reserve army'. Veronica Beechey has provided a systematic account of the advantages to capital that married women workers present — they are, she concludes, a 'preferred source' of the industrial reserve army.[11] I have already discussed these arguments, in considering the use of the concept of 'reproduction', and I want here to recapitulate briefly some key points. First, it should be noted that the application of a 'reserve army' model to female wage labour should not be regarded as an adequate explanation of the general characteristics of women's work in capitalism. No such claims are, in fact, made in this analysis and Beechey explicitly states that the advantages to capital she has explored rest on the presupposition of the family and its ideology. Although this point is left unexplored in her two articles, it is an important one, indicative of a Marxist feminist rather than a conventionally 'Marxist' approach. Second, although the 'industrial reserve army' model may usefully elucidate some mechanisms controlling women's participation in wage labour it cannot, as presently constituted, explain why it should be women who *necessarily* occupy a particular place in it. It may to some extent be able to do this, if it can specify the conditions which make particular groups of women comparatively insecure as workers, but such arguments would need to be supported at greater length than has so far been done.

There are a number of problems with the argument Beechey puts forward to support her view that married women present particular advantages to capital (because when unemployed their costs of reproduction are met within the family and not by the state). Obviously it is the case that women's domestic labour does reduce costs of reproduction of the working class generally, and it can be seen that such work is intensified to offset the effects of unemployment and recession. However, the parallel between the married woman and the semi-proletarianized migrant worker cannot be pushed too far: her costs of education and upbringing before marriage, and of reproduction generally afterwards are met *within* the capitalist economy itself through the state, her parents' wages and her husband's wage or state benefit. As

11. Veronica Beechey, 'Some Notes on Female Wage Labour in Capitalist Production', in *Capital and Class*, no.3, 1977, and 'Women and Production: a Critical Analysis of Some Sociological Theories of Women's Work', in *Feminism and Materialism*.

160

such, these costs (however much lowered by her domestic
labour) are met by collective capital, as well as through
wages and taxation, and this is an important difference,
from the point of view of capital, between her and a migrant
worker whose costs can be met entirely by the peripheral
economy. Approaching the problem from a different angle —
empirical evidence on women's unemployment in the present
British recession — it is also relevant to note that
unemployment among single women has, because of
increasing youth unemployment, in fact, risen faster than
among married women.[12]

The most serious problem with the 'industrial reserve
army' model, however, is that although it can help with the
analysis of women's participation rates and women's
unemployment, it precisely cannot explain the other features
of female wage labour described earlier. In two important
respects, this model is, in fact, in conflict with predictable
consequences of the form taken by female wage labour in
contemporary British capitalism. These concern women's
lower pay and their concentration in particular sectors of the
workforce. The low rates of pay customarily received by
women may lead to the possibility that in a recession they
will not be made redundant, but rather will be used to
undercut the higher wages demanded by male workers. Job
segregation will mean that the female workforce is too
inflexible to be disposed of as the 'reserve army' model would
suggest.

Taking first the question of substitution, it is clear that at
various points female labour has been used as a cheaper
alternative to male, even where this implies male
redundancy. Both Ruth Milkman and Jane Humphries, in
their work on the Great Depression, suggest that this was in
fact the case.[13] Such studies draw attention to the ideological

12. See Irene Bruegel, pp.15, 21.
13. Ruth Milkman, 'Women's Work and Economic Crisis', *Review of
   Radical Political Economics* vol.8, no.1, 1976; Jane Humphries,
   'Women: Scapegoats and Safety Valves in the Great Depression', in the
   same issue.

construction of the division of labour, since this 'role-reversal', by which the woman becomes the breadwinner and the husband an unemployed dependant, appears to create considerable familial tension. In fact it resembles the situation described by Engels in 1845, where cheap female and child labour was preferred by factory owners to more expensive male labour. Engels complains that this situation, as in the case of unemployed parents supported by their children, is degrading and 'unsexes the man and takes from the woman all womanliness'. Yet he demonstrates an insight into the ideological processes that produce this response when he correctly adds that *either* we must see this 'insane state of things' as a 'mockery', *or* we must admit that such a reversal reflects a false relation between the sexes in the first place: 'If the reign of the wife over the husband, as inevitably brought about by the factory system, is inhuman, the pristine rule of the husband over the wife must have been inhuman too'.[14]

If women's lower wages encourage a process of substitution that cuts across the 'reserve army' hypothesis, the profoundly sex-segregated nature of the workforce must also mitigate the redundancies among women that this hypothesis would predict. This is stressed by Milkman, who argues that this segregation protects women from expulsion from the workforce in times of contraction of production. The point can be put very simply: if all typists and cleaners are female (which is virtually the case) it is implausible to suggest that they can all be dispensed with.

Irene Bruegel has explored the reserve army hypothesis in relation to the unemployment created by the present recession and has proposed a useful distinction within it. She suggests that we can distinguish between two possible implications of the hypothesis: on the one hand that women's employment opportunities, taken as a whole, will deteriorate relative to men's in times of contraction, on the other that individual women are more vulnerable to

14. *The Condition of the Working Class in England*, London 1977, p.163.

redundancy than comparable men. She concludes from analysis of the data that the second prediction is borne out by the facts, doubtless through discriminatory processes as well as the principle of seniority, but that the overall concentration of women in particular sectors has a 'cushioning' effect.[15] Bruegel notes, however, that this degree of protection may be under threat in the near future. In particular, the clerical sector is one where the advantages to capital of a relatively cheap and amenable female labour force are soon to be transcended by the even cheaper and more docile technology that microprocessing has produced. The automation of clerical work has already posed a considerable threat to a major female occupation. In addition to this, the rationalization of office work has contributed to 'de-skilling' of women's work and has highlighted the similarities between clerical work and some forms of manual labour.

Definitions of skill, and the divisions in the working class that they generate and support, have played an important role in the historical struggles through which the division of labour of contemporary capitalism has developed. Within this process definitions of 'masculine' and 'feminine' work, and 'appropriate' hierarchies of skill, have been extremely significant. I want now to consider the role of gender ideology in the construction of the division of labour in the capitalist workforce and the consequences of this for the development of a divided working class.

II

The division of labour between men and women is not only oppressive for women but divisive for the working class as a whole. A divided working class is a weakened working class and it is important to explore the extent to which the sexual division of labour is integral to, and generated by, specifically capitalist processes, and the extent to which it

15.   Irene Bruegel, p.19.

involves external factors. The central point I am making here is that although the division of labour itself in capitalism is created by the economic requirements of capital accumulation, the *form* it takes incorporates ideological division to a considerable extent. A prime example of such ideological division is the division between men and women (although this does not imply that we should locate women's oppression exclusively at the level of ideology).

The division of labour in contemporary capitalism should be understood in terms of the labour theory of value. One of Marx's greatest achievements was to explain the real relations of exploitation underlying the capitalist wage system as the source of the division of labour. Capitalism is grounded in the accumulation of capital, which occurs through the extraction of surplus value from wage labourers. Workers do not sell products to capitalists, they sell their ability to labour for a certain amount of time, in return for a wage. In the time actually worked, workers produce goods to a value which is greater than the equivalent value of their wages. Wages are set, not according to the value of the goods produced, but according to the cost of reproducing the workers (food, clothing, shelter and so on). These costs of reproduction determine the value of labour power, and will vary historically. The difference between the value of labour power (roughly speaking, what the capitalist will have to pay out in wages), and the value of the goods produced, constitutes surplus value. When the capitalist exchanges the goods on the market, this surplus value is realized as profit.

The accumulation of capital rests on the attempt to increase the rate of surplus value extraction — the ratio of exploitation. Marx suggests that there are broadly two ways for capitalists to do this. They can increase surplus value in an absolute form by simply extending the time worked without raising wages; this strategy will eventually founder on the physical limitations of the working class. Or they can attempt to intensify labour and make it more productive, thus increasing relative surplus value. In either case it is

164

obviously in capital's interests to keep the cost of wages down. The attempt to increase the relative form of surplus value has historically involved the introduction of machinery and its effect of 'de-skilling' the workforce; the division of the labour force into differentiated groups, to whom more and less wages may be paid; and the stripping from the labourer of control over the production process. The intensification of labour has involved splitting the labour process into the smallest possible component parts. This has two advantages for capital: it is more efficient, and it allows the capitalist to pay wages which exactly correspond to the skill needed for the job. If the labour process is not divided up in this way, the capitalist is paying a skilled worker's wage for a worker who is at times undertaking unskilled work. Marx, and other nineteenth-century observers, regarded this 'detail' division of labour as dehumanizing.[16]

Gender has played a profoundly important part in this division of labour. At the level of a general social division of labour, in which occupationally derived groups of workers are divided from each other, the sharply sex-segregated character of the workforce has crucial implications. In terms of 'detail' work and de-skilling women have consistently been constructed as a differentiated and more vulnerable group than men. In terms of the mental/manual distinction women have, despite appearances to the contrary which I shall discuss below, consistently suffered from a severe loss of control over the labour process.

The question arises, to what extent the specifically sexual division of labour is determined by the logic of the capitalist division of labour itself. We can approach this question by considering two examples. Capitalist relations of production necessarily involve the establishment of two principles which are different from those structuring pre-capitalist production. The first is the separation of home and workplace, brought about by the development of large-scale production under the wage labour system. The second is the

16. In *Capital*, vol.1, Marx writes that the manufacturing division of labour 'attacks the individual at the very roots of his life' (p.357).

creation of a labour force divided along the lines in which the labour process itself is broken down by the capitalist drive for increased productivity of labour: it is divided along the lines of differentiation by level of skill. In both cases it is clear that the general tendencies are not merely attributable to capitalism but are essential preconditions for capital accumulation; and insofar as both have been disastrous for women workers, the argument that women's oppression is directly attributable to the organization of specifically capitalist relations of production is apparently a strong one. In my view this argument is mistaken, for it conflates a general tendency with its particular historical form. To argue, for instance, that capitalism requires the separation of home and workplace, and that therefore the relegation of women to the home and their exclusion from wage labour is an effect of capitalism is, in fact, precisely to accept the biologistic assumption that this outcome was inevitable. A more historical approach, however, indicates that this situation developed in a long and uneven process, one element of which was a struggle between male and female workers in which the better-organized male craft unions succeeded in over-riding the interests of women workers, many of whom themselves were responsible for dependants. So although the general tendency towards the separation of home and workplace has proved oppressive to women, this is because the problem is so starkly posed — who was to be primarily responsible for childcare? — was resolved, according to an ideology of gender that pre-dated capitalism, in the interests of men.[17] Hence, the question of capitalism's separation of home and workplace as a determinant of women's oppression cannot adequately be tackled without a consideration of family organization.

Similarly, it cannot be doubted that the differentiation within the labour force developed on the basis of definitions of skill has made a substantial contribution to women's

17. See Heidi Hartmann, 'Capitalism, Patriarchy and Job Segregation by Sex', in M. Blaxall and B. Reagan, eds., *Women and the Workplace*, Chicago 1976.

oppressed situation as wage workers. Women have frequently failed to establish recognition of the skills required by their work, and have consequently been in a weak bargaining position in a divided and internally competitive workforce. This is difficult to construe as simply an effect of capital's need for a differentiated workforce, since we need to know precisely how and why some groups of workers succeed in establishing definitions of their work as skilled. Some light is thrown on this problem by looking at the ways in which the capitalist labour force developed during the long transition period. In particular we need to consider the wages commanded by different categories of workers in relation to tasks requiring particular skills. Braverman has drawn attention to the rates of pay cited by Charles Babbage in his account of a pin factory. From these it can be seen that men's wages varied from 3s 3d per day (drawing wire) to 6s 0d (tinning or whitening). Women's wages varied from 1s 0d to 3s 0d. The most interesting aspect of these figures, however, is that they demonstrate Marx's point that wages depend on costs of reproduction rather than the value of goods produced. The man's highest wage of 6s 0d and the woman's highest wage of 3s 0d were paid for the *same task*. Similarly, although the task of twisting and cutting heads commanded a fairly high rate of pay for a man (5s 4½d), when undertaken by a boy it commanded only 0s 4½d.[18] This huge difference is not accounted for by variation in output; it reflected the assumption that some workers require more wages to reproduce themselves than others and

18. See Harry Braverman, *Labor and Monopoly Capitalism*, New York 1974, p.80:—

Drawing wire	Man	3s 3d per day
Straightening wire	Woman	1s 0d
	Girl	0s 6d
Pointing	Man	5s 3d
Twisting and cutting heads	Boy	0s 4½d
	Man	5s 4½d
Heading	Woman	1s 3d
Tinning or whitening	Man	6s 0d
	Woman	3s 0d
Papering	Woman	1s 6d

suggests that Marx was correct to point to the 'historical and moral element' in the determination of the value of labour power.

Thus, although the general tendency towards differentiation of the labour force by skill has had important consequences for women, it has not of itself determined the level of their wages. In addition to this it is important to question the objective status of definitions of skill. This is a particularly difficult task when skill has played a double edged role in the struggle between labour and capital: on the one hand it has provided capital with a weapon to divide and rule the working class, but on the other it has provided organized sections of the working class with a lever which has successfully been brought to bear on capital in struggles over wages and has been the instrument through which many major achievements have been won. Furthermore, insofar as differentiation by skill has played an important part in working-class consciousness, it must be examined as a crucial ideological as well as political element of the working class, and it is here that the question of gender assumes considerable importance. Before discussion of the general implications of this question, it is necessary to look more closely at what is meant by 'skill' in this context.

I do not wish to dispute that socially agreed definitions of skill are frequently based on objective criteria — a shorthand-typist, an electrician or a surgeon, for instance, have skills that I do not possess and which require considerable training and aptitude. There are, however, important ideological dimensions to the question of skill and these relate to the organization of capitalist relations of production and the concomitant divisions within the working class. These may be seen in several different ways.

First, it can be shown that skill, in the sense of technical expertise, may often be used to give legitimation to the control or authority of particular individuals. André Gorz has explored this in his very interesting account of 'technical supervisors': he points out that the training and skills which legitimate the authority of such junior managers are frequently quite irrelevant to the work in hand and may often be learnt on the job if they are relevant. Gorz argues that such training may bear no relation to efficiency or productivity — it is a training for 'superiority' over other workers and as such mystifies and occludes the shared class interests of the two categories of workers.[19] This process of legitimation of control by skill can be seen in the 'professions' too. A particularly glaring case to take is the medical profession: because doctors have the technical skills required to perform abortions, for instance, they are often held legitimately to control the decision as to whether a woman should have an abortion or not.[20]

Second, because acquired skills play such an important role in wage negotiations, there have developed a number of exclusionary practices which serve to protect the bargaining position of particular groups of workers. Training and recruitment may be highly controlled, and skills rendered inaccessible, for the purposes of retaining the differentials and privileges of a 'labour aristocracy'. This, it may be noted, frequently operates to the disadvantage of groups of workers, such as women, conventionally excluded from skilled trades. Furthermore, the extent to which a particular trade is recognized as 'skilled' will depend on the ability of its members to insist on that definition as much as on a more objective evaluation. To take a controversial example, this may be seen by considering the response of printing workers to the introduction of new technology in the newspaper industry. Compositors have traditionally been successful in establishing their work as highly skilled, and there is considerable sympathy for them in a situation where automation is threatening to strip these workers of a bargaining position that rests on these skills. Yet the same technological developments also threaten to radically 'de-skill' many secretaries, since word processors render

19. André Gorz, ed., *The Division of Labour*, Brighton 1976, p.176, in his own paper, 'Technology, Technicians and Class Struggle'.
20. See Michèle Barrett and Helen Roberts, 'Doctors and Their Patients: the Social Control of Women in General Practice', in Carol and Barry Smart, eds., *Women, Sexuality and Social Control*, London 1977.

obsolete the editorial and layout functions formerly required
in typing. Typists, however, have not achieved the same
success in gaining commensurate recognition for these
skills. If the compositors stand to suffer from these
developments, the secretarial workforce faces the threat
from a far weaker position.

A third instance of the ideological dimension of skill
concerns the distinction between 'mental' and 'manual'
labour. Marx's original point, that mechanization and the
introduction of a 'detail' division of labour stripped the
worker of mental control of the labour process, has been
misrepresented in the sociological assumption that 'white
collar', 'mental' labour is more skilled than manual labour.
This is merely an example of the illusory character of the
division of labour in capitalism. For while control over the
labour process may rest in managerial hands, it is certainly
completely absent from most work normally regarded as
'mental' labour. This point hardly requires elaboration. A
large proportion of clerical work, for instance, is undertaken
by women and, as Braverman has demonstrated, has been
rationalized and de-skilled in a manner exactly paralleling
the detail division of labour in factories.[21] Yet the pervasive
assumptions about mental and manual labour have proved
difficult to dispel. In the Registrar General's classification of
occupations, non-manual occupations figure consistently as
denoting a 'higher' class position than manual ones, giving
rise to the anomalies I discussed in the previous chapter.
These sociological assumptions are symptomatic of a failure
to challenge an ideology of skill which bears a tenuous
relationship either to any possible objective evaluations of
skills, or to definitions that industrial action has succeeded
in establishing.

The question of skill is central to any understanding of
how gender has been incorporated into the division of labour.
It has historically played a crucial role in working class
struggle and lies at the heart of the labour movement's

21.   Braverman, pp.301, 319.

failure to take up in any adequate manner the interests of women workers. It therefore plays a significant role in dividing the working class. This problem can be considered by posing two different strategies which the labour movement could pursue. The first would be to build upon the bargaining power of groups of workers whose skills and essential functions enable them to successfully raise wages and conditions of work, not only for themselves, but in such a way as to pull up the groups less powerful in these respects. This strategy depends upon differentials and exclusionary practices, but it is argued that in the long run it raises the standard of living of the working class as a whole. The second strategy is to attempt to establish a minimum wage for all workers, irrespective of skill and sectional bargaining power, and thereby reduce the likelihood of undercutting and substitution of cheaper labour.

These two strategies are, to some extent at least, incompatible. The labour movement in Britain has tended to concentrate its energies on the former rather than the latter, and in so doing has reproduced and reinforced the vulnerable position of women workers. Marx, in fact, can be taken to endorse this strategy. In his discussion of the substitution of female and child labour for male, with its attendant dilution of skill, he argued that organized male workers could successfully resist these tendencies.[22] Such a strategy has, in my view, not only incorporated unreflectively sexist assumptions of the male workforce, but is also inadequate to meet the present and future threats to the standard of living of the working class.

A number of issues lead to this conclusion. The degree of technological innovation envisaged for the future is such as to erode many areas of skilled work presently thought to be well protected. The effects of the new technology will not be restricted to clerical work but are already impinging on manufacturing and cannot be withstood by the short-term defence of obsolete skill differentials. The threat of

22. See *Capital*, vol.1, p.361.

unemployment on a scale never previously encountered renders the problem of competition and undercutting of wages particularly acute. The forms of work undertaken by women, and also to some extent by migrant labour (home-work and part-time work at low rates of pay) will represent an increasing threat to a labour movement strategy which relies on sectional bargaining power and the attempt to enforce practices of excluding weaker groups of workers. If the labour movement continues to press for a 'family wage', as earned by a male breadwinner, rather than for equal pay for women workers, the processes of substitution are bound to worsen.

In this context the current debate about the 'protective legislation' governing women's work is important. It would be difficult to acquit the labour movement of complicity in this legislation as a strategy for reducing competition for male workers. As Sally Alexander has noted, such legislation was introduced in areas of competition rather than in all areas of work.[23] Yet the solution to this problem now would not be to endorse the present government's proposal to repeal this legislation, but to argue for its extension to the hours and conditions of work of male workers too.[24] Such strategies are of course now being actively canvassed within the British labour movement, and a welcome aspect of this change has been an insistence on the reduction of the working day. The failure of the labour movement in the past to take up the interests of women workers has not merely resulted in the oppression and exploitation of women. It has militated against a unified working-class consciousness and unified militant action. In short, it has constituted a failure to resist the political division in the working class that capital's division of labour creates and profits from. Although the form taken by the division of labour between men and women owes much to the family structure and to an ideology of gender that pre-dates

23. 'Women's Work', p.63.
24. See Angela Coyle, 'The Protection Racket?', in *Feminist Review*, no.4, 1980.

capitalism, it has been incorporated into the political organization of the working class with consequences that capital can benefit from.

III

The previous two sections of this chapter have considered the differences between men and women as wage labourers and the ways in which these differences with regard to social production engender division in the political consciousness of the working class. Marxists have found it difficult to explain this at the level of social production itself, since it has proved impossible to specify, with reference to a Marxist theory of capitalist wage labour, why women and men should occupy these positions. Increasingly, in recent Marxist and Marxist feminist work, there has been a tendency to turn to the question of domestic labour in the family as a possible source of an explanation.

This development has been constructive in that it rests on the important recognition of a relationship between the structure of gendered wage labour relations and family structures as they have evolved under capitalism. This, as I argue throughout this book, is an essential starting point for an adequate analysis. There are, however, several problems inherent in the terms in which the 'domestic labour debate' has been posed and these discussions taken as a whole reveal the difficulty of applying Marxist categories to the question of gender. Put most strongly, the problem is that the object under discussion — women's domestic labour in the home — is seen only from one point of view: what functions does it perform for capital? This assumption has tended to dominate Marxist thought on domestic labour, which is accordingly characterized as a mechanism whereby the interests of capital are served. This approach, although usefully insisting on a connection between domestic relations and social production, tends to deprive us of any adequate analysis of familial ideology. The very object that posed a major problem for Marxist analysis of gendered .

wage-labour relations (the family) is incorporated into the existing framework as a precondition of social production rather than adequately addressed. Indeed it is not a coincidence that the limitations of the 'domestic labour debate' have led to the emphasis on ideological processes and the familial construction of gendered subjects, with accompanying claims for the 'autonomous' character of these systems.

The problem of how to develop a more adequate analysis of the family, avoiding both the functionalism of reducing it to an agent for the reproduction of capitalism and the analytic paralysis of elevating it to a completely autonomous structure, will be the subject of Chapter 6. Before tackling this, however, I want to look briefly at the arguments that domestic labour can be understood in terms of its functions for capital; that this form of women's oppression is dictated by 'the logic of capitalism' and constitutes an important element of the sexual division of labour from which capital benefits.

There now exist several excellent general discussions of 'the domestic labour debate'[25] and I shall restrict my account to a few major points. In particular, I want to examine what I consider to be the two principal points put forward in the various writings on domestic labour — that it concerns the reproduction of labour power, and the reproduction of the relations of production of capitalism.

These two points are perhaps most clearly outlined in one of the earliest works in this debate, Wally Seccombe's 'The Housewife and her Labour under Capitalism'.[26] Although a number of Seccombe's arguments have subsequently been challenged and qualified,[27] these two points constitute the

---

25. The most recent, and useful, of these being Maxine Molyneux, 'Beyond the Domestic Labour Debate', in *New Left Review*, no.116, 1979. See also S. Himmelweit and S. Mohun, 'Domestic Labour and Capital', *Cambridge Journal of Economics*, vol.1, 1977.

26. *New Left Review*, no.83, 1974.

27. See the two articles in *New Left Review*, no.89, 1975 — Jean Gardiner, 'Women's Domestic Labour'; and Margaret Coulson, Branka Magaš and Hilary Wainwright, '"The Housewife and Her Labour Under Capitalism" — a Critique'.

framework for the ensuing discussion and have dominated the general change in Marxist thought on domestic labour. Seccombe stresses early on in his article that Marxist analysis of production has concentrated on the observable phenomena of wage labour and ignored the preconditions which make them possible. It is as if, he argues, Marxists were analysing a play entitled 'The Working Day', whose action takes place as the workers arrive at the factory gates. The Marxist drama critics in the audience have been content to review and analyse the production, without explaining how the performance itself depends upon preparatory and back-stage labour — rehearsals, props, lighting, the box office and so on. Seccombe sees domestic labour as similarly essential to, yet 'behind the scenes' of, capitalist production. He argues that women's domestic labour in the family fulfils two vital needs. One is the economic need for the regeneration of labour power. This takes place on a generational basis in the production of new labourers, and encompasses all the work involved in bearing and rearing children. It also occurs on a daily basis in the form of servicing the wage labourer so that he (that is, the husband) can appear for work fed, clothed, laundered, soothed and untrammelled by responsibilities for childcare. Although these tasks could be dealt with by others — the labourer himself or paid workers — the cost is much lower if they are undertaken by the housewife.

The second major point Seccombe establishes is that domestic labour plays an important ideological role in the reproduction of the relations of production of capitalism. The housewife herself has a central role in this, since it is she who socializes the children into the 'appropriate' place in a division of labour organized into dominant and subordinate groups. She also plays the role of normative linch-pin in the family, providing an incentive for the man's motivation to work as a breadwinner and cushioning him against the alienation of his wage labour. This work, like the reproduction of labour power, is privatized within the family but provides an important, possibly essential, form of support for the relations of production in which the family is located. Of the many disputed points in the consideration of domestic labour I want to mention only one or two. Perhaps the most general theoretical dispute concerns the question of who benefits from this work. A functionalist Marxist approach has tended to argue that men as men benefit only incidentally from domestic labour, since it functions ultimately to keep down the value of labour power and reproduce the class relations of capitalism and hence directly benefits the capitalist class. Insofar as autonomy is granted to domestic relations *vis à vis* capitalist relations, it is argued that men benefit directly from this work. To some extent this basic theoretical disagreement governs the choice of emphasis between the generational and daily aspects of the reproduction of labour power. Radical feminists, for instance, have tended to stress the way in which men benefit from the daily services of their wives for their personal gratification and have seen this in terms of patriarchy or male dominance. Many Marxist feminists, on the contrary, have argued implicitly or explicitly that the labour of child-care understood in terms of capital's long-term needs for future labour power, constitutes the more intractable aspect of women's oppression. Thus the debate as to whether women are principally oppressed as *wives*, from which child-care and other domestic responsibilities follow, or as *mothers*, reflects this underlying difference of emphasis.

A further general question posed by domestic labour concerns whether it could be socialized and if so under what conditions. A corollary of seeing domestic labour as a functional prerequisite of capitalist production will obviously be that it is not amenable to socialization under capitalism, and this view is frequently argued by Marxists or Marxist feminists, notably by Adamson and her collaborators.[28] Yet this claim rests to some extent on the simple assertion that domestic labour is necessarily privatized, and also on the assumption that under capitalism it is

28. Adamson *et al.*, 'Women's Oppression Under Capitalism', *Revolutionary Communist*, no.5, 1976.

conceptually incorrect to speak of any 'socialization' since capitalist relations will still apply. The more precise question is in fact to what extent domestic labour need be privatized, and to what extent it might be 'collectivized', or 'capitalized', in capitalism. Some writers have pointed to the difficulty of approaching this question at the level of theory alone; it is, after all, strange to rule out the possibility of collectivized domestic labour when we know that periods of expansion and high female employment bring increased use of convenience foods, laundries, restaurants and so on, and that periods of recession bring an intensification of domestic labour in the home.[29] Consideration of empirical evidence of this kind is essential and suggests that we may usefully approach the argument that domestic labour — indeed the sexual division of labour generally — is required by 'the logic of capitalism' by developing an historical perspective. Answers to the questions of who benefits from women's domestic labour and whether it could be collectivized may rest, at least partially, on historical rather than solely theoretical work. I therefore want to consider these two questions by looking at the division of labour, and particularly the division of labour within the household and its relation to production as this has been affected by changes in the mode of production generally. This involves considering, albeit briefly, the transition from feudalism to capitalism, which I shall look at in relation to Britain, and the effect of changes made in those countries which have attempted to make a transition to socialism.

The argument that sees domestic labour as functional for capital rests on certain assumptions about the character of the pre-capitalist household. It suggests that the labour of the 'housewife' in feudal households contributed to social production, was not privatized and was undertaken in a relationship of equality with her husband. Furthermore, it suggests that familial ideology as encountered in capitalism

29. See Gardiner, 'Women's Domestic Labour', p.57.

did not exist then or was less oppressive to women. It rests, in short, on an idealization of the pre-capitalist household, and indeed one of the problems of this historical exercise is that the descriptions given of feudal households tend to vary according to the interpretation or theoretical analysis offered.

There are, however, a number of features of pre-capitalist households which can be differentiated from the forms that have developed under capitalism. The first of these concerns the character of production prior to a system based on the wage relation. It seems clear that feudal relations of production tied the whole household rather than the individual to socially productive labour and that there was therefore a less sharp distinction between the labour of men and women. Although agricultural systems of production often exhibit customary divisions of labour between men and women as regards particular tasks, these are not necessarily very salient; we find instead the existence of *common* productive labour within the household.[30] As well as this common household production, in which men and women, the old, the young and the sick could contribute more evenly than is the case under capitalism, feudal relations of production to some extent may have facilitated what Roberta Hamilton has called a 'unity of production and consumption'. Although Hamilton ignores the appropriation of serf-labour in her romantic statement that rich and poor families alike '... ate most of what they grew and grew most of what they ate, made most of what they used and used most of what they made', the remark has still some resonance.[31] The development of wage labour had profound effects upon this 'unity'. As goods were produced for the market rather than for use the consumption of the household began to rely on the incoming wage(s) rather than on

30. Max Weber, *Economy and Society*, trans. G. Roth, New York 1968.
31. Roberta Hamilton, *The Liberation of Women*, London 1978, p.25. Christopher Middleton's discussion of 'Sexual Divisions in Feudalism' includes, *inter alia*, a useful critique of Hamilton's account (*New Left Review*, nos. 113/114, 1979).

internal production. Hence although households under capitalism have not been completely stripped of their productive functions (as sociologists are wont to argue), notably because they have retained the production of labour power, it is certainly clear that in comparison with their predecessors under feudalism, they have become to a far greater extent units of consumption bearing no *direct* relationship to social production.

Second, and distinct from the consequences of the wage labour system, we have to consider the effects of the separation of home and workplace brought by capitalism. This separation is not actually a categorical *sine qua non*, but rather a tendency, of capitalism. In the early textile industry wage labourers worked in their own homes for several decades until the introduction of machinery which was simply too large for this arrangement. In our own time capitalist wage relations are alive and well in the ('anachronistic') case of contracted home-work. It is not implausible to suggest that future developments in micro-technology may create a situation where many workers operate from a computer terminal in the front room. The separation of home and workplace is not analytically coterminous with capitalist relations of production, but was historically brought about in the development of capitalism. The drive towards capital accumulation leads to mass production and mechanization and, given technological factors and logistics, it became more and more likely that such production would take place in sites outside the household. A further respect in which capitalism effects a separation of home and workplace lies in its demand for a mobile labour force. This ensures that the separation is not necessarily merely a local one, but may take wage labourers away from their families and into the areas where work is available; this frequently involves a long-term move to a metropolitan industrial city, which is however not secure enough to permit relocation of the family, which remains in the agricultural hinterland — a pattern noted in the nineteenth-century drift towards the towns, in Irish emigration to England, in migration from the Bantustans to South African centres of production and among migrant workers in Europe.

The consequences of the separation of home and workplace for the family, and for gender relations, have been very marked. This is because the situation raises the problem of caring for children and other members of the working class not in a position to undertake wage labour (the disabled and old for instance). This question has, as we know, customarily been resolved by ascribing these responsibilities to women and cutting them off from equal participation with men in wage labour. The accompanying ideological processes have involved the establishment of the privatized domestic area of 'the home' as the particular province of women and of 'femininity' and maternalism. Women have become dependent upon the male wage in capitalism and this mediated dependence upon the wage is circumscribed by an ideology of emotional, psychical and 'moral' dependence.

A third major consequence of the transition to capitalism on the household has been to increase the degree to which relations between men and women vary between classes. Hamilton suggests that all the feudal classes (nobility, yeomanry, peasantry and so on) shared the characteristic of absorbing both men and women into a relatively equal participation in production (or appropriation).[32] Although this argument again courts the danger of idealizing feudal households, it would seem reasonable to conclude that gender divisions were somewhat less differentiated between classes than they became under capitalist production. This is difficult to assess over such a long period. We know, for instance, that courtly-love ideology among the nobility in the twelfth century indicated very sharp gender division. On the other hand the power of women in the medieval church indicates opportunities for public responsibility denied subsequently to women of comparable classes. Clearly there are dangers in posing a radical distinction between the

32. Hamilton, Chapter 2.

proletarian and the bourgeois family in this regard; Engels's view that there was equality for women in the former and complete dependence for women in the latter is a gross over-simplification. It ignores, for instance, the extent to which an ideology of domesticity took hold in the proletarian family, and is unsatisfactory as a characterization of the contemporary bourgeois family where a greater degree of financial independence for women obtains. It remains the case, however, that the character of women's oppression differs greatly between the classes of capitalism, and that this represents a significant element of any understanding of the changes wrought by the transition from feudalism to capitalism.

Recognition of these general differences between feudal and capitalist households has led many Marxists to the conclusion that the advent of capitalism created privatized domestic labour for women as a precondition of capitalist production. This view underlies much of the work on the political economy of the household which comprises the 'domestic labour debate', and also underlies analyses such as Zaretsky's argument that the logic of capitalist development is ultimately the source of the privatized family.[33] These approaches to the form of the household under capitalism tend to attempt to explain domestic labour and familial ideology with reference to specifically capitalist needs and imperatives. Other writers have argued the opposite. Margaret Benston, for instance, sees domestic labour as essentially 'pre-capitalist' in character — a relic from a feudal mode of production which has survived into capitalism.[34] Many others have seen domestic labour, or even a 'domestic mode of production' as an autonomous set of relations operating within capitalism.

I am not really convinced by any of these arguments, especially when they are posed at the level of theoretical generalization. It has yet to be proved that capitalism could

33. Eli Zaretsky, *Capitalism, The Family and Personal Life*, London 1976.
34. 'The Political Economy of Women's Liberation', *Monthly Review*, vol.21, no.4, 1969.

not survive without the present form of domestic labour. On the other hand it is equally difficult to regard the development of the family as unrelated to the changing needs of capitalist production. The available historical evidence suggests that neither generalization is adequate. It might be more useful instead to consider the ways in which pre-capitalist gender divisions have been incorporated, possibly entrenched and exaggerated, into the structure of capitalist relations of production. The two major features of female wage labour in capitalism provide an interesting point of departure for a less dogmatic and more historical approach to the question of the relationship between domestic relations and social production: the uneven distribution of women workers into particular sections of the labour force, and the typically poor working conditions and insecurity of female wage labourers. Although both of these are clearly beneficial to capitalism, neither can be explained without reference to a pre-capitalist sexual division of labour.

Let us take job segregation first. Many feminists have commented that the areas where female workers are concentrated correspond to ideological divisions between men and women that relate to the family. Women are over-represented in service work and the 'caring' occupations, and in manual work such as cleaning which resembles domestic work in the home. Sally Alexander has pointed out the extent to which the distribution of the predominantly female occupations effectively represents an extension of the division of labour within the patriarchal family.[35] Studies of the early period of industrialization point to similar conclusions, in that occupations such as charring, domestic service, spinning, weaving, millinery and so on were very common for women, while their major engagement in factory and mining work lasted only for a short while.[36] Evidence from an earlier period, notably Alice Clark's well-known

35. 'Women's Work', p.73.
36. See the Appendix (Occupations of Women in 1841) printed in Pinch-beck, *Women Workers and the Industrial Revolution 1750-1850*, London 1977.

study,[37] suggests that even where goods were being produced in the household there was a division of labour according to which certain aspects of the work were undertaken by men and others by women. It is, of course, difficult to establish the extent to which this division of labour within the household existed in feudal family structures, but the available evidence suggests that there was a differentiation of tasks. What should be added, however, is that a simple differentiation of tasks (as between not only men and women, but also children and old people) may not necessarily be inegalitarian or divisive when all the labour is directed towards common household production. The difference between this division of labour and that of capitalism is that capitalism not only took over and entrenched the differentiation of tasks, but divided the workforce itself into wage earners and those dependent upon the wage of others. Capitalism did not create domestic labour, or the 'feminine' areas of wage labour, but it did create a set of social relations in which pre-existing divisions were not only reproduced but solidified in different relations in the wage-labour system.

This can be seen more clearly when we consider the other major aspect of female wage labour to which domestic relations are connected — that of women's pay, working conditions and security of employment. The entire history of women's work, including their function as an industrial reserve and their role as cheap substitutes for male labour, rests on the fact that from the earliest years of capitalist production it has been possible to insist on this differential. Put another way, it could be said that the situation depends upon the assumption that the value of women's labour power — the cost of their reproduction — was customarily lower than men's. Why should this be the case? It seems clear that male workers were more successful in organizing themselves, into craft unions for example, and this gave them an advantage at the outset of industrialization. In addition,

37. *Working Life of Women in the Seventeenth Century*, London [1919] 1968.

records of wage levels from the early period of industrial capitalism show quite plainly that women, and children, could be hired for cheaper wages than men — as in the case of wages in the pin factory mentioned earlier. This discrepancy can be related to ideological definitions of the basic element of food consumption. The early capitalists appear to have anticipated Marx's account of the relationship between wages and costs of subsistence and, assuming that women ate less than men (and children less still), settled wages accordingly. Studies of food consumption do in fact show that women frequently have consumed less than men, and often gone short (even when pregnant) in order to feed their husband and children.[38]

There can be no doubt that capitalism has encouraged and benefited from such customs and assumptions. Nevertheless the existence of such divisions in the very earliest period of capitalism does suggest that we cannot attach too much weight to specifically capitalist processes in understanding their origins. To say that capitalism has benefited from customary assumptions about the lower wages payable to women and the assignment to women of domestic and child-care responsibilities is not necessarily to fall into the error of concluding that this explains why such assumptions exist today. Nor, indeed, is it implied, by insisting on the existence of a pre-capitalist sexual division of labour, that capitalism does not subsequently benefit from it. As I have attempted to show in these remarks, the relationship between domestic labour and female wage labour in capitalism has evolved through a process in which pre-capitalist distinctions have become entrenched into the structure of capitalist relations of production. This being the case, it is not to be expected that societies which have attempted to abolish or transform capitalist relations of production will necessarily have made significant changes in either the division of labour between

38. See Laura Oren, 'The Welfare of Women in Labouring Families: England, 1860-1950', in *Clio's Consciousness Raised*, M. Hartman and L. W. Banner, eds., New York 1974; and Christine Delphy, 'Sharing the Same Table: Consumption and the Family', in C. C. Harris, ed., *The Sociology of the Family*, Keele 1978.

men and women within the household or the relationship between domestic labour and wage labour.

I am aware that any discussion of this point raises the question of whether any genuinely 'socialist' society exists at present. This, although a central question for any substantive analysis of gender division in non-capitalist countries, is not an issue which need concern us unduly here. The reason why I am holding the definition of a socialist society in suspension is that I am considering here solely the argument that capitalism requires a particular form of women's oppression, and not a proposed general position that socialism will inevitably bring women's liberation. The societies in point — Cuba, China, the Soviet Union and so on — are certainly not capitalist countries in the sense that Britain and the USA are. All have self-consciously undergone revolutionary transformation of the mode of production and have attempted, however successfully, to implement socialist goals. Although many of them are organized on a wage system not unlike that of western capitalism, they do at least provide us with some comparative data on which we can base consideration of the role of the household in non-capitalist systems of production.

There is now a growing literature on the position of women in these societies,[39] and I want here simply to make a few general observations. First, it is clear that the phenomenon of job segregation so familiar in western capitalism has to some extent been eroded. Although claims about Soviet women doctors and Chinese women high-tension wire engineers, for instance, are now known to be less representative than might have been thought previously, there is evidence to suggest that women in these societies do undertake work which was previously defined as 'masculine'. We should, however, bear in mind that the preponderance of women engaged in heavy manual labour may also reflect a different history of gendered divisions of

39. A selection of references can be found in Mary Evans and David Morgan, *Work on Women: A Guide to the Literature*, London 1979, pp.56-7.

labour from that which we are familiar with in Western Europe.

In other important respects the general picture is not dissimilar from that described in the British context. Women's pay and working conditions are generally inferior to men's. It would be difficult to find an example of any adequate socialization of domestic labour. In the Soviet Union, for instance, domestic labour is undertaken almost exclusively by the housewife, frequently on top of waged work, and is more time-consuming than domestic labour in capitalist countries.[40] Although developments in China have at certain periods involved a drive towards collective child-care, it is noted by various observers that this rarely brought men into active participation.[41]

Furthermore, there is little evidence so far of any thorough and permanent challenge to familial ideology. Although post-revolutionary governments have frequently liberalized the laws on divorce, homosexuality, abortion and so on, these reforms have tended to be eroded or reversed over time. Indeed, in many of these societies the family is seen as the essential unit of political and ideological cohesion and is, if anything, protected and reproduced by the state more actively than in capitalism. It is obviously relevant here to note that the ideology of gender in these societies, with a frequently oppressive construction of masculinity and femininity, cannot be viewed apart from the cultural history of the society in question: legacies of misogyny in Christian ideology, of Islamic doctrine and (in Latin cultures) of the cult of machismo, play an important part in the definition of gender in many socialist societies.

The tenacity and intractability of gender ideology, and the failure of socialist societies to socialize domestic labour and

40. See Alena Heitlinger's excellent study of *Women and State Socialism: Sex Inequality in the Soviet Union and Czechoslovakia*, London 1979, p.92.
41. See Judith Stacey, 'When Patriarchy Kowtows: the Significance of the Chinese Family Revolution for Feminist Theory', in *Capitalist Patriarchy*, pp.326-7; and Elizabeth Croll, *Feminism and Socialism in China*, London 1978.

childcare to any significant degree, must lead to the conclusion that these processes are not restricted to capitalist systems of production. As we have seen, family forms, and their relationship to social production, may vary. There are important differences between the form of the family in different classes of contemporary capitalism, in different periods of capitalist development, and between families in capitalist and non-capitalist societies. Furthermore, these historical differences are such that we cannot speak in any unproblematic way of 'the family' at all. It is more precise to refer to households, which have varying arrangements for the reproduction of the labouring and non-labouring population, and to the varying familial ideologies which accompany different household forms.

What is clear, however, and may usefully serve as conclusion to this chapter, is that the gender divisions of social production in capitalism cannot be understood without reference to the organization of the household and the ideology of familialism. This area represents the primary site of relations between men and women, of the construction of gendered individuals, and is closely related to the organization of social production. The structure and ideology of the family in contemporary capitalism is surely the most salient issue for any Marxist feminist approach to address. In the following chapter I shall investigate the progress so far made in attempting to provide an adequate analysis of this central institutional site of women's oppression.

6
Women's Oppression and 'the Family'

I have several times suggested that further understanding of 'the family' is essential to the solution of some of the analytic and practical problems encountered so far. In one sense it is ironic that this should be the case, since it is precisely in terms of 'the family' that women have always apparently been located. What could be odder than that feminists, let alone Marxist feminists, should be drawn back to give analytic pride of place to the very institution in which women have historically been immured? However, this paradox is more apparent than real. It depends upon an assumption that there is an entity recognizable as 'the family' which is the common object of the many different discussions about it — an assumption that this chapter seeks to challenge, arguing that it is precisely the characterization of very different family forms as 'the family' that has underwritten much of women's oppression.

'The family', in popular ideology and in a vast amount of historical and intellectual work, is posed as self-evidently the same whether we speak of it in feudal, slave or capitalist societies, in the West, in the Soviet Union, in Cuba. Even to conceptualize *the* family is to concede the existence of an institution that, in whatever historical context it is found, is essentially and naturally there. The difficulties in the context of 'family history' itself are spelled out very clearly by Rayna Rapp: 'much of the work on the history of the family is conceptually wedded to an acceptance of the distinction between the family itself, and the larger world....

It is this acceptance of "the family" as a natural unit existing in separation from the total social formation which *creates* the problem of its insertion into that world, at least at the level of theory. ... Unless we develop a more critical awareness of the family as a social, not a natural unit, we run the risk of mechanically assigning it to either "cause" or "effect" in the study of social change'.[1] In practice, of course, most theoretical perspectives on the family do slide into regarding it as a simple cause or effect of some wider structure. Conceptualizations of the family as an 'effect' of economic determinations have been extremely influential in both sociological and Marxist work; conceptualizations that present it as a biological 'cause' of patriarchy have been influential in both feminist and anti-feminist theories. Before going on to examine ways of transcending a concept of 'the family' as a pre-given entity, we should look at the implications of these existing approaches.

I

Many sociological and Marxist treatments combine naturalistic assumptions about 'the family' itself with reductionist and functionalist accounts of changes in family form. The classic example here is the thesis that the nuclear family form has developed because it is particularly well suited to industrial capitalism's need for a mobile labour force. There is, it is often argued, a 'functional fit' between the nuclear family and industrial capitalism.

Perhaps the most influential of such accounts is that provided by Talcott Parsons, who has fitted the family neatly into a functionalist account of contemporary society.[2] Parsons argues that the family of today has two main functions: to socialize children into society's normative

1. Rayna Rapp, Ellen Ross and Renate Bridenthal, 'Examining Family History', *Feminist Studies*, vol.5, no.1 (Spring 1979). Rayna Rapp's section of this paper contains many succinct observations on this problem and her ideas stimulated much of the discussion of this chapter.
2. See especially T. Parsons and R. Bales, *Family, Socialization and Interaction Process*, London 1956.

system of values and to inculcate 'appropriate' status expectations, and to provide a stable emotional environment that will cushion the (male) worker from the psychological damage of the alienating occupational world. Within the family these functions are carried out by the wife and mother. It is she who plays the affective, 'expressive' role of nurturance and support, and it is the husband who plays the 'instrumental' role of earning the family's keep and maintaining discipline. Parsons concedes a problem of 'role conflict' for the educated wife, but otherwise poses this as a functional family form developed to suit the structure and values of modern industrial society. His thesis has, however, been criticized from a number of points of view. Not only does it reproduce conventional attitudes towards the supposedly primary 'home-making' role of women, it also denies the economic importance of the household.[3] Furthermore, the historical evidence on which the thesis rests has now been convincingly challenged.[4]

Parsons's formulation, although an influential one in sociology, is only one of many accounts of the family that reduce it to an effect of external factors. The Marxist tradition has tended to share this view. Marx himself, as I have indicated earlier, operated with assumptions about biological differences between men and women and the 'naturalness' of the family unit. Engels's account of the history of changing family forms looks at this question far more critically, but concludes that inequality within the modern family is essentially the product of the development of private property. The privatized family is seen by Engels as a creation of private property and one not to outlast the relations of production that brought it into being — in the proletarian family, where wife as well as husband are engaged in wage labour, the material foundations for such inequality are said not to exist.

3. Veronica Beechey 'Women and Production: a Critical Analysis of Some Sociological Theories of Women's Work', in *Feminism and Materialism*.
4. Colin Creighton 'Family, Property and Relations of Production in Western Europe', *Economy and Society*, vol.9, no.2, 1980.

It is, in fact, characteristic of Marxism's tendency to reduce the family to an effect of relations of production that many Marxists have followed Marx himself in the rash prediction that the family could be abolished. All the evidence from societies in a period of transition to socialism points to the improbability of this development. Recent work on the family has sought to understand some of these problems by looking in much more detail at the development of the family in capitalism and, in particular, has attempted to come to grips with the relationship between the private and the social in contemporary capitalism. Such work — I am thinking particularly of Zaretsky and Foreman[5] — has tried to develop an understanding of both the economic importance of the family in capitalism and its psychological and emotional role.

Zaretsky argues that capitalism, in socializing the production formerly undertaken in household units, created the idea of the family as 'a separate realm from the economy'. Furthermore, it constructed a realm of the 'personal' — a subjective preoccupation with relationships, individuality and the meaning of fulfilment, much of which takes place within the family. Zaretsky sees this construction of familial and personal life as an extension to the masses of a self-cultivation formerly only available to the leisured classes, but argues that it resulted in the devaluing of women's work in the household and the identification of femininity with the realm of the personal. He seeks to establish that our very notions of 'the personal' are constructed by capitalism and that the form of the family is a part of the capitalist mode of production itself.

Zaretsky is clearly right to emphasize the dangers of assuming a split between the personal and the social, and some of his criticisms of feminists such as Firestone and Millett point correctly to weaknesses in this respect. However, his own analysis courts this danger too, by failing

5. Eli Zaretsky, *Capitalism, the Family and Personal Life*, London, 1976; Ann Foreman, *Femininity as Alienation: Women and the Family in Marxism and Psychoanalysis*, London, 1977.

to distinguish between the ideology of individualism in different family structures and in different periods of history. 'Personal life' and 'the family' are historicized only in the sense that as constructions they are located as the product of a particular mode of production, and this leads to a rather static analysis. Perhaps more importantly, in designating these areas as effectively the necessary outcome of capitalist relations of production, Zaretsky's treatment of familial relations and ideologies tends to empty them of any specific content. He rightly inveighs against the claims of psychoanalytic theory, but does not engage substantively with the arguments it has put forward. His book is interesting in that it does recognize the importance of the social construction of personal life, but is ultimately frustrating in that it collapses the object of his inquiry into an 'effect' of capitalism.

A similar danger is apparent in Ann Foreman's attempt to provide an account of *Femininity as Alienation.* As the title of the book suggests, we are invited to see femininity, the construction of gender, as a product of particular tendencies of capitalist development. Foreman is more sympathetic to the Engels-Reed position — that early human societies were matrilineal — than to Freud's account of the primal patriarchal scene.[6] (This point is often a good index of an author's position on the causes of women's oppression, for if you are going to argue the 'effect-of-capitalism' approach it helps to evoke either early human society or at least pre-capitalist society as less oppressive of women. This is one reason why it is so difficult to establish the 'origins' of women's oppression: historical evidence is not neutral.) Foreman sees the rise of the capitalist wage labour system as breaking down the subjective existence of the individual as a labourer at the same time as it broke down the organization of household production. Yet this subjectivity was not destroyed, it was transposed into the area of non-labour, the family. Quoting Marx's observation on the worker — 'He is at

6. Ibid., p.19.

home when he is not working, and when he is working he is not at home' — Foreman argues that 'the importance of the individual's existence within the family increased with the intensification of alienation within the workforce'.[7]

Foreman argues that femininity is the product of the private/social split generated and reproduced by capitalism. Men struggle to succeed in the public world of business and industry, but failing that they rule in the family. Femininity is constructed as a reaction to this — women provide men with relief from their alienation. Inevitably women are relegated to the sphere of emotionality and cannot escape the intimate oppression of being foils for men. For women this was a disastrous development, a 'body blow' to their position in the social workforce and one that can be perceived in terms of Simone de Beauvoir's concept of 'alterity' — man as subject, woman as other.[8]

Much of this argument is similar to Zaretsky's, although Foreman stresses the identification of femininity with living exclusively through personal relations to a greater extent, and hence risks falling more deeply into the very public/private split with which these books are concerned. Where Foreman differs from Zaretsky, however, is in her attempt to re-pose both Marxism and psychoanalysis in a more adequate synthesis. This is potentially the most useful aim of her book and it begins with an interesting critique of why previous writers have failed to reconcile these two bodies of thought. Foreman herself sees this as the failure of Marxism to understand the unconscious, and to incorporate it into a theory of political action. In particular, Marxist theories of ideology have tended to explain ideology as a set of (wrong) ideas, whereas it would be better to see ideology as based on a partial understanding of real experience. The unconscious comes in here as 'the process of reification [the process by which social relations take on the appearance of relations between things] structurally excludes a level of

7. Ibid., p.73.
8. Ibid., p.93.

reality from thought' and ensures that the experience of women is different from that of men.[9]

Foreman's attempt to understand femininity in terms of unconscious as well as conscious elements of the psyche represents a potentially useful historical and materialist appropriation of psychoanalytic concepts. It is, however, somewhat mechanistic in its assumption that the construction of gender is the straightforward effect of alienation and reification. She argues that a Marxist concept of freedom in a world that had transcended the reification characteristic of capitalist relations of production would entail a rejection of masculine appropriation of women as sexual objects and would lead to 'polymorphous sexuality'.[10] This is mechanistic in the sense that, as was indicated in Chapter 2, it is very difficult to prove such a strong causal connection between given modes of production and erotic behaviour. In the light of our knowledge of sexuality in societies which are not capitalist, the argument is also somewhat utopian.

Foreman's argument raises the question, to what extent Marxism has in fact failed to engage with the concept of the unconscious in its treatment of ideology. In the first place, it is something of a caricature to suggest that Marxist theory has traditionally restricted the term ideology to 'ideas' of a cognitive kind. Certainly in post-Althusserian Marxist theory this would be untrue (Althusser having characterized ideology as a 'lived relation to history'), but even before that ideology has commonly been treated as pertaining to 'consciousness' rather than strictly in terms of ideas. Furthermore, it would be rash to posit too radical a break between consciousness and the unconscious, since although the latter term was not available to or created by early Marxists (including Marx), their work in certain respects probes beneath the level of conscious thought to which this polarization of the terms confines them. Even the rather crude notion of 'false consciousness' implies the structural

9. Ibid., p.105 (the definition of reification inserted here is given by Foreman on p.104).
10. Ibid., p.109.

'exclusion of a level of reality from thought', which Foreman sees as characterizing the unconscious. A considerable amount of attention is paid by Marx to questions of the apparent and the real, the phenomenal forms of labour and the underlying, but disguised, wage relation that creates the illusory character of our experiences. So although one would not want to underestimate the significance of Freud's 'discovery' of the unconscious, it is incorrect to argue that all previous thought necessarily constructed ideology at the level of conscious thought.

Ann Foreman's book is suggestive and interesting, but ultimately does not resolve these difficulties. In its ambitious attempt to historicize the insights of psychoanalysis it succeeds in locating phenomena such as the recent definitions of masculinity and femininity as the product of tendencies inherent in capitalist relations of production. This does not, however, constitute a satisfactory reconciliation of Marxist with psychoanalytic theory, for the latter's conceptual framework is completely negated in the merger. Once again, though the argument is sophisticated and interesting, 'the family' is posed as the privileged and exclusive home of femininity and is seen as an effect of capitalism, without any specific content or dynamic of its own. Although this type of analysis appears to avoid the problem of functionalism in its treatment of the familial construction of gender identity, it is not clear to me that it really does so. Nor, indeed, is it clear why things should have fallen out in the way they have. For although the alienation of the wage labourer does apparently suggest a need for an area of emotional compensation, it is not self-evident that the labourer should be male and the source of comfort female. As Foreman acknowledges, a substantial proportion of women have always been engaged in wage labour and the attempt to secure a 'family wage' system based on a male breadwinner has been a process of struggle. It is debatable whether that struggle was necessarily the product of men's desire to seek relief from alienation in the form of sexual appropriation of their wives.

I have discussed some of the problems of analysing 'the family' as constructed to suit the needs of a particular mode of production. Such arguments often claim to 'explain' changes in the structure or ideology of the family as the effect of historical changes in the system of production. Yet despite the insistence on changing forms in such analyses, it is clear that underlying the argument there is some notion of an essential family whose internal structure may vary and whose relations to the system of production may vary, but which nevertheless persists across these historical transformations. This is the difficulty referred to by Rayna Rapp at the outset — that theories of 'the family' try to insert a pre-given natural unit into analysis of the wider social formation. As a conceptual problem, it can be seen even more clearly in analyses that, instead of seeing 'the family' in terms of its external conditions, pose it as a *determinant* of processes beyond it. In practice such arguments frequently rest on assumptions about a pre-given sexual division of labour, a 'natural' set of relations between men and women, and on the social implications of biological differences between the sexes. In their strongest form these arguments encounter the problem of biologism — the assumption that gender divisions are the natural and inevitable outcome of biological differences.

The arguments to which I am referring have been discussed in earlier chapters and I shall merely recapitulate the main points here. Perhaps the clearest example of this tendency would be those radical feminist analyses which locate patriarchy as the outcome of divisions between men and women in 'the family'. Shulamith Firestone, for instance, argues that the nuclear family is merely one development from a basic 'biological family' which 'has existed everywhere throughout time'. 'Natural' patterns can be transcended by 'human' agency in Firestone's view, but she dismisses the 'anthropological sophistries' of the '"cultural relativity" line'. She characterizes the biological family as the reproductive unit and asserts that it rests on the 'facts' that 1. women are at the mercy of their reproductive biology and are therefore dependent upon men for survival; 2. human infants are dependent upon adults for a long period; 3. a basic mother/child interdependency is universal; and 4. the natural reproductive division between the sexes is the origin of all divisions of labour, economic and cultural classes, and possibly of castes.

These 'facts', then, are the intractable and universal material to which human arrangements must adapt — the procrustean bed of reproductive biology. Because of women's dependence on men, the 'biological family is an inherently unequal power distribution'.[11] It is interesting to consider the extent to which, although Firestone puts forward a feminist polemic and is concerned to show how advances in reproductive technology could liberate women, her analysis incorporates popular assumptions about the family. The 'facts' of which she speaks are culturally and historically variable. Childbirth, for instance, is considerably more disruptive to women's lives in some societies than in others. The dependence of children upon adults has varied widely at different points in time, with contemporary capitalism reaching the apogee of decades of financial and emotional dependence. As Ariès has convincingly demonstrated, the concept of 'childhood' itself is an historically specific one.[12] The universality of mother/child interdependence has been challenged by anthropological evidence of different cultural child-rearing practices.[13] These first three 'facts' are all no more than a description of beliefs about the family in contemporary capitalism that Firestone has generalized into universal biological imperatives. The fourth 'fact' is a theoretical assertion bearing no obvious relationship to the premises it is supposed to follow. We can conclude nothing more from all this than that the ideology of the family has succeeded, with this writer at least, in presenting historically

11. *The Dialectic of Sex*, pp.17-18.
12. Philippe Ariès, *Centuries of Childhood*, New York 1972.
13. A review of this literature is provided by Ann Oakley's *Sex, Gender and Society*, London 1972.

variable structures and meanings as 'natural' and therefore inevitable.

Firestone's is perhaps the clearest case of the representation of fundamentally different practices as expressions of one essential, biologically determined 'family'. Yet assumptions about the causal role of biology are contained in many analyses from a radical feminist perspective, and lead to some of the problems already isolated in use of the concept of 'patriarchy'. Kate Millett, for instance, characterizes men as a group who rule 'by birthright'. More controversially, however, I want to suggest that psychoanalytic approaches to the familial construction of gender operate with the same assumptions. In my discussion of Juliet Mitchell's 'reading' of Freud I addressed this question briefly. Some basic points should be noted. First, Freud's own work is not amenable to being rescued from biological determinism. As I tried to show, his entire theory of female psychosexual development falls away if we refuse the construction he puts upon the (male) phallus. Second, attempts to integrate a psychoanalytic with a materialist perspective have been notably unsatisfactory. Annette Kuhn's attempt to do so encounters problems raised in Chapter 1; Ann Foreman's, as I argued earlier, is a synthesis which deprives psychoanalysis of any explanatory weight. Third, when challenged on the universalistic claims made for the significance of psychosexual determinants, psychoanalytic theorists have tended to render their arguments more abstract rather than limit their sphere or period of application. No substantial work has yet been produced that historicizes the processes outlined in psychoanalytic theory, and the debate has repeatedly taken the form of defensive psychoanalytic response to the 'cultural relativity' challenge. The Lacanian rendering of psychoanalytic theory, by substituting 'the bearer of the law' for 'the father' and so on, manifestly increases rather than decreases the universal claims of the theory. Indeed it would not be unfair to argue that the object of psychoanalytic theory is, precisely, to establish that relatively inevitable patterns of psychosexual development are the source of social arrangements in general. Melanie Klein puts this very directly: 'a group — whether large or small — consists of individuals in a relationship to one another; and therefore the understanding of personality is the foundation for the understanding of social life'.[14]

Klein's naive 'therefore' reveals the methodological individualism of psychoanalytic thought in general. It is not a biologistic theory in the way that Firestone's is, but it is grounded in the supposedly inevitable implications of human anatomy and in the assumption that human civilization takes its form from these familial processes of gender construction rather than *vice versa*.

It may seem strange to draw a parallel between the assumptions of radical feminists and those of psychoanalysis, and it is one which adherents of either would undoubtedly reject. Yet the charge of parallel assumptions is substantiated by the fact of parallel consequences. Both tendencies have arrived at comparable, and in my view retrogressive, revaluations of gender differences. Radical feminism has undoubtedly inspired that assertion of 'female principles' which is evident in a great deal of feminist culture. We have frequently seen celebrations of women's lives, past and present, in feminist art and culture generally, based uncompromisingly on the biological rather than the social aspects of what is 'female'.[15] Feminist psychoanalytic work, with the notable exception of Nancy Chodorow's more sociological perspective,[16] has not managed to shake off the legacy of its founding fathers. Although it has obviously shed the blatantly pejorative stance towards women conventionally found in psychoanalytic theory and clinical practice, feminist psychoanalysis would seem to have opted for a reassertion of 'difference' and a re-valorization of femininity and maternity.

14. Melanie Klein, *Our Adult World and Its Roots in Infancy*, London 1962.
15. Judy Chicago's exhibition, *The Dinner Party*, represents women in this way.
16. *The Reproduction of Mothering: Psychoanalysis and The Sociology of Gender*, Berkeley 1978.

This is partly, I suspect, an inherent danger of working with conceptual frameworks that privilege exclusively questions of biological sex and the social construction of gender. Although it is understandable that the 'invisibility' of women in Marxism and social science should have led to an interest in the work of those who did attach weight to the question of gender (Freud and Lévi-Strauss for instance), there is a danger of feminist use of these double-edged conceptual weapons. For just as some of the weaknesses of bourgeois literary criticism has been to an extent reproduced in feminist literary criticism, there has been a tendency for feminist work on gender division in the family to incorporate the naturalistic assumptions made by earlier systems of thought.

One such naturalistic assumption is the very concept of 'the family'. Shulamith Firestone's description of 'the biological family' embodies the central feature of contemporary ideology of the family unit; women are defined in terms of their anatomy and hence assumed to be 'naturally' dependent upon men. 'The family', however, does not exist other than as an ideological construct, since the structure of the household, definition and meaning of kinship, and the ideology of 'the family' itself, have all varied enormously in different types of society. It would in fact be better to cease to refer to '*the* family' at all, and in the following discussion I shall concentrate instead on *households*, and on *familial ideology*, as terms that avoid some of the naturalism and mystification engendered by 'the family'.[17]

II

There is not the space here to consider in any detail the vast literature now existing on household structure and familial ideology, from the point of view of 'family history'. It is,

17. These issues are explored in Jaques Donzelot's very interesting book which, although referring constantly to 'the family', characterizes it as a shifting terrain rather than an institution. (*The Policing of Families*, New York 1979).

however, essential to define the present situation in relation to earlier, significantly different, forms.

First, it is important to note that our present concept of the family depends upon the conflation of two elements that in earlier periods were quite separate: kinship and co-residence. 'The family' is popularly thought of as a group of people, related by blood, who share the same household and yet this particular combination is, to some extent at least, an historically specific one. The meaning of kinship ties has varied enormously; indeed any study of anthropology reveals that the social significance of particular kinship links differs dramatically in cross-cultural comparisons. In Western Europe it is only comparatively recently that it has been established as 'natural' for residence in households to be based on ties of kinship. This point can be shown by looking at historical definitions of the family, which reveal that the two distinct aspects of blood relations and co-residence in a household were formerly much more strongly separated.

Jean-Louis Flandrin has provided a fascinating history of these definitional changes, on which the following account is based. Flandrin argues, from a study of French dictionary definitions of the term 'family', that in the sixteenth, seventeenth and eighteenth centuries the two meanings of the term (kinship and co-residence) were clearly dissociated: 'the word "family" more often referred to a set of kinsfolk who did not live together, while it also designated an assemblage of co-residents who were not necessarily linked by ties of blood or marriage'.[18] Flandrin quotes evidence to suggest that in the seventeenth century it was common to refer to a 'family' as including all members of the household in so far as they were all subject to the authority of its male head: wife, children, servants, domestics, officials were all included. This, indeed, was the principal definition of the term in this period, but during the course of the eighteenth century the concept began to be restricted to those members

18. Jean-Louis Flandrin *Families in Former Times: Kinship, Household and Sexuality*, Cambridge 1979, p.4.

of the household who were related by blood. The interesting example is given of definitions of 'the Holy Family', which until about 1740 always comprised 'Our Lord, the Virgin, Saint Joseph and Saint John', but after that period was limited to the three main protaganists, with Saint John's presence no longer automatic. Today Saint John has entirely disappeared. It was of course a particularly tortuous ideological labour to secure a 'natural family' in this case, since, if the Bible is to be believed, Saint Joseph's biological role in the creation of the family was minimal.

Flandrin argues that over this period the notion of the family became restricted to kin relations only and that it was only subsequently the case that it also suggested co-residence in a household. 1869 furnishes the earliest definition he could find that assumed it to be 'persons of the same blood living under the same roof, and more especially the father, the mother and the children'.[19] It is clear, then, that when we speak of the family we should take care to distinguish what it is that we are referring to: an aggregation of kinsfolk or a household of co-residents.

A second major point to be drawn from historical studies concerns differences between the household structures of different social classes. Mark Poster has suggested that we can work with four models: the peasant and aristocratic forms of the sixteenth and seventeenth centuries, the working-class family of the early industrial revolution and the bourgeois family of the mid-nineteenth century.[20] Poster tends to concentrate on the psychic and emotional differences between these different models of the family, drawing on material about sexual practices such as those documented in Lawrence Stone's researches.[21] An important element of any historical discussion of these models would be consideration of the extent to which the different household structures characteristic of these classes might relate to

19. Ibid., p.9.
20. Mark Poster, *Critical Theory of the Family*, London 1978, p.166.
21. L. Stone, *The Family, Sex and Marriage in Britain 1500-1800*, London 1977.

patterns of property relations and inheritance. Colin Creighton has argued that factors connected with changing property relations in the transition from feudalism to capitalism exercised an important influence on aspects of the peasant household, making joint ownership and sub-division of land give way to the 'stem family' household in which one child (preferably a son) inherited the land intact.[22]

The structure of the household among the peasantry has generated considerable debate, in the context of the argument that the process of industrialization encouraged a 'nuclear' family structure. Peter Laslett has produced evidence to suggest that this nuclear structure existed and was widespread among the rural working population long before industrialization and the development of an urban proletariat, but his findings have proved extremely controversial.[23] These disputes are as yet unresolved and it is not clear what relation exists between the structure of peasant households and those of the industrial proletariat. What does seem clear, however, is that the ideological construction of the meaning, or significance, of household arrangements for the notion of 'the family' was sub-stantially affected by the developing bourgeoisie. At this point it is relevant to reconsider the arguments put by Zaretsky and Foreman, although I would want to pose them rather differently. For if it is difficult to establish that capitalism itself requires, and so constructed, a realm of privatized family and personal life, it certainly appears to be the case that the bourgeoisie as a class articulated this ideology very strongly. I would suggest that it is more useful to pose these arguments in terms of a struggle between the familial ideology of the emergent bourgeoisie and the practices of other classes, than in terms of a strictly necessary logic of capitalism.[24]

It appears that the bourgeoisie placed a construction upon the meaning of 'the family' that was absent from the peasant and aristocratic household structure. Although this is

22. Creighton (see footnote 4 above).
23. P. Laslett, *Household and Family in Past Time*, Cambridge 1972.

frequently discussed in the context of the high point of bourgeois familialism — the mid-nineteenth century — it is clear that this ideology has its roots much further back. Flandrin cites an encyclopaedia entry in the eighteenth century, which makes absolutely explicit (at least in the French context) the difference between the bourgeoisie's practice and ideology and the more public context of kinship and household for the aristocracy and the working people. It shows that the 'family' was quite distinct from aristocratic lineage on the one hand and ramshackle labouring households on the other: 'pride has ... decreed in our language, as in past times among the Romans, that the titles, the great dignities and the great appointments continuously held by people of the same name should form what one calls the *houses* of the people of quality, whereas one describes as *families* those of citizens who, clearly distinguished from the dregs of the populace, perpetuate themselves in an Estate, and transmit their line from father to son in honourable occupations, in useful employments, in well-matched alliances, a proper upbringing, and agreeable and cultivated manners'.[25] *Families*, in short, are an achievement of industriousness, respectability and regulation, rather than a pre-given or natural entity, and it was only later than these aggregations of co-residing kin came to be seen as the only natural form of household organization.

Mark Poster stresses, in my view correctly, the distinctive character of the bourgeois family as an historical phenomenon. He also argues that the bourgeois conception of the family has become dominant — that, in fact, the imposition of the bourgeois family onto the working class is 'one of the unwritten aspects of the political success of

24. For this reason, although it tends towards class reductionism, Poster's approach avoids the dangers courted by Zaretsky and Foreman. Catherine Hall's work points to the importance of bourgeois ideology, and specifically the influence of religious ideas in it, in the development of domestic ideology. See 'The Early Formation of Victorian Domestic Ideology', in S. Burman, ed., *Fit Work for Women*, London 1979.
25. Flandrin, pp.6-7.
26. Poster, p.196.

bourgeois democracy'.[26] This is an important point, and one that I shall return to in discussing contemporary family structure. Yet it does raise again the problem of collapsing the ideology of familialism into the structure of households. At an ideological level the bourgeoisie has certainly secured a hegemonic definition of family life: as 'naturally' based on close kinship, as properly organized through a male breadwinner with financially dependent wife and children, and as a haven of privacy beyond the public realm of commerce and industry. To a large extent this familial ideology has been accepted by the industrial working class and indeed has proved effective as motivation for male wage labour and the male 'family'-wage demand. Yet there is a disjunction between the pervasiveness of this ideology (from about the mid-nineteenth century onwards) and the actual household structure of the proletariat in which it exists. Few working-class households have historically been organized around dependence on a male 'breadwinning' wage and the earnings of other family members have usually been essential to maintain the household. Understanding of this disjunction — between the economic organization of households and the ideology of the family — is essential for an analysis of the contemporary family.

III

In this section I want to introduce the processes which take place in the system of household organization that has developed in twentieth-century capitalism. Although there are important links between economic aspects of the household and the ideology of the family it is analytically important to bear in mind the distinction between the two. I shall begin, therefore, with the process of the construction of gendered individuals, which I locate in terms of family ideology; then turn to the area of housework and childcare, posed in terms of household structure and its relation to the economic system of production; and, third, look at the combined role of the two, which I see as a stabilizing and conservative one. What follows is not an account of any supposed 'functions' of the household or of family ideology — at the moment I want simply to describe the processes involved, as a basis for subsequent discussion.

It is not necessary to accept the entire corpus of psychoanalytic theory to argue that gender identity and the definition of masculinity and femininity that pervades our culture are pre-eminently constructed within the ideology of the family. Furthermore, it is here more than anywhere else that we can see most clearly an ideological process by which supposedly 'natural' relations between parents and children, men and women, are struggled for. 'The family' provides the nexus for the various themes — romantic love; feminine nurturance, maternalism, self-sacrifice; masculine protection and financial support — that characterize our conception of gender and sexuality. It is, however, an ideological nexus rather than any concrete family system which is involved here and there are many connections between these processes within and outside the locus of the family home. Familial definitions of appropriate gender behaviour often rely strongly on general social definitions to such an extent that families strive to achieve the characteristics attributed to 'the family' by representations of 'it' in, for example, the media. It seems at least possible that much of the pressure exerted on individuals to conform to various indices of behaviour relate more to fear of social disapproval of 'the family' than to strictly internal family demands. (White weddings, indeed weddings at all, might be a good example here, since many parents appear to desire these for reasons of 'the family's' social respectability even if they themselves have accepted their child's loss of virginity, principled opposition to marriage, homosexuality or whatever.) Families are enmeshed in and responsive to the ideology of 'the family' as well as engaged in reproducing it.

The construction of gender identity does not take place exclusively in terms of familial relations. Parents who try to raise their children in such a way as to avoid gender-stereotyping soon find their efforts confounded by the school, peer group and the media, which reproduce and strengthen the very meanings that they have attempted to subvert. This is because gender identity is not created once and for all at a certain point in the child's life but is continually recreated and endorsed, modified or even altered substantially, through a process of ideological representation.

The point I am emphasizing here is that we can make a distinction between the construction of gender within *families*, and the social construction of gender within an *ideology of familialism*, and we can conclude that the latter formulation is the more accurate one. Whatever criteria we use to define the contemporary structure of family organization (father, mother and children, or even adult and dependant) we find that many individuals are in fact socialized in domestic situations that do not fit the definition, however loosely it may be framed, and we have therefore to consider how they acquire a gender identity which conforms broadly to that created in our typical 'family' structure. It is interesting to note that residential institutions in which children are reared frequently adopt, in a highly self-conscious manner, strategies to reproduce what are seen as the essential components of the nuclear family structure. Children's homes, orphanages and boarding schools commonly operate by means of surrogate parental figures, and the term 'in loco parentis' has substantial content in institutions for children and adolescents.

It is, therefore, in an ideology of family life, as distinct from concrete families, that gender identity and its meaning is reproduced. Nevertheless, the ideology of the family is perhaps most pervasively and intensively articulated in the processes of gender socialization that take place in families themselves. Feminists have paid considerable attention, and quite rightly, to these intimate and oppressive processes whereby little girls are enjoined to be helpful, dependent and caring and little boys to be active, independent and protective. The intense emotional and psychological forces deployed in family life clearly play an important role in bringing pressure to bear on children to internalize appropriate gender identities and in structuring our consciousness of gender. Ideologies of domesticity and maternity for women, of breadwinning and responsibility for men, are articulated very strongly in families themselves in contemporary society and it is unsurprising that feminists should have pointed to 'the family' as a prime agent of gender socialization and hence women's oppression. Families clearly play a crucial role in constructing masculinity and femininity and in providing pressures which encourage a disposition towards heterosexual conformity.

These processes are not in dispute here, but neither are they universal. Sources cited earlier document the historical variability of the meaning of gender identity and of the incidence of and social significance attached to different patterns of erotic behaviour. It may well be the case that the present structure and ideology of the family has created an institution more effective as an agent of gender socialization than earlier arrangements were, but this effectiveness is to be explained rather than assumed. We could take for instance the 'mother-child bond', which Shulamith Firestone saw as an immutable, biologically given, element of 'the family'. Bourgeois family ideology proposes that this bond rests, at least in part, on the 'natural' relationship of breast-feeding. Yet we know that the aristocracy has often delegated this particular chore to wet nurses and that the exigencies of factory work forced many mothers in the proletariat to fob their babies off with 'Godfrey's Cordial'. Much of the propaganda for 'natural feeding' emanating from Dr. Spock onwards has been directed towards persuading other classes of the rectitude and desirability of bourgeois notions of child-care. It may be that some methods of child-rearing are self-evidently 'better' than others, but it is also true that the ideological framework in which they are purveyed is specific to particular classes and historical periods. The 'mother-child bond' is a good example of this. It undoubtedly creates an opportunity for very effective socialization and therefore strengthens the ideology which insists upon it.[27] It forms, however, an element of contemporary ideology of the family and is not a universal or unchangeable aspect of human reproduction.

The second major area I want to introduce briefly concerns the household itself as a material institution. Although there are dangers in rigidifying analytically the division of labour within the household — we need to be aware of several qualifying factors — it is possible to distinguish distinct areas of work and responsibility for men and women. Women are primarily responsible for all the tasks connected with housework and children. As is now well known, even when women work outside the home they normally carry the burden of household organization and labour at home as well. This work is by no means restricted to the servicing of the male, although this remains predominantly the house-wife's responsibility. She also must service herself and care for three major categories of people who require considerable labour — children, the sick and disabled, the elderly.

Women's responsibility for childcare is widely recognized as labour-intensive, requiring extraordinarily long hours of work, and fatiguing. It is perhaps less widely recognized, although Hilary Land has correctly drawn attention to it,[28] that the work involved in caring for other members of the household can be equally onerous. Often the birth of a disabled child, or the advancing disabilities of a parent, means that a woman gives up her job to stay at home and care for them. Frequently it arises that women in middle age, having just seen the last of their children into a state of independence, find an elderly relative reaches the stage where constant care is needed. It is predominantly women who will take up the slack as the social services cuts result in

27. Nancy Chodorow comments that 'exclusive and intensive mothering, as it has been practised in Western Society, does seem to have produced more achievement-oriented men and people with psychologically monogamic tendencies'. (*The Reproduction of Mothering*, p.75).
28. Hilary Land, 'Who Cares for the Family?', *Journal of Social Policy*, vol.7, part 3, 1978.

a reduction of facilities for the disabled and elderly.

Such labour is undertaken by women in a relationship of financial dependence upon a man. The degree of this dependence, although obviously not total in all cases, is far greater than the dependence of women in a household where all adults engaged in social production, or in the early decades of capitalism. The household is consequently not merely a site in which a division of labour exists, but a set of relations between household members by which women are / systematically dependent upon, and unequal to, men. This inequality has been described in sociological terms as resulting in, for instance, women's lack of power over major / household expenditure decisions.[29] Feminist critiques of sociological assumptions about the internal equality of the contemporary family form have rightly pointed to a material conflict of interests within the household.[30]

Any brief description of the division of labour within the household raises a number of disputed issues and I will mention what I consider to be the three most important ones to return to in later discussion.

First, there is dispute as to the role played by the state in the construction of these structural relations of the household — how important has it been and whose interests does it serve? These questions will be dealt with in more detail in Chapter 7. Second, there is controversy about the extent to which the picture I have drawn is empirically correct or an exaggerated one. Feminists such as Hilary

29. See Dair Gillespie 'Who Has The Power? The Marital Struggle', in H. P. Dreitzel, ed., *Family, Marriage and the Struggle of the Sexes*, New York 1972; and Pauline Hunt, 'Cash-Transactions and Household Tasks', *Sociological Review*, vol.26, no.3, 1978.

30. One element of potential material conflict within the household is that of food consumption. Although Oren and Delphy (see above) are mainly concerned with inequalities in food distribution in poorer households, Mrs Beeton's *Household Management* is redolent of inegalitarianism in the bourgeois customs. Of snipe she writes, 'one of these small but delicious birds may be given whole to a gentleman; but in helping a lady, it will be better to cut them quite through the centre, completely dividing them into equal and like portions, and put only one half on the plate'. London 1906, p.1273.

Land and Leonore Davidoff suggest that the division between 'male breadwinner' and 'dependent wife' is a more fluid one than has been implied by, for instance, Marxist contributors to the domestic labour debate. On the one hand women have historically played a crucial role in wage-earning for the financial support of the household,[31] and on the other the attempt to characterize domestic labour as privatized labour has occluded the extent to which women's household labour has contributed to the household's maintenance. Leonore Davidoff, in a study of the landlady-lodger relationship, rightly suggests that such 'intermediate forms of enterprise' are ignored in Marxist theorizing, which assumes a rigid split between social and privatized labour.[32] Third, there is controversy on the general question — which also surfaces in the two issues just mentioned — as to whose interests are served by women's labour in the household. On the one side Marxists argue that it serves capital, by reproducing labour power at very low cost; on the other side feminists argue that it serves men's interests by providing personal services and relieving them of family obligations.

The structure of the household and the ideology of the family combine to form a system that has important effects on the consciousness of the working class and hence on the possibilities for political action. So, although I have insisted on the need to differentiate the material relations of the household from the ideological construction of familialism and gender, it is possible to speak of a system in which these two aspects operate in conjunction with one another in relation to other elements of the social relations of capitalism. Mary McIntosh's phrase 'the family-household system' conveys the combination of two distinct elements quite clearly and serves as a useful shorthand term with which to explore their joint operation.[33]

31. Hilary Land, 'Women: Supporters or Supported?', in D. Leonard Barker and S. Allen, eds., *Sexual Divisions and Society*, London 1976.
32. 'The Separation of Home and Work? Landladies and Lodgers in Nineteenth and Twentieth-Century England', in S. Burman, ed., *Fit Work for Women*, London 1979 (see p.66).

The family-household system of contemporary capitalism constitutes not only the central site of the oppression of women but an important organizing principle of the relations of production of the social formation as a whole. This, as I have suggested before, is not necessarily inevitable, since the argument that it would not be possible for capitalism's relations of production to be organized in other ways has yet to be proven. Furthermore, it is evident that the contemporary family-household system has incorporated a substantial element from struggles between the interests of men and those of women, by and large in favour of the former. However, it still remains the case that the specific combination of gender and class relations that characterizes this system has entrenched gender division in the fabric of capitalist social relations in a particularly effective way.

The family-household constitutes both the ideological ground on which gender difference and women's oppression are constructed, and the material relations in which men and women are differentially engaged in wage labour and the class structure. Women's dependence on men is reproduced ideologically, but also in material relations, and there is a mutually strengthening relationship between them. It is not simply that an ideology of the family causes women to be used as 'reserve army' labourers and as cheap reproducers of labour power; nor is it simply that capitalism creates an ideology of gender difference to legitimate the exploitation of women. The ideological and the material cannot be so neatly separated as either of these formulations would imply.

The family-household system is effective, or has become so, in a number of ways. Not least of these is its role in securing one major division in the working class. The

33. McIntosh describes the 'family household' as a system in which 'a number of people are expected to be dependent on the wages of a few adult members, primarily of the husband and father who is a "bread-winner", and in which they are all dependent for cleaning, food preparation and so forth on unpaid work chiefly done by the wife and mother'. ('The Welfare State and the Needs of the Dependent Family', in *Fit Work for Women*, p.155).

division between the perceived and real interests of men and women in the working class has proved of major importance to capital, and undoubtedly the establishment of women, children and others as dependent upon a male wage has contributed to this. Such a system maximizes motivation to work on the part of the wage labourer and reduces the likelihood of militancy that might jeopardize the maintenance of non-labouring household members. The tendency of the family-household system is to encourage conservatism and militate against protest, and the close relationship between the economic aspects of household support and highly intense personal and emotional relationships is an important factor in this. These relationships, between parents and children, husbands and wives and so on apparently constitute what Christopher Lasch has called the 'haven in a heartless world' of capitalism.[34] They are not, of course, any such haven, although they may appear as such experientially. The material site on which they take place is located in the relations of production of capitalism and their private, intensely individual character draws on the ideology secured by the bourgeoisie as well as pre-capitalist notions of gender and sexuality.

The family-household system provides a uniquely effective mechanism for securing continuity over a period of time. It has proved a stable (intractable) system both for the reproduction of labour power, and as an arrangement to contain personal life, in the face of major social upheavals. The family-household system, as Mary McIntosh points out, characterizes societies of different kinds where reproduction occurs through a wage system,[35] and indeed the similarities between the system in Britain and, say, the Soviet Union are apparent.

If the family-household system of contemporary capitalism is oppressive for women and divisive for the working class the question arises as to who does benefit from it (if anyone) and how and why it is maintained. We can tackle

34. Christopher Lasch, *Haven in a Heartless World*, New York 1977.
35. 'The Welfare State and the Needs of the Dependent Family', p.170.

this question directly by looking at the various arguments that identify one or another group as its beneficiaries, and then attempt to reach an adequate answer.

IV

There is of course a null hypothesis to be tested here: it is possible that this family-household system benefits no-one. The possible candidates as beneficiaries might be listed crudely as: men, women, the working class and the bourgeoisie. Each of these categories poses problems that render it difficult, some would say impossible, even to pose this question.

An obvious difficulty occurs with the categories 'men' and 'women'. If we want to assess whether either of these groups benefits from the present family-household system we need to define the group in such a way as to make it clear that such a group could, collectively, do so. Are these categories biological, ideological or social? Writers such as Parveen Adams and Rosalind Coward have warned us of the dangers in assuming that men and women are pre-given categories, and have insisted that these categories are discursively constructed. My own view is that these insights are more appropriately directed to ideological constructs such as 'the family', and this present chapter has drawn on some elements of their approach. The categories of 'men' and 'women', however, are not ideological constructs devoid of concrete reference. Biological differences between male and female are the basis upon which specific gender identities of masculinity and femininity are constructed, and these identities are coherent and recognizable, despite the existence of occasional biological ambiguity and the lack of continuity between biological sex and social gender. Hence the categories of men and women (as opposed to males and females) are socially and ideologically constructed, rather than naturally given, but they are in a real sense historically 'there' as concrete collectivities. It should be added, however, that groups such as men and women are not thereby accorded the same analytic status as social classes, which can be located in specified relations to a mode of production and class structure, and it is this which gives rise to a second major difficulty: that of separating categories of gender from classes in an exclusive way. It is possible that the family-household system of contemporary capitalism benefits men, and men of all classes, or benefits one class, men and women equally, but it is also possible that it might, say, benefit men of one class but not another. This problem will emerge in more detail in the discussion that follows.

Perhaps the easiest category to dispose of is that of women, since it is difficult to argue that the present structure of the family-household is anything other than oppressive for women. Feminists have consistently, and rightly, seen the family as a central site of women's oppression in contemporary society. The reasons for this lie both in the material structure of the household, by which women are by and large financially dependent on men, and in the ideology of the family, through which women are confined to a primary concern with domesticity and motherhood. This situation underwrites the disadvantages women experience at work, and lies at the root of the exploitation of female sexuality endemic in our society. The concept of 'dependence' is perhaps, the link between the material organization of the household, and the ideology of femininity: an assumption of women's dependence on men structures both of these areas. It is possible to analyse this link in straightforward materialist terms and Virginia Woolf, for instance, saw women's struggle for mental independence of men as directly related to the difficulties of shaking off the burden of financial dependence.[36] Woolf's analysis, however, was explicitly couched in terms of the bourgeoisie, and cannot be transferred unproblematically onto the case of working-class women who have traditionally played an important part in the financial support of the household. Yet it seems to be the case that even in households where women contribute

36. *A Room of One's Own*, Harmondsworth 1972.

considerably to the budget (whether professional 'dual-career families' or lower-paid workers) the ideology of women's dependence remains strong.

The assumption of women's dependence constitutes a central aspect of the oppressive character of the contemporary family-household. All women are oppressed by this, albeit in different ways, and there are significant aspects of women's oppression that cut across the boundaries of class. There are, however, arguments that could be put forward to suggest that women of particular classes do in fact benefit from this system. For instance, it can be argued that female capitalists benefit materially from a system that enables them to employ cheap female workers and to employ men at wage levels that are lowered by their wives' unpaid domestic labour. It has also been argued that in so far as this family-household system has been defended by the working class, on the basis of a correct perception of its advantages, it serves the interests of working-class women as well as those of men.[37] This latter point falls away if we do not accept that the working class as a whole benefits from this family-household system, and I shall take this position when dealing with the general argument on this point. The question of the female capitalist is more complicated. If it is the case that the bourgeoisie as a class benefits from this system, then *qua* bourgeoise, she clearly does do so. This poses important problems for feminist political action, which must then seek to overcome objective class differences among potential female supporters. On the other hand, although women capitalists are not as rare as is sometimes supposed, in an important sense they represent a struggle against the principles which have historically structured the bourgeois household and family ideology. We should note here that the past hundred and fifty years have seen a prolonged struggle by bourgeois women against these principles, beginning with campaigns going back to the 1830s. Bourgeois women have fought for financial indepen-

37. Jane Humphries, 'Class Struggle and the Persistence of the Working-Class Family', *Cambridge Journal of Economics*, vol.3, no.1, 1977.

dence, control of their property, a right to a share in the
marital assets on divorce, for divorce itself, for contraception and abortion law reform, for the right to control over
children after marital break-up, and also for political rights
and access to the professions. All these campaigns represent
an onslaught on the principle of the bourgeois married
woman's dependence, and they suggest that the bourgeois
family-household has been resisted with some strength by
organizations of its female members.

Feminists, and particularly radical feminists, have argued
that the real beneficiaries of the family-household system
are men, whose interests are directly served by the
oppression of women. In one sense this argument is true.
Most men benefit from the material advantage of having
women undertake various servicing roles, care of relatives
and so on. Many women are tied to the home through looking
after their husband's relatives, cooking for his friends and
colleagues. Furthermore, the construction of gender identity
ensures that all men benefit from the privileges of
masculinity in a society where this brings many advantages.
This is not a question of individual intention, for just as any
individual white person may be fervently anti-racist, yet
benefit as all whites do, from the oppression of blacks, so
progressive or pro-feminist men will nonetheless benefit
from the privileges that masculinity bestows on them — with
or without their consent.

Although it is clearly true that men benefit, as men, from
women's oppression in general, it is not so clear that they
benefit specifically from the present organization of the
household. If we take the assumed dependence of women
upon a male breadwinner, it is not self-evident that the role of
'breadwinner' is intrinsically a desirable one. Clearly men
have perceived it as more desirable than that of dependant,
since the exclusionary practices by which men have sought
to preserve their jobs and skills indicate considerable
tenacity in pursuit of this advantage, but it may have
entailed consequences that are not so desirable. For one
thing, the assumption of the male breadwinner locks men

effectively into wage labour, with considerable pressure to remain politically docile in order to safeguard their jobs and hence provision for their households. Second, although many men evade domestic labour and responsibility for childcare by assigning this work to women, there is now a growing expression of dissatisfaction with the degree to which this has deprived men of significant access to their children. There are very few jobs where men can, if they wish, take time off to care for children or other relatives. Similarly if a man wants custody of children in a divorce case, he is unlikely to get it unless he can prove that their mother is 'unsuited' to motherhood. Increasingly, in recent years, the male homosexual movement, and heterosexual men's groups, have argued that a rigid definition of masculinity is oppressive to men.[38]

These considerations limit the extent to which men can be said to benefit exclusively from the present organization of the household and ideology of the family. Christine Delphy's picture of the husband as a self-conscious appropriator of his wife's labour power, responsible for the exploitation of her labour in the home,[39] does confront the undoubted existence of male dominance and control, but it misplaces the material significance of this labour. For while men undoubtedly do wield considerable power in the household and the relations of domestic labour are incontrovertibly oppressive and restricting for women, it is not clear to me that the 'breadwinner's' position is as privileged as she suggests.

A further set of problems is encountered in considering the argument that the family-household system developed under capitalism reflects the material and political interests of the working class. Historians have long been interested in the reasons why the labour movement supported the legislation of the 1840s which not only 'protected' women from the excesses of capitalist exploitation, but effectively consolidated job-segregation between men and women and reinforced the role of women in the working-class family

38. See magazines such as *Achilles Heel, Gay Left.*
39. Christine Delphy, *The Main Enemy*, London 1977.

structure. Jane Humphries suggests that the struggle of the working class for these ends in the nineteenth century, and the fight for a 'family wage' to be earned by a male breadwinner, was part of a rational defence of the family. She sees this as a positive strategy for the labour movement, since she considers the family to serve the interests of the working class in several major respects. Notably, it provides a form of support for non-labouring members of the working class that is not degrading in comparison with state support; it raises the standard of living of the working class by giving it a lever on the supply of labour (hence counteracting the pressure towards a fall in the value of labour power); finally, it has provided an important means for transmitting working-class militancy.[40] These arguments have been considered elsewhere in some detail by Mary McIntosh and myself, and I want here briefly to recapitulate some central points of our disagreement with this thesis.[41] First, as was indicated in the previous chapter, the divisions in the labour-force to which the relations of the family household contribute are politically divisive for the working class. The substitution of cheaper female labour for male creates competition between men and women as wage labourers and creates the conditions for conflict within the household. Nor is it clear that women's domestic labour in the home raises the standard of living of the working class as a whole; on the contrary it would tend to lower it by enabling lower wage levels to be secured. The additional question of dependence on a male wage has to be considered, for although state support is inevitably extracted in dehumanizing forms it is at least arguable that such provision is an advance on the complete dependence upon the wage assumed by a 'family-wage' system. As far as the present theme is concerned, perhaps the most important point of all is that this 'family-

40. See Humphries, 'Class Struggle and the Persistence of the Working-Class Family', and also her 'The Working-Class Family, Women's Liberation and Class Struggle', *Review of Radical Political Economics*, vol.9, no.3, 1977.
41. 'The "Family Wage": Some Problems for Socialists and Feminists', *Capital and Class*, no.11, 1980.

based' system has never been thoroughly established, and even if it had would be severely constricting for working-class women. Predicated as it is on their financial dependence on men, it has proved oppressive for women living with men they have to depend upon, and disastrous for the interests of all other women. The family-household system has resulted in the 'double shift' of wage labour and domestic labour for many working-class women, and the assumption of their household dependence has left many 'unsupported' women in a very vulnerable position. All the evidence in my view points to the conclusion that the family-household system has not been of great benefit to the working class, as a class, although within the working class its establishment can be traced to a struggle of male interests over female interests.

If, then, the present organization of the household and its accompanying family ideology cannot be said unequivocally to benefit women, men or the working class we are left with the possibility that it reflects the interests of capital. This, however, is a contentious argument, when considered carefully. There are a number of reasons why we might want to argue that it benefits the bourgeoisie. First, it is obviously relevant that the structure of male breadwinner and dependent wife emanated historically from the bourgeoisie, and, second, that it was imposed upon and accepted by the industrial working class. Third, the argument has been put forward that this system had, for the bourgeoisie, a material base: that of protecting the inheritance of capital, and hence Engels's argument that this family structure rests on the need for legitimate transmission of private property.[42] Fourth, our attention has been drawn to the enormous effort expended by the state in the support of this household structure and ideology, a degree of support which might be tantamount to active construction rather than mere endorsement.[43] Why should the state invest so heavily in this system if it were not to the advantage of the bourgeoisie?

42. *The Origin of the Family, Private Property and the State*, New York 1972.

These points are all, in fact, difficult to sustain in depth, and this is so partly because a number of contradictory forces are at play. One way of conceptualizing these contradictions is suggested by Irene Bruegel in her attempt to answer the question 'what keeps the family going?' She writes: ... 'the relationship of capitalism to the family is contradictory: it tends both to destroy it and maintain it. As a means of expanding the forces of production, capitalism tends to take over many of the productive and reproductive functions of the family; as a means of preserving capitalist relations of production, it tends to reinforce the traditional family, increasingly, ... through the state'.[44] Bruegel argues that preservation of the 'traditional family' was in the interests of working-class men (but *not* working-class women), and in the interests of the bourgeoisie in so far as it provided a cheap labour supply and an industrial reserve army of women, and also in that it provided the illusion of a sphere of individual emotion not penetrated by market relations and hence facilitated the political passivity of the working class. Although it would be wrong to pose a sharp distinction between the forces of production as an economic category and the relations of production as an ideological and political one, Bruegel's argument does suggest that it would be fruitful to explore possible distinctions between economic, political and ideological factors in relation to the bourgeoisie's interests in the family. In particular, the political factors have been somewhat neglected. Such an exploration might throw some light on the rather unsatisfactory arguments as to why the bourgeoisie supported so strongly the male breadwinner/dependent wife household and ideology.

The argument that support for this type of household was economically beneficial, some would say the only option, for

43. See Elizabeth Wilson, *Women and the Welfare State*, London 1977; and Mary McIntosh, 'The State and the Oppression of Women', in *Feminism and Materialism*.
44. Irene Bruegel 'What Keeps the Family Going?', *International Socialism*, vol.2, no.1, 1978.

the bourgeoisie has been discussed already. Although it clearly does present advantages which capital has fully exploited, I am not convinced that this household structure is potentially the most beneficial for capital. If we compare it to a system where migrant workers live virtually in barracks with their costs of reproduction largely borne in the hinterland we can see that the overall costs incurred in reproducing the working class through the present system are not as low as they might possibly be. So from the point of view of capital's need for the reproduction of labour power, the family household system is perhaps a good one, but not necessarily the cheapest, although this partly depends upon the outcome of struggles over wages and state benefits.

One area in which this form of household is beneficial for capital — and this is a point that the emphasis on domestic labour as 'functional for capital' has tended to occlude — is that of consumption. The purchase of consumer goods such as washing machines, refrigerators and so on is undoubtedly maximized in a situation where households of two, three and four people are thought to require a large range of such items, even if they are frequently not actually in use. The privatized nuclear family has proved an excellent market for commodities of this kind, and there is a certain amount of evidence to suggest that high rates of consumption are facilitated by or may even depend upon the full-time housewife. J. K. Galbraith has in fact argued this position with some force,[45] although the evidence has been somewhat neglected by Marxists in the field.

A different way of approaching the bourgeoisie's interest in the family-household is to see it not in terms of a concern to control and hegemonize the working class but in terms of the material conditions of the bourgeoisie itself. Engels's argument is the most influential here, since he attempted to spell out precisely the material basis of the bourgeois family. Although his argument, that the need to secure legitimate inheritance of property underlies the dependence of the

45. J. K. Galbraith, *Economics and the Public Purpose*, Harmondsworth 1975.

bourgeois wife, has considerable appeal as a materialist analysis of the ideological configuration of the family (monogamy and a double standard of sexual morality for men and women), it raises a number of serious difficulties. First, it is not self-evident from Marxist theory that legitimacy and established paternity are in fact required for the reproduction of capital. On the contrary, as far as capital accumulation is concerned, the inheritor's legitimacy or otherwise is irrelevant, and it is more likely that the insistence on legitimacy characteristic of the nineteenth-century bourgeoisie has its roots in the puritanical ideology of Christian morality in which it flourished. Second, Engels's analysis cannot adequately explain why it was that the proletarian family, far from disintegrating through lack of a comparable material basis for the inequality between husbands and wives, was not only strengthened but increasingly came to approximate the bourgeois model. Third, given the extent to which bourgeois women have succeeded in breaking down some of the dependent immobility of the role of wife — without necessarily losing the advantages of being members of the bourgeoisie — it is not clear in what sense the bourgeoisie now rests on this 'material foundation'.

It is, therefore, difficult to argue rigorously that the bourgeoisie's interests lie with the family-household, either as the best possible system for the reproduction of labour power or as an essential structure of the reproduction of themselves as a class. Of the economic arguments on this point, I find the significance of the privatized family in relation to maximizing consumption more telling in the twentieth-century context. However, the difficulty in separating economic from political and ideological considerations becomes apparent if we look at the extent to which the family-household operates to stabilize and strengthen capitalist relations of production and therefore the conditions of existence of capitalism itself. The bourgeoisie has a considerable interest in the consolidation of a family-household that divides and weakens the working class and reduces its militancy. Thus, although the bourgeoisie, primarily through the state, has invested enormous resources in the economic support of this form of household, the reasons for this are essentially concerned with ideological and political struggle in relation to long-term economic interest. Throughout the nineteenth and twentieth centuries the bourgeoisie has consistently advo-cated the moral desirability of 'the family', invoking an ideology of familialism that assigns financial support to the husband and father, sexual fidelity and domesticity to the wife and mother, and obedience to children. This ideology can, I think, be viewed in terms of a long-range collective interest of the bourgeoisie as a class, and certainly it has proved a burden to individual members of the bourgeoisie (notably politicians) who have been mercilessly destroyed as and when their deviations became public scandals.

The question as to who benefits from the family-household in contemporary capitalism has, then, no very clear answer. Women clearly do not. The working class does not, or if so it is working-class men rather than the class as such who do, and in any case the 'gain' is a divisive one. The bourgeoisie appears to have benefited from this system, but not unambiguously. With no easy answer to hand we are left with the problem of accounting for the pervasiveness and strength of the ideology of the family, and in the final section of this chapter I want to set out the conclusions we can draw from the discussion.

V

I began by considering the essentialism implicit in current uses of the term 'the family' and showed how the notion of 'the family' as a small group of co-residing blood relatives is a comparatively recent one. Despite its recentness, this model of the household as coterminous with immediate kin has achieved a remarkable degree of hegemony, and Irene Bruegel's question — 'what keeps the family going?' — needs to be answered historically as well as theoretically.

It seems that although the common household production slowly eradicated in the long and uneven development of capitalism may have been more egalitarian between men and women than the present form, there was a division within it based on gender. We have to return here to the role of biology in these historical divisions and I am inclined to agree with Mark Poster that, in the absence of adequate knowledge, we must remain 'agnostic' on the salience of biological differences to the organization of earlier family forms.[46] Certainly social divisions based on biological differences preceded capitalism and as far as we know represent an oppression of women that, although perhaps less pervasive than that found in capitalism, provided men with specific advantages on which to build. It should be noted, however, that developments of a technological kind (contraception particularly) have now rendered biological differentiation a much less plausible basis for exhaustive social gender division than may have been the case for previous societies. Furthermore, an historical approach indicates that developments during the transition to capitalism saw an exaggeration and an entrenchment of divisions which were previously less profoundly integrated into the relations of production, and in this sense the social construction of gender division massively outweighs any basis in biological differences.

Specific processes in capitalism, notably the wage-labour system and the tendency towards the separation of home and workplace, contributed to the construction of the family-household. In addition, however, the struggles between the interests of working-class men and those of women, and the coinciding interests of working-class men and the bourgeoisie, played a crucial role. So although the development of the family-household contained many, and serious, contradictions, there was considerable force acting in this direction.

46. Poster, p.149. Timpanaro, in fact, suggests quite rightly that any such abdication should be a temporary one, pending more scientific exploration of the relationship between biclogy and psychic and social patterns (*On Materialism*, p.46).

The gradual establishment of this system involved the substantial labour of restructuring the household and consolidating an ideology of familialism centred on the family as the 'natural' site for the fulfilment of supposedly 'natural' emotional needs. This came about partly through an important process of defining as 'marginal' people who did not fall within the confines of immediate nuclear family relations. At one level, as Leonore Davidoff has pointed out in relation to the early nineteenth century, institutions were created for '. . . all those who did not come under the domestic rubric: workhouses, hospitals, orphanages and purpose-built barracks for soldiers'.[47] In the twentieth century we have seen 'homes' for the old added to the list. This structural re-organization was complemented by the process of definition of personal identity in relation to immediate familial relations. As was noted in Chapter 2, the 'homosexual role' as we know it today did not exist as an identity until comparitively recently — possibly not before the late nineteenth century. Parallel histories could be drawn for the identity of childhood, adolescence, old age, disablement and so on, and all relate to the elevation of the nuclear parent-child bond and the marginalization of other members of the household.

Feminist work on the ideology of the family, for instance as embedded in the Beveridge proposals and in Bowlby's research on 'maternal deprivation', has demonstrated the ways in which ideological constructions are represented as natural and inevitable. It is important to understand ideological configurations such as 'the family' in terms of the production and reproduction of meaning, rather than through some notion of 'false consciousness'. Although I have spent some time treating the family-household from the point of view of who might benefit from it or not, it does not follow that all women, or the entire working class, suffer from some simple false consciousness as to where their interests really lie. Gender identity and the ideology of the

47. 'The Separation of Home and Work?', p.78.

family are embedded in our subjectivity and our desires at a far more profound level than that of 'false consciousness'. That being the case, the question arises as to how the present organization of the family household might be changed. Nancy Chodorow, in her refreshing formulation of psychoanalytic theory, calls for a conscious break in the cycle of 'mothering' by which contemporary femininity and masculinity are reproduced. It is absolutely correct, I think, to conclude that the possibility of women's liberation lies crucially in a re-allocation of childcare, and this is why the erosion of gender division in the sphere of wage labour will not bring an end to women's oppression. It remains to be said, however, that the organization of production under capitalism has historically been structured around the assumption that childcare is not divisible in this way. Hence no voluntaristic attempt to change these relations of childcare is likely to succeed, for the reason that the sexual division of labour of which they are a part is now deeply entrenched in the relations of production of capitalism.

7
Feminism and the Politics of the State

The state occupies a curiously contradictory position in the theory and practice of the British women's liberation movement. The question of how feminism should approach the state is of the utmost political importance, yet it remains controversial. Consideration of the strategic issues involved in this debate also highlights some of the ways in which the British women's movement has tended to differ from its sister organizations in other countries.

On the one hand, feminists in Britain have long been aware of the importance of the state in maintaining and enforcing women's financial dependence on men and in supporting and legitimating the various dimensions of women's oppression in this society. One indication of actual complicity in this oppression is the fact that the Sex Discrimination Act exempted 'statutory provisions' from its sphere of influence, leaving the state coolly free to discriminate massively against women in the basic systems of welfare and taxation. As I shall show in more detail below, the state plays an important role in constructing and regulating the processes described in earlier chapters of this book as well as contributing to the oppression of women through its own specific structure and operation.

On the other hand the women's liberation movement here has not in any unified way launched a major assault on the state. Although various groups and campaigns have received a certain amount of support, there is an underlying fear in many sections of the movement that direct engagement with state policy and constitutional politics would lead to liberal reformism. The politicization of personal life that is the hallmark of contemporary feminism has led to a critical stance on 'civil rights' politics and campaigns based on formal constitutional questions. It is symptomatic of this that the suffragette movement is remembered by many feminists more for its formal, constitutional aims than for the militancy with which it sought to achieve them. At one level this refusal to engage with the state can be seen in parliamentary politics, where the women's liberation movement is characterized by an absence only partially caused by the prejudice of party selection committees. Unlike countries such as Belgium, which has a feminist political party, or the United States, which has large women's political caucuses and conventions, or Australia, where systematic feminist lobbying has occurred, the parliamentary issues that attract widespread feminist support in Britain are restricted to a few major questions such as the abortion legislation.

It is, in fact, unclear to what extent the seven demands of the British women's liberation movement are directed explicitly towards the state, and there is considerable room for different interpretations of them in this respect.[1] From a socialist feminist point of view, these issues are compounded by current theoretical and strategic problems in Marxist approaches to the state, and I shall return to these difficulties later on. As a basis for that discussion I want now to indicate some of the ways in which the state is currently involved in different aspects of women's oppression.

I

If we look back at the various topics already considered it is clear that the role of the state in maintaining particular, and

1. The demands call for (in brief): equal pay; equal education and job opportunities; free contraception and abortion on demand; free twenty-four-hour childcare facilities; legal and financial independence; an end to discrimination against lesbians and the right to a self-defined sexuality; an end to rape and all violence against women.

for women oppressive, structures and ideology is very important. The case is perhaps most apparent in state support for the household system, where women and children are supposedly dependent upon a male bread-winner's 'family wage'. As Rosalind Delmar has pointed out, the contrast drawn by Engels between a bourgeois family form in which women's dependence was legally and juridically supported and a proletarian form where women's earnings gave them material independence is less useful now that the law has been extended to regulation of the working-class family.[2] How and why this regulation has come about forms part of the answer to Mark Poster's question as to how the bourgeoisie succeeded in hegemonizing the working class family under its own rubric.[3] Several feminists have suggested that the welfare provisions developed in the twentieth century, and in particular as they were codified in the legislation emanating from the 1942 Beveridge Report, represent a major link in the chain of women's dependence. Angela Weir writes: 'one of the effects of these reforms, even though they were paid for largely through working-class taxation and insurance contributions, was to provide the material basis for working-class family life. It meant that the working class adopted patterns of familial relations which had hitherto been exclusive to the upper-middle classes. In short, they created a more efficient structure for the reproduction of labour power based on the family unit and women's labour as wives and mothers'.[4]

The pattern established hinged upon the notion that a man had 'an obligation to maintain' his wife and any dependent children. The obligation has never been rigorously enforced by the state but it is the basis on which benefits are withheld. Since it was thought wrong to encourage immorality by releasing from this duty a man living 'as man and wife' with

2. 'Looking Again at Engels's *Origin of the Family, Private Property and the State*', in *The Rights and Wrongs of Women*.
3. Poster, p.126.
4. 'The Family, Social Work and the Welfare State', in S. Allen, L. Sanders and J. Wallis, eds., *Conditions of Illusion*, Leeds 1974.

a woman, the principle was extended to cohabiting couples. This gave rise to the now notorious practice of social security officials attempting to ascertain a woman's sexual relations with men with a view to enforcing the 'cohabitation rule' and depriving her of the right to benefits. The principle of a woman's financial dependence upon any man with whom she has sexual relations thus goes beyond the idea of dependence within marriage that underlies provisions such as the 'married man's tax allowance' and arrangements for national insurance payments. As feminists campaigning on these issues have repeatedly stressed, it represents nothing less than institutionalized prostitution.

Elizabeth Wilson's work in this area has emphasized that the construction by the state of this particular family form is an essential element of the 'ideology of welfarism' characterizing the post-war British state.[5] Certainly it is impossible to understand the state's assumptions about women's dependence without an adequate grasp of its ideological character since, as Hilary Land has demonstrated, these assumptions simply 'do not accord with the evidence'. Economic activity rates are such that the number of households fitting the stereotype of the male breadwinner/full-time dependent housewife is at any given time very small, and in addition to this married women are also obliged to maintain dependent husbands in certain circumstances.[6] In the light of the state's efforts to use its welfare provisions to enforce women's dependence within the household, there is heavy irony in the Department of Health and Social Security's current argument against feminists that to phase out this principle would offend public opinion.[7]

One point of debate in this area is why the state should so

5. *Women and the Welfare State*, London 1977.
6. Hilary Land 'Social Security and the Division of Unpaid Work in the Home and Paid Employment in the Labour Market', Department of Health and Social Security, 1977 (reprinted from *Social Security Research Seminar*, pp.43-61).
7. See 'Disaggregation Now! Another Battle for Women's Independence', *Feminist Review* no.2, 1979.

firmly have upheld the principle of women's dependence. Running through Marxist feminist analysis of state involvement in the household is the notion that, as Angela Weir put it, this model is 'more efficient' for the reproduction of labour power. This idea is elaborated in the thesis of Elizabeth Wilson's book and given a further twist in Mary McIntosh's argument that state policy in this respect denotes precisely a recognition of the inadequacy of the family as a means for the reproduction of the working class. Other feminists, insisting equally strongly on the centrality of the state in maintaining these patterns of dependence, have tended to interpret the same evidence in terms of its benefits for men rather than for capital. This debate raises again the question of functionalism in Marxist analysis, and has tended to be posed in terms of a dispute as to whether state involvement in the household is really concerned with motherhood (and the reproduction of labour power) or with marriage (and the interests of men). I shall return to this question in the discussion later in this chapter.

Related to the question of the state's involvement in the family-household is that of its role in the division of labour at work. Numerous examples might be cited of ways in which the state regulates terms and conditions of employment in such a way as to reinforce women's subordination in the sphere of wage labour. Obviously the protective legislation that specifies occupations (such as mining) from which women are barred, and limits their hours of work, is important here and can partially be construed as a mechanism to protect male workers from competition. The legislation on sex discrimination at work contains elements that are inexplicable except in terms of state support for an ideology of the family and women's primary allegiance to it. For example, although it is illegal for an employer in Britain to discriminate against a woman on the grounds of her being married, it is not illegal — for instance in respect of maternity leave — to discriminate against her on the grounds that she is not married. At the time when the legislation was being drafted, a case was made, and the government accepted it, that institutions might want to withhold maternity benefits from unmarried mothers.

Phenomena such as these illustrate a general relation between the state, the family household and the wage-labour system. The principle of dependence has been instrumental in forcing women's wages down and means that the state can exercise some control over the deployment of their labour.[8] This can be seen in the effects of current government expenditure cuts. The closure of facilities for old and sick people, for handicapped children and so on, means that many women will have to give up employment to care for these members of the family. As feminists have noted, the welfarist concept of 'community care' usually means that a woman is found to look after the person concerned.[9] In addition to this, cuts in the public sector, where a very large proportion of the female workforce is employed, will mean disproportionally high unemployment for women. Further still, many women workers depend upon the already meagre facilities (such as state nurseries) enabling them to combine wage work with family responsibilities and will not be able to continue their jobs at all.

This general relation between the state, the household and wage labour can be seen perhaps most clearly in the case of women, particularly those with dependent children, who are not in fact themselves dependent upon the hypothesized male breadwinner. Hilary Land quotes the 1909 Royal Commission on the Poor Laws as saying: 'relatively low relief is granted and the mother is expected to earn something in addition. This is the common practice. Guardians do not insist on the mother working but they give an allowance so small that either she must work or the home

8. This is not, of course, to suggest that the state enjoys a unitary relation with the capitalist class as a whole or with particular fractions of capital. The debates in Marxist theory on the 'autonomy of the political level' are summarized with admirable brevity in an appendix to Ian Gough's *The Political Economy of the Welfare State* (London 1979). See also Bob Jessop 'Marx and Engels on the State', in S. Hibbin, ed., *Politics, Ideology and the State*, London 1978.
9. See Cynthia Cockburn, *The Local State*, London 1977, p.179.

must suffer'.[10] It is not difficult to see how this practice, still operating today, further weakens the already poor bargaining position of women doing irregular or part-time work, however necessary such work might be for the upkeep of their dependants. Mary McIntosh argues that the level of state provision for such women in fact defines their relationship to the labour market; 'a generous and unconditioned provision could keep them out of employment altogether', while 'a meagre provision could force them to seek work at whatever wages'. She concludes that welfare policy is thus 'potentially a fairly flexible instrument keeping women more or less in reserve for wage labour'.[11] The qualifying 'potentially' is important here, since it is not clear to what extent such policies are deliberately varied as a means of controlling the labour supply, and in any case the ability of the state to do so will depend on the degree of resistance offered in national and local struggles by and on behalf of claimants. Although I think we can reasonably assume a degree of planned control by the state, such policies operate within a framework defined historically through the struggle of the working class to protect erosion of its standard of living.

State provision and regulation of education clearly plays an important part in structuring the different opportunities open to men and women, the ideology of women's dependence upon a male breadwinner, and in constructing women's 'dual relationship' to the class structure. This role may be interpreted in different ways. Some writers have sought to emphasize it as part of the material conditions of existence of capitalism; Joan Smith, for example, considers the educational system as part of a 'mode of reproduction' of capitalism.[12] Others have emphasized the ideological role of the state, representing in its official documents and reports the pervasive ideology of gender division characteristic of

10. 'Social Security and the Division of Labour', p.56.
11. 'The State and the Oppression of Women', in *Feminism and Materialism*, p.280.
12. 'Women and the Family', *International Socialism*, no.100, 1977.

contemporary capitalism. As such, the ideology of the state reproduces this division anew in a form that adds legitmating force to it. Recent work in this area has explored the possibility of 'reading' state reports as ideological practices, or discourses, in which particular configurations of meaning are articulated.

One such study is that of Lucy Bland, Trisha McCabe and Frank Mort, who examine three reports commissioned by state agencies (Beveridge, 1942; Newsom, 1948; and Wolfenden, 1957) bearing on the inter-relations of marriage, the family, sexuality and procreation.[13] Although these authors are concerned with the expression in these documents of an ideological construction of procreation, which they see as 'partially autonomous' of capitalism's need to reproduce labour power, their work in itself poses the question as to how a 'reading' of this kind would relate to an analysis of the state's regulation of sexuality and procreation. State reports may well encapsulate in their discursive assumptions the complexities and contradictions of, for instance, an ideology of procreation, but we need to approach this in the context of a broader understanding of the role of the state in this respect. The state does not only articulate the ideology of a link between sexuality and procreation; it also regulates and sanctions our behaviour accordingly. Very severe punishments for infringement of these codes have in the past included capital punishment and may still entail a prison sentence. On such matters, however, the state is fascinatingly reflexive — engaging with 'public opinion' as a means of monitoring its legal and juridical regulations. The extent of state regulation of sexual behaviour is indicated by the terms of reference of the Criminal Law Revision Committee, which is currently reviewing all aspects of the law on sexual offences, including its internal coherence. After it has methodically collected evidence from a vast array of interested parties we can expect it to make legislative recommendations on a range of

13. 'Sexuality and Reproduction: Three "Official" Instances', in Michèle Barrett *et al.*, eds., *Ideology and Cultural Production*, London 1979.

topics including the heterosexual age of consent, the age of legal homosexual relations, incest, intercourse with mental defectives and many more.

In addition to controlling the legal codes by which sexuality is regulated, the state exercises some control over the ideological and cultural representation of sexuality. The British state is at present involved in protracted debate on questions of pornography and obscenity, and the criteria upon which censorship should rest. Indeed, this is an area where, at the margins, the cultural production and reproduction of gender is itself circumscribed by state regulation. An example of this might be the recommendation of the recent Williams Committee report that 'snuff movies' should be unavailable for legal public consumption.[14] It is worth noting in passing that although the state has for some while not hesitated in banning works deemed to be obscene, the increasing proportion of work now produced under state patronage will tend to extend its influence in such matters.

The question of sexuality, and its relation to procreation, is merely one of many areas in which the state plays an important role in gender division. Every chapter of this book has provided instances where the processes described are at least monitored by the state and at most actively constructed through its particular operations. In addition to this there are specific mechanisms by which the state in its more repressive aspects controls and enforces other dimensions of women's oppression.

One way of approaching this is to consider the workings of the law, the judiciary and the penal system. The police force operates according to particular assumptions about gender; they are, for instance, reluctant to intervene in cases of even the most brutal marital violence because they see themselves as respecting the privacy of 'the family'. In rape cases the police are well known for subjecting the victim to an offensive and degrading inquisition in which her own sexual history is on trial. It is the police, too, who enjoin women not

14. See the Home Office Report of the (Williams) Committee on Obscenity and Film Censorship (London, HMSO 1979).

to go out alone at night when they have difficulty in tracking down a still-active rapist or murderer, thereby adding a secondary element of control to the original threat. The police are charged with interpretation of the law where, as in offences related to prostitution, a double standard applies; their harassment of prostitutes and reluctance to pursue kerb-crawlers is revealing.

The law itself encodes fundamental assumptions about gender division and it is salutary to consider how recently it is that women have been recognized as legal subjects in their own right. Albie Sachs and Joan Hoff Wilson have provided an enlightening account of 'male bias' in British case law on this question. They consider the cases brought by feminists wishing to vote, enter the professions and be elected for public office. The appropriate statutes indicated that 'persons' with the right qualifications should have access to these opportunities and cases were brought to establish whether the word 'person' should be held to include women. Numerous judgments went against the feminist appellants and it was not until 1929 (ten years after parliament had passed legislation removing the disqualifications on women holding public office) that a court ruling conceded that the term 'person' should include women.[15]

A general feature of the judicial and penal systems is that by and large the involvement of women in the entire sphere of criminality is substantially less than that of men. As is common knowledge, the number charged with crimes, the rate of conviction, the likelihood of prison sentences and so on, is lower for women than for men. Conversely, the incidence of mental illness is in general higher for women than it is for men and this overall picture has led some feminists to suggest that these two types of behaviour might be regarded as 'functional alternatives'. I shall return to this argument later, but first I want briefly to note some aspects of the practice not only of the medical and psychiatric professions but also of that of social work.

15. *Sexism and the Law*, London 1978, p.38.

These practices all represent fields of work where an ideology of professionalism coexists, at times uneasily, with a high degree of state regulation and in this respect they are not unlike the educational system. Feminists and socialists in these areas have to struggle with an ideology of 'caring' that mystifies the processes by which conformity to definitions of femininity and family life is secured, where necessary by coercion. Social workers, for example, are expected to cooperate with magistrates in their treatment of the sexual behaviour of adolescent girls. This involves, as Lesley Smith has pointed out, the perception of female juvenile delinquency as a threat less to law and order than to accepted sexual morality. She argues that non-sexual misbehaviour in such girls is frequently overlooked or underplayed while sexual promiscuity that in boys would be an irrelevancy often results in corrective measures. The willingness of the state to deem such girls as in need of its 'care, protection and control' is symptomatic of a sexualization of female delinquency which is clearly related to a particular definition of women's role in society.[16]

Feminist social workers must also contend with the more explicit ways in which the state, both nationally and locally, tends in its policies to reinforce a specific definition of the household. Housing policy by and large massively privileges the 'nuclear family' and is inflexible in meeting the needs of those who do not conform to this stereotype. Struggles against such policies entail conflict and contradiction for social workers who attempt to break down a professional relationship with their 'clients' and ally themselves to struggles of local community groups.[17]

Feminists in the medical, psychiatric and related health services fight a similar battle, and one which is increasingly becoming connected to that in social work. These areas have overlapped for some time (for instance in the person of the psychiatric social worker) but in recent years there has been

16. Lesley Shacklady Smith, 'Sexist Assumptions and Female Delinquency', in *Women, Sexuality and Social Control.*
17. See J. Cowley *et al.*, eds., *Community or Class Struggle?*, London 1977.

a greater tendency to institutionalize formal links between the two professions, for example in the attachment of social workers to health centres. This development might have the welcome effect of facilitating recognition of the social bases of medical and psychiatric problems, but in my view it is more likely to contribute to the insidious process by which social problems (and 'anti-social' behaviour) are accommodated to a medical model of individual pathology. This has already taken place, most disturbingly, in the use of drugs to control prisoners. It is interesting in this context to note that a large proportion of female offenders when sentenced to prison are destined for Holloway, which is 'psychiatric in orientation, emphasizing the treatment of inmates and concentrating on their individual needs and psychological problems'.[18]

The lengths to which medical practice will go to secure the 'correct' definition of femininity are now widely recognised by feminists, particularly those active in health campaigns. This is not so much a strategy (although the level of misogynism in this profession might lead one to think so), but rather an absorption of gender ideology into the definition of health. An extreme instance: a woman was referred by her general practitioner to a psychiatrist, who corroborated his diagnosis by immediately admitting her to a mental hospital and treating her with electro-convulsive therapy, for a 'breakdown' which took the form of the patient's waking up one morning saying that she was not going to do the housework any more.[19] It is, of course, difficult to ascertain how widespread such practices have been or still are, but research has shown that the criteria on which psychiatric judgments of male and female mental health are based lean heavily towards stereotypical

18. Carol Smart, *Women, Crime and Criminology*, London 1977, p.147 (Holloway is Britain's only secure women's prison).
19. This incident took place in the early 1960s but was discussed with the GP's successor in 1975 who regarded the treatment as perfectly appropriate for 'stress' of this kind. See 'Doctors and Their Patients: the Social Control of Women in General Practice', by Michèle Barrett and Helen Roberts, in *Women, Sexuality and Social Control*.

definitions of masculinity and femininity.[20] Furthermore, medical decisions on matters such as contraception, abortion and sterilization rest frequently on the assumption that women's reproductive capacities outweigh all other considerations of health and well being.

II

I have given merely a few examples of the ways in which the state, through its own repressive mechanisms and through the practices of the semi-autonomous professions that it closely regulates, plays a part in the structures and ideology of women's oppression. It can clearly be seen that the state is closely concerned with the form of the household developed in contemporary British capitalism and, more generally, with the reproduction of women's dependence. The means employed to these ends differ considerably from the overt manipulation that characterizes other types of state activity, and rely heavily on the construction of privatized familial dependence. Feminists have recently paid attention to the character of the state's role in this respect and have developed a useful analysis of its tendency towards the 'coercion of privacy' in relation to women.

This phrase is used by Annika Snare and Tove Stang-Dahl in their account of the way in which the state constructs the home as a private prison for women. They argue that the state's refusal to intervene in family matters such as domestic violence, its failure to protect women from sexual abuse, its immobilization of women as dependants within the household and its attempt to treat women offenders as normatively sick, add up to a form of 'house arrest' no less coercive than the more usual incarceration in public penal institutions. In this way the state need not fall back on secondary means of repression and control, but can operate

20. See I. K. Broverman *et al.*, 'Sex Role Stereotypes and Clinical Judgments in Mental Health', *Journal of Consulting and Clinical Psychology*, 34, 1970.

through the construction of a family form which exercises primary, informal control.[21]

This argument relies on a recognition of the role of the state in maintaining the myth of a separation of the public from the private sphere, according to which women are held to occupy a privileged (albeit at the same time restricted) place in the private arena. Diana Leonard Barker, stressing the ways in which the state purports to 'protect' the weaker party in its regulation of the marriage contract, refers to this as 'repressive benevolence'. Similarly Mary McIntosh points out that the relation of the state to women is, compared with its relation to men, more indirect, less interfering, apparently more benevolent than punitive: 'the state frequently defines a space, the family, in which its agents will not interfere but in which control is left to the man'.[22] These arguments suggest a more satisfactory answer than the 'functional alternatives' thesis to the question as to why the deviance of women should frequently take the form of in-turned psychiatric problems and household-related crimes such as shoplifting. More importantly perhaps, they suggest why this difference between male and female patterns should be exaggerated and codified in the perceptions of the relevant authorities, hence rendering the official statistics particularly difficult to interpret.[23] It is possible, too, that this perspective could usefully be applied to the problem I raised in Chapter 2 as to why it should be the case that lesbianism has escaped the punitive sanctions imposed on male homosexuality.

The 'coercion of privacy' thesis raises a number of issues about the ideological construction of the public/private

21. 'The Coercion of Privacy: a Feminist Perspective', in *Women, Sexuality and Social Control*.
22. Diana Leonard Barker, 'The Regulation of Marriage: Repressive Benevolence', in G. Littlejohn *et al.*, eds., *Power and the State*, London, 1978; and Mary McIntosh, 'The State and the Oppression of Women', p.257.
23. The statistics relating to women and deviance are notoriously difficult to interpret. On mental illness see the fascinating discussion by Dorothy Smith, 'Women and Psychiatry', in Smith and S. J. David, eds., *Women Look at Psychiatry*, Vancouver 1975.

distinction, and Albie Sachs has explored some of these in
his discussion of 'the myth of male protectiveness'. Sachs
argues that underlying the refusal of the British judiciary to
recognize the existence of women as 'persons' was the
conviction that far from thereby doing an injustice to women
these judges were in fact merely endorsing women's favoured
position as elevated spiritual beings. This view of women is
neatly encapsulated in the grounds on which Gladstone
refused the vote to women: he thought it would degrade their
moral purity and lower them to the mundane level of men.
Sachs sees this myth as a legal prejudice that can be related
to the desire of bourgeois men to demonstrate their class
position by displaying an unemployed wife. It depended
upon an ideology of gender in which men and women were
seen as different, but complementary. He points out that the
restrictions against bourgeois women's occupational aspira-
tions were differently motivated from those limiting the
employment of working-class women, and he attributes the
former to the desire of bourgeois men to maintain a
dependent wife as manager of the household.[24] This
argument relating legal to familial dependence can be
illustrated through the particular case of one of the feminist
litigants in the 'persons' cases. Sophia Jex-Blake figures in
the history of feminism not only as a protagonist in these law
suits, but also through her preserved correspondence with a
father whose desire to enforce her dependence (financial and
emotional) on himself, and subsequently on a husband to be
approved by him, is made fascinatingly clear.[25]

It is important to identify the strong correspondences
between the ideology of gender enshrined in various
operations of the state and the structure and ideology of the
family-household. The state is involved in the endorsement
and enforcement of a particular household structure which

24. Albie Sachs, 'The Myth of Male Protectiveness and the Legal Subordi-
    nation of Women', pp.28-34 in *Women, Sexuality and Social Control*.
25. Mr Jex Blake offered to pay his daughter's teaching salary himself if
    she would oblige him by refusing it from the college. His contortions
    are mercilessly described by Virginia Woolf in *Three Guineas*,
    pp.239-40.

in its turn is entrenched in the division of labour that capitalist relations of production have historically developed. A question which poses itself at this point is: how do we analyse the role of the state in this nexus of processes structuring women's oppression? Are we to see the state as representing the interests of capital, or of men? This is not a productive question in my view. In the first place it rests on the assumption that these categories of people are in some sense comparable, whereas I have tried to show that they are not. Women do not constitute a class and furthermore it would be difficult to argue that even a substantially increased representation of women in positions of political power would automatically benefit the interests of women in general. A distinction must be drawn here between the possible effects of more *women* holding political power and women attempting to use such power for *feminist* ends. Although an increased representation of women in parliamentary politics is clearly something to be struggled for, the present situation is to a large extent the product of a sexual division of labour rather than a cause of it. This point hardly needs elaboration in the case of Britain's first woman prime minister, whose policies cutting public expenditure on housing, hospitals, schools, nurseries and so on have already had particularly disastrous consequences for women.

In practice, the debate as to whether the state, and particularly in its welfare policies, should be understood as representing the interests of capital or of men has been posed in terms which transcend the reductionist view of the state which either answer would imply. It has been displaced onto the question as to whether state support for the assumed male breadwinner/dependent wife household should be construed as endorsement of woman's role as mother, or as wife. The various protagonists in this debate agree to a large extent on the identification of the processes involved, but tend to differ in that Marxist feminists put more emphasis on the state construction of motherhood (with a view to the reproduction of labour power) while those inclining more to a radical feminist approach emphasize the subordination of the wife to the husband as the object of a patriarchal state's policy. In so far as this debate is a displacement of a long-standing dispute between radical-feminist and Marxist accounts of the family in capitalism, it encounters the familiar problems. An analysis that stresses state regulation of wifehood is forced into the absurdity of seeing child care as work undertaken by the wife for the husband (the children being 'his' rather than hers); that which stresses state involvement as a mechanism for improving the reproduction of labour power is forced, on the other hand, to reduce the oppressive daily routine of servicing and caring for men to a supposedly essential need of capitalism. It is only if we recognize the elements of male domination that have been incorporated into the particular family-household system that the state has supported and structured that we can avoid either of these unsatisfactory options.

III

The question of reformism is a crucial one for the women's liberation movement in Britain and it has been raised in many contexts, particularly those of strategy and organization. Although it is difficult to generalize in this way, I think it would be right to comment that a preoccupation with, an alertness to the dangers of, sliding into reformism is more intense among feminists in Britain than in countries that have pushed ahead with the institutionalization of feminist politics. American feminists who criticize the British women's movement for 'failing' to establish alternative power structures — from party-political groups to networks of academic 'experts' — sometimes themselves fail to recognize that this reluctance is based on a reasoned critique of such strategies.

Several arguments underlie this position of opposition to reformism, only some of which are analogous to the classic socialist ones. Firstly, there is the justified view that if feminism were to engage in the systematic infiltration of hierarchies of power it would become vulnerable to careerism on the part of women who selected it as a platform for personal advancement. This would inevitably incur the more general danger of recuperation, and feminism's accommodation to the status quo. Experience in Britain has provided us with salutary evidence to justify this fear. The Equal Opportunities Commission, set up to monitor and enforce the 1975 sex discrimination legislation, has proved particularly pusillanimous and ineffective. Although it has many committed feminists working within it, they struggle against a leadership that is unwilling to pose any fundamental challenge to accepted definitions of women's position. When the Conservative government was elected in 1979 and Sir Geoffrey Howe made Chancellor of the Exchequer, Lady Howe resigned from her post as vice-chairperson of the EOC because, she said, she felt it would be impossible to combine such an important job with her responsibilities as the wife of a man holding such high national office.

A second reason for fearing that engagement with formal state politics would be reformist is that the state is so ineluctably committed to the representation of men's interests that any changes secured would merely extend and institutionalize its control over women. Hence, it could be argued, we should not press for further state provision of nurseries, for instance, since this would only increase the power of the state over women and would be less desirable than alternative sources. The strongest example here is the (in my view justified) case against the demand for a state wage for housework. Feminists rightly point out that were such a wage to be negotiated it would in practice confirm women in low-paid work and institutionalize their relegation to the home.[26] A rather less obvious, although analogous issue, is that of the demand for a 'guaranteed minimum income' from the state. The Claimants Union's support for a 'GMI' has been criticized, for instance by Ruth Lister, as

26. The suggestion that 'wages for housework' be adopted as a formal demand of the British women's liberation movement has been rejected by the national conference every time it has been raised.

tending to reinforce women's role in the household and as not providing a fundamental challenge to the state's assumptions concerning women's dependence.[27]

A third element in feminist hostility to directing campaigns against the state is that to do so is merely to tinker with the administration of a power structure whose roots lie elsewhere. Just as some socialists have argued that the state would 'wither away' in the transition to a communist society, so some feminists have viewed the state as an instrument of male control that would fall away with the destruction of patriarchy. This perspective can be maintained irrespective of how patriarchy is defined and where its dynamic is located (in biological reproduction, in the exploitation of women's labour by men, or whatever) as long as a highly reductionist view of the state as determined by these structures is adhered to.

Finally, I think it can be noted that the emphasis in women's liberation on the politics of the personal, and its organizational basis in small-group grass-roots work, as well as its antipathy to structural hierarchies, contribute to a tendency to play down the importance of attacks on the state at a national level. Increasingly women's liberationists have played an important role in attacks on 'the local state', in community struggles over housing, the law, battered women and so on, and this has tended to deflect attention from attempts to influence the state at the level of national policies.

Notwithstanding all this, the women's movement has in specific campaigns and groups launched major assaults on aspects of state policy and the importance of these should not be under-estimated. The campaign for free, legal and safe abortion is an outstanding example of massive mobilization. In other areas, too, many groups have submitted evidence and proposals to government committees of various kinds and have exerted pressure on agents of the law. Organizations such as the National Women's Aid Federa-

27. 'Some Thoughts on an Independent Income for Women', *Scarlet Woman*, no.8, 1978.

tion, Rights of Women, and the Campaign for Legal and Financial Independence, regularly bring their arguments to bear on the relevant state decision-making bodies. This work is essential and I want to argue that in spite of the arguments mentioned earlier, the charge of reformism need not apply to it.

First, it is not appropriate to transpose onto the struggle for women's liberation those socialist perceptions of the state which have reduced it to the mere expression of economically determined class relations. Political and ideological processes carry considerable weight in the construction of women's oppression and should be attacked in their own right; and this involves a systematic attack on the state.

Second, the state is not a pre-given instrument of oppression, but is a site of struggle and to some extent at least responsive to concerted pressure. Although it would be just as ridiculous to claim that such pressure could of itself bring about women's liberation as to think it might bring about socialism, to reject this level of struggle altogether is to lapse into the romance of anarchism.

In the present situation the state is particularly important for women's liberationists, since the evidence suggests that public sector cuts are likely to increase women's dependence on men in the household. In the first place, much of the huge increase in public sector employment this century has been the employment of women, and the protection of their jobs and wages is essential. In the second, many employed women rely on state provision for dependent family members (the old, the sick, children) to maintain their ability to undertake wage work at all. One example of this is the suggestion made to cut the education budget by sending children home for lunch or ending the school day at 2pm. How many employed women will have to give up their jobs to cope with such changes?

Finally, I am unconvinced by the argument that familial dependence is less degrading for women than dependence on the state. However inadequate and oppressive the conditions of state support, they do not carry the implications of emotional and personal subordination associated with the personal dependence of a woman on a male wage, and indeed this is why the state's support of this relationship is so insidiously coercive. State provision of welfare benefits, as well as the mechanisms of the state generally in relation to women, have contributed substantially to the oppression of women and should be contested on their own ground.

8
Capitalism and Women's Liberation

In conclusion I want briefly to return to the conceptual problems raised in the first chapter and the political issues mentioned in the preface. What light has this discussion thrown on the usefulness of the concept of patriarchy or the attempt to analyse women's oppression in terms of the reproduction of capitalism? To what extent are we justified in regarding the oppression of women as an ideological process? What are the possibilities for achieving women's liberation in capitalism and what relationship does or should the political mobilization of women have with a revolutionary socialist movement?

I have argued that it is inadequate to attempt to grasp the character of women's oppression in contemporary capitalism in terms of the supposed needs of capitalism itself. The reasoning in favour of this analysis has tended to be couched in terms of capital's support for a system of the reproduction of labour power, through domestic labour in the household, that operates at the lowest possible cost and provides a cheap and flexible reserve army of married women workers to lower the price of wages in general. Although these are undoubtedly important points in any explanation of capital's support for a household in which a wife and children are assumed to be dependent upon a male breadwinner, the argument leaves unexplained many aspects of women's oppression. The charge that this argument is a functionalist one is not in my view as important as the fact that it tends towards a reductionist account of women's oppression and denies specific aspects of women's subordination to men in the pre-capitalist period, in socialist societies and within the different classes of contemporary capitalism.

I have argued that this particular form of household, and its accompanying ideology of women's dependence, is not the only possible form for an efficient reproduction of labour-power in capitalist relations of production. It is the product of historical struggles between men and women, both within the working class and the bourgeoisie. Furthermore, the 'reproduction' thesis can deal only in a very mechanistic way with the complexity of the ideological construction of gender as it has developed in capitalism. A consideration of the areas of sexuality and the cultural representation of gender demonstrates a need to understand the force of ideology in the production and reproduction of the categories of masculinity and femininity on which such an analysis implicitly depends, but tends not to explore.

These arguments need not be ruled out altogether, but it is necessary to historicize them. A model of women's dependence has become entrenched in the relations of production of capitalism, in the divisions of labour in wage work and between wage labour and domestic labour. As such, an oppression of women that is not in any essentialist sense pre-given by the logic of capitalist development has become necessary for the ongoing reproduction of the mode of production in its present form. Hence, the oppression of women, although not a functional pre-requisite of capitalism, has acquired a material basis in the relations of production and reproduction of capitalism today.

It follows that although important dimensions of women's oppression cannot be accounted for with reference to the categories of Marxism, it is equally impossible to establish the analytic independence of a system of oppression such as the category of 'patriarchy' suggests. The resonance of this concept lies in its recognition of the trans-historical character of women's oppression, but in this very appeal to longevity it deprives us of an adequate grasp of historical change. How useful is it to collapse widow-burning in India with 'the coercion of privacy' in Western Europe, into a concept of such generality? What we need to analyse are precisely the mechanisms by which women's oppression is secured in different contexts, since only then can we confront the problem of how to change it.

Feminists who employ the concept of patriarchy vary in the extent to which they ground it in biological differences between the sexes or in inevitable power structures stemming from these differences. A number of writers have inquired into the historical origins of patriarchy and, related to this, the question of whether these origins are biologically determined. No one would want to deny that there are physiological differences between the sexes, but what is at issue is how these natural differences are constructed as divisions by human social agency. Racists who attempt to provide 'scientific' apologias for the oppression of blacks are treated with the contempt they deserve and we should be equally wary of apologias for gender division, including those emanating from feminist quarters. The valorization of the female principle that a biologistic use of the concept of patriarchy encourages should be rejected at all levels.

I would not, however, want to argue that the concept of patriarchy should be jettisoned. I would favour retaining it for use in contexts where male domination is expressed through the power of the father over women and over younger men. Clearly some societies have been organized around this principle, although not capitalist ones. Insofar as feminist appropriations of psychoanalytic theory have attempted to cast this principle as a primary psychic dynamic of contemporary gender construction, I have dissented from their conclusions. Nevertheless, there remain elements of what might properly be called patriarchal power in the recent history of women's oppression and these can usefully be identified, for instance in some aspects of fascist ideology and the relations of the bourgeois family in the nineteenth century. Hence I would argue for a more precise and specific use of the concept of patriarchy, rather than one which expands it to cover all expressions of male domination and thereby attempts to construe a descriptive term as a systematic explanatory theory.

The discussion throughout this book has emphasized the importance of ideology in the construction and reproduction of women's oppression. A particular household organization and an ideology of familialism are central dimensions of women's oppression in capitalism and it is only through an analysis of ideology that we can grasp the oppressive myth of an idealized natural 'family' to which all women must conform. It is only through an analysis of ideology and its role in the construction of gendered subjectivity that we can account for the desires of women as well as men to reproduce the very familial structures by which we are oppressed. To argue this is not to suggest that needs for intimacy, sexual relations, emotional fulfilment, parenthood and so on are in themselves oppressive. What is oppressive is the assumption that the present form of such needs is the only possible form, and that the manner in which they should be met is through the family as it is today. We can have little knowledge of the form such personal needs have taken in the past, and still less of what form they might take in a future society. What feminism requires, however, in order to reach out to a wider group of women, is a more perceptive and sympathetic account not only of how or why a dominant meaning of femininity has been constructed, but how or why women have sought, consciously and unconsciously, to embrace and desire it. This requires not simply an analysis of collusion or false consciousness, but a much deeper analysis of subjectivity and identity, which presents us with the task of carrying on where earlier feminists such as Simone de Beauvoir have begun.

If we accept the importance of ideology in an analysis of women's oppression the question arises whether we should see that oppression as located solely at the ideological level. Some feminists, and many socialists, have arrived at this conclusion and I have tried to differentiate my position from theirs. To argue that women's oppression rests exclusively on ideological processes would involve one or other of two alternative assumptions. Either you need to hold that ideology is absolutely autonomous of the economic relations of capitalism, in which case it is plausible that a completely dissociated ideology of gender could exist independently of those relations; or you need to hold that ideology is always grounded in material relations but that gender ideology is grounded in economic relations between men and women that exist independently of capitalism. The first view is idealist, divorcing ideology entirely from material conditions; the second view is materialist but poses a different set of material determinants from those specified by Marxism. (A third possibility, that the ideology of gender is necessarily determined by the material relations of capitalist production, appears to me to be untenable and I have argued against it in several contexts.)

It is, perhaps, possible to resolve this problem without recourse to the analytically paralysing thesis of 'absolute autonomy', or to a form of materialism that displaces the labour/capital contradiction from its centrality in the analysis of capitalist society. First, we can note that the ideology of gender — the meaning of masculinity and femininity — has varied historically and should not be treated as static or unified, but should be examined in the different historical and class contexts in which it occurs. Second, we can note that the meaning of gender in capitalism today is tied to a household structure and division of labour that occupy a particular place in the relations of production, and that, therefore, this ideology does, concretely and historically, have some material basis. Third, we can recognize the difficulty of posing economic and ideological categories as exclusive and distinct. The relations of production and reproduction of contemporary capitalism may operate in general according to exploitative capital accumulation processes that are technically 'sex-blind', but they take the form of a division of labour in which ideology is deeply embedded.

Thus I would want to argue that ideology is an extremely important site for the construction and reproduction of women's oppression, but I would resist the suggestion that this ideological level can be dissociated from economic relations. Here I would take some distance from the feminist appropriation of post-Althusserian theories that seek to locate all aspects of women's oppression in terms of a theory of discourse. Although I have drawn on a modified form of some of these ideas, notably in order to analyse the changing definition of 'the family', I would not be prepared to argue that men and women themselves represent discursive categories in which differences are produced. Masculinity and femininity obviously are categories of meaning in one sense, but men and women occupy positions in the division of labour and class structure which, although not pre-given, are historically concrete and identifiable. The general claim that women's oppression is to be located at the level of ideological production alone is either unduly restricting in our analysis, or rests on an unacceptably expansionist definition of the scope of 'ideology'.

These arguments come together around the question of historical analysis. A major problem in the development of Marxist feminist work has been a tendency to try to resolve questions such as the independence or otherwise of women's oppression from the capitalist mode of production, or the degree to which women's oppression is to be seen as ideological, by posing them as strictly theoretical issues to which a correct formulation can provide an answer. It is, however, unlikely that such a formulation will materialize, since the questions themselves are historical rather than exclusively theoretical.

One way of illustrating this point would be to pose the question: was capitalism progressive for women or not? Marxists and feminists have attempted to answer this question by a process of theoretical deduction and within both approaches the answer has varied extremely. If we pose the question historically, the issues become clearer. Feudal households were not, in any class, egalitarian as between men and women, but the development of capitalism brought an exacerbation of these divisions, a far greater degree of dependence of women on men within the household, and constructed a wage-labour system in which the relationship of women to the class structure came to be partially mediated by an assumed or actual dependence on a male wage. These developments, however, are only partly attributable to forces internal to capitalist production and also reflect a struggle within the working class.

Once the problem is posed in this way, it becomes clear that there is no programmatic answer to the question of whether women's liberation might be achieved within capitalism. We can, however, come to some conclusions. The liberation of women would require, first, a redivision of the labour and responsibilities of childcare. Whether privatized or collectivized, it would be mandatory that this be shared between men and women. Second, the actual or assumed dependence of women on a male wage (or capital) would need to be done away with. Third, the ideology of gender would need to be transformed. None of these seem to me to be compatible with capitalism as it exists in Britain and comparable societies today. The widespread and profound job-segregation characterizing the social division of labour will prove intractable. Male employment is predicated upon the assumption that domestic and childcare responsibilities are unimportant for them, and this holds true in all classes. State provisions, although not entirely inflexible, constitute at present a leaden weight of support for the male-breadwinner system of household maintenance. The ideology of gender and sexuality is deeply engrained in our consciousness.

These divisions are systematically embedded in the structure and texture of capitalist social relations in Britain and they play an important part in the political and ideological stability of this society. They are constitutive of our subjectivity as well as, in part, of capitalist political and cultural hegemony. They are interwoven into a fundamental relationship between the wage-labour system and the

organization of domestic life and it is impossible to imagine
that they could be extracted from the relations of production
and reproduction of capitalism without a massive transformation of those relations taking place. Hence, the slogan
'No women's liberation without socialism; no socialism
without women's liberation' is more than a pious hope.
Although both parts of this slogan properly call for an active
political intention and commitment to achieve these
objectives, both also indicate the reality of the situation in
which we now struggle.

At the same time, it must be emphasized that the
conditions affecting improvements in women's position vary
with changes in capitalism. It is more plausible to look for a
lifting of the burden of domestic labour from women in times
of high female employment and capitalist expansion. It is
not altogether impossible that capital might wake up to the
'wastage of talent' involved in the present educational
system and attempt to reduce the channelling of girls away
from useful technological subjects. The effects of new
technology may create a situation where the relationship
between the household and wage labour is less crucial for
social production, and hence create the conditions for a more
equal distribution of childcare. These developments are
possible, even if we may deem them unlikely, but in any case
the situation would be analogous to that in socialist societies
where, for instance, policy on abortion and contraception is
influenced by projected labour needs.

It would be a foolish and doctrinaire stance to deny the
possibility of improvement and reform under capitalism.
Bourgeois women have already effected a dramatic change
in respect of their civil rights — to own property, to vote,
stand for public office and enter the professions. These are
sweeping changes, and a restructuring of the ideological and
political parameters of women's situation is not incon-
ceivable. It is perhaps less clear what changes we could
expect in the case of working-class women. The 'double shift'
of domestic labour and poorly paid wage labour is also
affected by variations in the strength of the capitalist

economy, and the present recession is likely to lower women's standard of living generally and force many women into particularly exploited jobs in order to maintain some contribution to the household budget. These issues bite deeply on the political project of socialist feminism. By generations of socialists we stand accused of bourgeois, diversionary, individualist reformism. By our sisters we are charged with betraying feminism in favour of a sexist, male class struggle. The rhetoric on both sides may have shifted a bit, but the questions still are: does the women's liberation movement have a 'middle-class' basis? Do existing forms of class struggle represent feminist demands? The accusation that the women's movement is 'middle class' in fact robs it of a justified recognition of the unique achievements in forging common objectives across the boundaries of class. The movement is by no means restricted to women of one class. Although class divisions may cause problems that need to be worked on internally, the concept of sisterhood does have some political reality within the movement. More accurately, though, it is undoubtedly the case that — certainly in the early years of the present movement — feminist political struggle was disproportionately engaged in by women who were highly educated, many of them university graduates. Although education is sharply divided by class, it is not completely reducible to it. This problem has not gone unnoticed in the movement, particularly in Britain. Rather, it has posed the question of how to make feminism relevant to women across a range of different experiences and situations. In particular, it means that without losing our vital emphasis on sexual politics we need to engage as much as possible in struggles over the conditions, hours, pay, security of women workers. These are areas which the labour movement has in the past severely neglected and we need to ensure that women's interests are fought for and feminist demands made.

What, then, might we conclude as to the relationship between women's liberation and the left? A politically autonomous women's liberation movement does not require elaborate justification, and indeed we have correctly assumed a right to organize independently of men, however sympathetic male supporters may be to our general objectives. The political and ideological processes that contribute so massively to women's oppression must be fought by those affected by them, and there has been little justification for the view that existing programmes for socialism will automatically bring about women's liberation. In addition to this, the battle within the trade-union movement — for instance, for equal pay and a shorter working day in opposition to men's demands for a family wage and a shorter working week — needs to be fought by a strong feminist presence with a base in an autonomous women's movement.

There are, however, fundamental political imperatives directing us not only towards a strong feminist presence on the left but towards some kind of alliance between the women's liberation movement and the left. This certainly does not mean that the women's movement should be subsumed under the left, nor that its function should be to radicalize and renovate an ailing organizational structure. In this respect I would tend to be somewhat critical of the view expressed by the authors of *Beyond the Fragments* that the libertarian, grass-roots style of the women's movement could be taken as a model for a new socialist organizational form.[1] Important though questions of organization are, I would not see the potential benefits of some kind of alliance as consisting in what each movement could learn from the other in these respects. The more urgent question to be asked is whether there are *political objectives* in common that might constitute a basis for a relationship.

At present there are, I think, some major areas of at best a difference of political emphasis, and at worst outright conflict. An obvious thorny example is that of biological reproduction. As Sue Himmelweit has pointed out, there is

1. Sheila Rowbotham, Lynne Segal and Hilary Wainwright, *Beyond the Fragments: Feminism and the Making of Socialism*, London 1980.

surely some conflict between a feminist insistence on the
right of each individual woman to decide when and whether
she will have a child and a socialist notion of collective
responsibility in relation to reproduction.[2] Problems such as
these cannot be evaded. There are, however, many issues
where objective interests might coincide and provide a basis
for greater unity. One such example would be the question of
women's wages and working conditions. As I suggested in
Chapter 5, the labour movement has in the past used
exclusionary practices to define women workers as less
skilled than men, thereby confirming women in low paid and
insecure jobs and facilitating capital's use of cheap and
flexible female labour as a means of keeping general wages
down. This has strengthened the divisions between men and
women within the working class, and it is a major task of
feminists and the left to challenge these practices and
assumptions and offer an alternative strategy. Such a
strategy could be grounded in shared objectives of both
socialism and feminism.

There are more general reasons underlying a drive
towards an alliance. Feminism seeks to change not simply
men or women, or both, as they exist at present, but seeks to
change the relations between them. Although the basis for
this will be provided by an autonomous women's liberation
movement the strategy must involve political engagement
with men rather than a policy of absolute separatism.
Socialist men, like other men, stand to lose political power
and social privilege from the liberation of women but, more
than other men, they have shown now and in the past some
political intention to support feminist struggle. This is not a
question of benevolence on their part. For if women's
oppression is entrenched in the structure of capitalism then
the struggle for women's liberation and the struggle for
socialism cannot wholly be disengaged. Just as we cannot
conceive of women's liberation under the oppression of

2. Sue Himmelweit, 'Abortion: Individual Choice and Social Control',
   Feminist Review, no.5, 1980.

capitalism so we cannot conceive of a socialism whose principles of equality, freedom and dignity are vitiated by the familiar iniquities of gender.

Select Bibliography

ADAMS, Parveen, 'A Note on Sexual Division and Sexual Differences', *m/f*, no.3, 1979.

ADAMSON, Olivia, Carol Brown, Judith Harrison and Judy Price, 'Women's Oppression Under Capitalism', *Revolutionary Communist*, no.5, 1976.

ALEXANDER, Sally, 'Women's Work in Nineteenth-Century London; a Study of the Years 1820-50', in Juliet Mitchell and Ann Oakley, eds., *The Rights and Wrongs of Women*, Harmondsworth: Penguin, 1976.

ALTHUSSER, Louis, *Lenin and Philosophy and Other Essays*, London: NLB, 1971.

BARRETT, Michèle, and Mary McIntosh, 'The "Family Wage": Some Problems for Socialists and Feminists', *Capital and Class*, no.11, 1980.

BARRON, Richard, and G. M. Norris, 'Sexual Divisions and the Dual Labour Market', in LEONARD BARKER and ALLEN.

BEECHEY, Veronica, 'Some Notes on Female Wage Labour in the Capitalist Mode of Production', *Capital and Class*, no.3, 1977.

___, 'On Patriarchy', *Feminist Review*, no.3, 1979.

BRUEGEL, Irene, 'What Keeps the Family Going?', *International Socialism*, vol.2, no.1, 1978.

BURMAN, Sandra, ed., *Fit Work for Women*, London: Croom Helm, 1979.

CHODOROW, Nancy, *The Reproduction of Mothering: Psychoanalysis and the Sociology of Gender*, Berkeley: University of California Press, 1978.

COULSON, Margaret, Branka Magaš and Hilary Wainwright, 'Women and the Class Struggle', *New Left Review*, no.89, 1975.

COWARD, Rosalind, 'Rethinking Marxism', *m/f*, no.2, 1978.

CREIGHTON, Colin, 'Family, Property and Relations of Production in Western Europe', *Economy and Society*, vol.9, no.2, 1980.

DE BEAUVOIR, Simone, *The Second Sex*, Harmondsworth: Penguin, 1974.

DELMAR, Rosalind, 'Looking Again at Engels's *Origin of the Family, Private Property and the State*', in Juliet Mitchell and Ann Oakley (see ALEXANDER).

DELPHY, Christine, *The Main Enemy*, London: Women's Research and Resources Centre, 1977.

EDHOLM, Felicity, Olivia Harris and Kate Young, 'Conceptualizing Women', *Critique of Anthropology*, nos. 9 & 10, 1977.

EISENSTEIN, Zillah, ed., *Capitalist Patriarchy and the Case for Socialist Feminism*, New York: Monthly Review Press, 1979.

ENGELS, Frederick, *The Origin of the Family, Private Property and the State*, New York: Pathfinder, 1972.

EQUAL OPPORTUNITIES COMMISSION, *Third Annual Report*, London: HMSO, 1979.

FIRESTONE, Shulamith, *The Dialectic of Sex*, London: The Women's Press, 1979.

FLANDRIN, Jean-Louis, *Families in Former Times: Kinship, Household and Sexuality*, London: Cambridge University Press, 1979.

FOREMAN, Ann, *Femininity as Alienation: Women and the Family in Marxism and Psychoanalysis*, London: Pluto, 1977.

FREUD, Sigmund, *On Sexuality*, Harmondsworth: Penguin, 1977.

GARDINER, Jean, 'Women in the Labour Process and Class Structure', in Alan Hunt, ed., *Class and Class Structure*, London: Lawrence and Wishart, 1977.

HAMILTON, Roberta, *The Liberation of Women*, London: Allen and Unwin, 1978.

HARTMAN, Mary, and Lois W. Banner, eds., *Clio's Consciousness Raised*, New York: Harper and Row, 1974.

HARTMANN, Heidi, 'The Unhappy Marriage of Marxism and Feminism: Towards a More Progressive Union', *Capital and Class*, no.8, 1979.

HEITLINGER, Alena, *Women and State Socialism: Sex Inequality in the Soviet Union and Czechoslovakia*, London: Macmillan, 1979.

HUMPHRIES, Jane, 'Class Struggle and the Persistence of the Working Class Family', *Cambridge Journal of Economics*, vol.1, no.3, 1977.

KUHN, Annette, and AnnMarie Wolpe, eds., *Feminism and Materialism*, London: Routledge and Kegan Paul, 1978.

LAND, Hilary, 'Who Cares for the Family?', *Journal of Social Policy*, vol.7, no.3, 1978.

LAPLANCHE, Jean, and J-B. Pontalis, *The Language of Psychoanalysis*, London: Hogarth Press, 1973.

LEONARD BARKER, Diana, and Sheila Allen, eds., *Dependence and Exploitation in Work and Marriage*, London: Longman, 1976.

MCINTOSH, Mary, 'The State and the Oppression of Women', in KUHN and WOLPE.

MILLETT, Kate, *Sexual Politics*, London: Sphere, 1971.

MITCHELL, Juliet, *Psychoanalysis and Feminism*, Harmondsworth, Penguin, 1975.

MOLYNEUX, Maxine, 'Beyond the Domestic Labour Debate', *New Left Review*, no.116, 1979.

OAKLEY, Ann, *Sex, Gender and Society*, London: Temple Smith, 1972.

PINCHBECK, Ivy, *Women Workers and the Industrial Revolution 1750-1850*, London: Cass, 1977.

POSTER, Mark, *Critical theory of the Family*, London: Pluto, 1978.

RAPP, Rayna, Ellen Ross and Renate Bridenthal, 'Examining Family History', *Feminist Studies*, vol.5, no.1, 1979.

ROWBOTHAM, Sheila, Lynne Segal and Hilary Wainwright,

Beyond the Fragments; Feminism and the Making of Socialism, London: Merlin, 1979.

RUBIN, Gayle, 'The Traffic in Women: Notes on the "Political Economy" of Sex', in R. R. Reiter, ed., *Toward an Anthropology of Women*, New York: Monthly Review Press, 1975.

SMART, Carol, and Barry Smart, eds., *Women, Sexuality and Social Control*, London: Routledge and Kegan Paul, 1978.

SNELL, Mandy, 'The Equal Pay and Sex Discrimination Acts: Their Impact in the Workplace', *Feminist Review*, no.1, 1979.

STONE, Lawrence, *The Family, Sex and Marriage in England 1500-1800*, London: Weidenfeld and Nicolson, 1977.

TIMPANARO, Sebastiano, *On Materialism*, London: NLB, 1975.

WILSON, Elizabeth, *Women and the Welfare State*, London: Tavistock, 1977.

WOLPE, AnnMarie, *Some Processes in Sexist Education*, London: Women's Research and Resources Centre, 1977.

WOOLF, Virginia, *Three Guineas*, London: Hogarth Press, 1938.

ZARETSKY, Eli, *Capitalism, the Family and Personal Life*, London: Pluto, 1976.

Index of Subjects

Index of Authors